地理标志与实现可持续发展目标

地理标志保护实务探讨与案例分析

（汉英对照版）

SDGs

刘红春 著/译

知识产权出版社
全国百佳图书出版单位
——北京——

图书在版编目（CIP）数据

地理标志与实现可持续发展目标：地理标志保护实务探讨与案例分析：汉英对照/刘红春著译. —北京：知识产权出版社，2023.1
ISBN 978-7-5130-8420-8

Ⅰ.①地… Ⅱ.①刘… Ⅲ.①地理—标志—研究—汉、英 Ⅳ.①F760.5

中国版本图书馆 CIP 数据核字（2022）第 197493 号

内容提要

本书具体阐述了地理标志在促进联合国可持续发展目标中能够发挥的作用，列举了国内外地理标志的成功案例，在总结成功经验的同时，很有针对性地指出地理标志产品成功须遵循的个案原则，具有很强的实践意义。

责任编辑：卢海鹰 王瑞璞	责任校对：潘凤越
封面设计：杨杨工作室·张冀	责任印制：刘译文

地理标志与实现可持续发展目标
——地理标志保护实务探讨与案例分析（汉英对照版）

刘红春　著/译

出版发行：	知识产权出版社 有限责任公司	网　址：http://www.ipph.cn
社　址：	北京市海淀区气象路 50 号院	邮　编：100081
责编电话：	010-82000860 转 8116	责编邮箱：wangruipu@cnipr.com
发行电话：	010-82000860 转 8101/8102	发行传真：010-82000893/82005070/82000270
印　刷：	三河市国英印务有限公司	经　销：新华书店、各大网上书店及相关专业书店
开　本：	880mm×1230mm　1/32	印　张：12
版　次：	2023 年 1 月第 1 版	印　次：2023 年 1 月第 1 次印刷
字　数：	330 千字	定　价：99.00 元

ISBN 978-7-5130-8420-8

出版权专有　侵权必究
如有印装质量问题，本社负责调换。

作者简介

刘红春,澳大利亚国立大学公共政策硕士,2001年起,先后在原国家质量监督检验检疫总局通关业务司、科技司从事原产地和地理标志管理工作。参与《原产地标记管理规定》的实施管理和《地理标志产品保护规定》的起草发布和实施管理工作。参与中欧地理标志协定谈判和中欧10+10地理标志互认试点项目(China-EU 10+10 Pilot Project)的磋商交流,以及原国家质量监督检验检疫总局与欧盟贸易总司地理标志合作备忘录的起草和磋商工作。作为中国代表团成员,多次参加世界贸易组织知识产权理事会(WTO/TRIPS Council)例会暨地理标志特会,以及中欧、中美、中瑞(士)知识产权工作组会议,中国-东盟、中国-智利、中国-秘鲁等自由贸易区原产地规则和地理标志谈判。担任国际标准《ISO/DIS 20671-3 地理标志及相关品牌评价导则》中方项目负责人。参与联合国框架下金伯利进程国际证书制度(Kimberley Process

Certification Scheme)技术磋商及其在我国的实施管理工作。2013~2020年援藏,先后任西藏自治区质量技术监督局和西藏自治区市场监督管理局副局长,分管标准化(含地理标志)、计量等业务。

About the Author

Hongchun Liu, Master of Public Policy of the Australian National University, engaged, since 2001, in the administration of origin-related trade affairs and geographical indications for the former General Administration of Quality Supervision, Inspection and Quarantine of the People's Republic of China (AQSIQ). He was involved in the implementation of the *Regulation of the Mark of Origin*, the drafting and administration of the *Regulation of the Geographical Indication Product*. In addition, he participated in the negotiations of China-EU Agreement on Geographical Indications and China-EU 10+10 Pilot Project as well as the MoU signed between AQSIQ and DG-Trade of the European Union. Being a member of the Chinese delegation, he participated in multiple sessions of regular meetings of WTO/TRIPS Council and special sessions on geographical indication, as well as the working group meetings of China-EU, China-US, China-Switzerland on intellectual property rights. Meanwhile, he was involved in the negotiations on rules of origin and geographical indications of China - ASEAN, China - Chile and China - Peru Free Trade Agreement, and the drafting team for *ISO/DIS 20671 - 3*: *Brand evaluation- Guidelines for brands related to geographical indications*. Furthermore, he was head of two working groups on behalf of China for the Kimberley Process Certification Scheme, engaging in technical meetings for implementation purposes. Between 2013 and 2020, he served as Deputy Director of the Bureau of Quality and Technical Supervision and the Bureau of Market Regulation of Tibet Autonomous Region, in charge of the regional development of standardization and geographical indications.

序

  地理标志保护制度起源于19世纪的法国，其前身是法国针对葡萄酒等具有地域特色的产品所实施的原产地命名监控制度，后逐渐被包括欧盟各国在内的世界上大多数国家所接受。1994年，世界贸易组织（WTO）《与贸易有关的知识产权协定》第22条首次明确将地理标志作为一种知识产权形式进行保护。1999年，原中国国家质量技术监督局颁布《原产地域产品保护规定》，率先从产品角度入手在中国推动地理标志的保护。之后，原国家出入境检验检疫局、原农业部、原国家工商行政管理总局等部门也从不同角度参与了地理标志在中国的保护工作。2018年国务院机构改革后，地理标志保护工作确定由国家知识产权局统一负责。

  作为一种特殊形式的知识产权，地理标志权的"公共性"特征尤为突出，它所代表的产品的品质、信誉除了取决于当地的自然因素外，也是该地劳动者生产、经营多年，共同努力、创造的结果，是一种名副其实的集体财富，甚至成为国家无形资产和文化遗产，因此需要由国家出面进行保护和监督。当前，地理标志作为一项重要的知识产权得到许多国家的关注和保护，充分说明了其价值所在。

本书作者曾长期从事国家地理标志产品保护管理工作，亲身参与了地理标志保护制度在中国的建立和发展，在近20年的工作过程中积累了十分丰富的实践经验和案例研究成果，对国内外地理标志保护的历史、发展进程及现状有着非常深入的认识和独到的见解。在工作过程中，作者敏锐地意识到，地理标志保护制度的独特性使得它在人类可持续发展中具有意想不到的积极作用。可持续发展的概念，最先是在1980年《世界自然资源保护大纲》中正式提出并讨论的，是人类对工业文明进程进行反思的结果。联合国于2015年通过了《2030年可持续发展议程》并设定了17项可持续发展目标，呼吁所有国家行动起来，在促进经济繁荣的同时保护地球。经过分析，作者惊讶地发现17项目标中有11项与地理标志保护制度存在关联性，这使得作者产生了写作本书的想法。本书作者除了对地理标志制度（第一章）和可持续发展理念（第二章）进行介绍外，还创新性地把11个目标依照其内涵划分为四个类别：①减贫脱贫与粮食安全（第三章）；②实现经济增长与社会公平（第四章）；③保护生态环境，应对全球气候变化（第五章）；④开展国际合作（第六章），然后逐一结合案例具体分析了地理标志保护制度对于实现这四类可持续发展目标的作用和积极意义。

可持续发展是全人类面临的一个至关重要的问题，关系到生存和未来。虽然关于可持续发展的文章和论著非常多，但尚未见到有论著从地理标志保护角度出发，论述该制度对于实现可持续发展目标的作用和意义。独特的视角和出发点使得本书具有非常重要的参考价值。

丰富的案例让本书的可读性极强,对于全国从事地理标志保护的管理人员、地理标志产品的生产人员、知识产权领域的研究人员等都具有重要的借鉴意义和实用价值。

开卷有益。希望所有读者都能从本书中有所收获。

中国农业大学教授
战吉宬
2022.4.22

Foreword

The protection system for geographical indication, which was derived from l'Appellation d'origine Contrôlée (AOC) governing characteristic products such as wines, originated in France in the 19th Century and has been adopted by many countries especially those in Europe. Geographical indication is provided by Article 22 of the *Agreement on Trade - related Aspects of Intellectual Property Rights* (TRIPS) as one of the intellectual property rights in 1994. Meanwhile, in 1999, the former State Bureau of Quality and Technical Supervision issued the *Regulation for the Designated Origin Product*, launching the protection of geographical indications in China. Thereafter, the former State Administration for Entry-Exit Inspection and Quarantine (SCIQ), the former State Administration for Industry and Commerce (SAIC) and the former Ministry of Agriculture (MOA) engaged in the protection of geographical indications in China as well within their own jurisdictions. Since the latest institutional reform in 2018, the China National Intellectual Property Admini Stration (CNIPA) under the State Administration for Market Regulation (SAMR) has been designated as the national authority regulating the protection of geographical indications in China.

Being a special form of intellectual property right, geographical indication is characterized by its 'public' feature. The quality and reputation of such a product are attributed to, apart from the natural factors of the producing areas, the yields created through long-term joint efforts of local producers. It is indeed a collective wealth or even national intangible assets and cultural heritage calling for authorized protection and supervision. The rising interests from many countries that consider geographical indication as one of the importatnt intellectual property rights are plain responses to its value.

The author of this book had a long career in the national administration of geographical indication products, engaging in the setting up and development of the GI system for almost two decades with extensive practical experience. He has considerable knowledge of the history and progress of the GI system combined with unique insights. He is keenly aware of the unexpected positive roles generated by the originality of the GI system for sustainable development, which, innitially appeared in the *World Conservation Strategy* published in 1980, was an introspection of global industrialization process. *The 2030 Agenda for Sustainable Development* adopted by the United Nations in 2015 has set 17 Sustainable Development Goals (SDGs) that called on all countries to take actions to protect our planet while promoting economic prosperity. Upon careful review of the SDGs, he surprisingly found that as many as 11 goals were in connection with the GI system, thus triggering his intent to write this book.In addition to his elaborations on the GI system (Chapter 1) and the SDGs (Chapter 2),the author creatively groups the 11 goals into four divisions,i.e.,1.eradicating poverty,ensuring health and food safety (Chapter 3);2.promoting economic growth and balanced development (Chapter 4);3.protecting biological environment and combacting climate change (Chapter 5);4.facilitating international partnership (Chapter 6).The discussions are unfolded accordingly on the roles and contributions of the GI system to the relevant goals.

Sustainable development is crucial for the survival and future of mankind.Despite plenty of literature on sustainable development,there have been few works targeting the roles and contributions of the GI system for achieving the SDGs.The author's peculiar perspectives add to the value of this book,whilst the abundant case analysis makes this book more readable.It is a practical guide for GI producers,managing staff engaging in the protection of geographical indications as well as researchers of intellectual property rights.

Reading is always beneficial.I hope that every reader may gain from this book.

Jicheng Zhan

Professor,China Agricultural University

22.4.2022

前　言

联合国于 2015 年通过了《2030 年可持续发展议程》(*The 2030 Agenda for Sustainable Development*)，并设定出 17 项可持续发展目标（Sustainable Development Goals，SDGs），要求世界各国为实现该目标而共同努力。可以说，实现可持续发展目标已成为 21 世纪全球瞩目的焦点，它考验着决策者的智慧和国家治理能力，并深刻影响着国际政治、经济关系。国内外关于可持续发展的论著可谓浩瀚，但有关地理标志保护制度对于实现可持续发展目标的正向意义和具体影响仍鲜有研究出炉。笔者作为曾长期从事国家地理标志产品保护管理工作的专业人士，在近 20 年的工作过程中积累了较为丰富的实践经验和业务素材，对国内外地理标志保护的历史、发展进程及现状有较深入的了解。本书结合对可持续发展目标的分析研究，从实务角度分析了地理标志保护制度对于实现可持续发展目标的价值和意义。对于关心地理标志的读者，尤其是从事地理标志管理或参与地理标志保护实操的读者来说，笔者试图提供较为直观的解读和分析，期望以此提高本书的参考意义和实用价值。对于关注可持续发展目标及其实现路径的读者而言，笔者围绕与地理标志直接相关的11个可持续发展目标进行了分析探讨，提炼归纳了地理标志保护制度对于实现相关可持续发展目标所发挥的积极作用，并辅以案例说明，希望有助于读者更好地理解二者之间的关系，深化对实现可持续发展目标的具体认识。

书中不乏个人观点，不代表任何官方或专家意见。与之相关的案例主要引自国内外文献资料，一部分源于论坛演讲或专业会议交流材料，还有一些来自官媒报道或个人亲身经历。个别案例发生时间较早，其发展现状或已有差异，列于本书仅反映当时情况。

总体而言，地理标志制度对于实现可持续发展目标具有积极意义。与此同时，也应清醒地认识到其局限性，例如：地理标志生产方式所强调和倡导的传统工艺和低密度种养殖等理念，在有利于保护环境、缓解气候变化影响、传承历史文化的同时，客观上或会造成产能不足、缺乏规模效应，难以满足市场需求等问题。在增加就业、促进实现男女平等方面，地理标志制度主要在相关农业人口中产生积极影响，但覆盖面仍较有限。换言之，地理标志制度并非普世良方，即使在农产品领域也多适用于自然条件特殊、不具备开展规模化生产条件，但产品质量特点显著的特色产业发展。

需要说明的是，尽管参阅了大量文献资料，但笔者水平有限，对地理标志制度的分析探讨仍显粗浅，对地理标志保护与实现可持续发展目标之间的关系研究不足，某些观点缺乏实证依据，敬请读者谅解并批评指正。

Preface

The United Nations adopted *The 2030 Agenda for Sustainable Development* in 2015, setting out 17 Sustainable Development Goals (SDGs) and calling on all countries to make concerted efforts to achieve the goals.The SDGs are the focus of global concerns of the 21st Century,testing decision-makers' wisdom and governance ability. It has profound impacts on international political and economic relations.Literature about sustainable development is abundant,yet studies on the positive roles and concrete impacts of the protection system of geographical indication (hereinafter referred to as the GI system) on the SDGs are relatively limited.Having been involved in the administration and study of geographical indications in China over the last twenty years,this author has accumulated rich practical experience and source materials, including knowledge of the history,progress and status quo of both domestic and international protection of geographical indications.By incorporating analysis of the SDGs,this book discusses the value and roles of the GI system for achieving the SDGs.For readers interested in geographical indications,especially those engaging in the management and protection of geographical indications,this author attempts to render straightforward analysis and interpretation with a view to enhancing the practical and reference value of this book.For readers concerned about the SDGs and their roadmap,this author deliberates the 11 sustainable development goals in connection with geographical indications, summarizing the positive roles of the GI system for achieving the relevant goals aided by case analysis.It is expected that readers would be well informed of the relevant sustainable development goals and their relations with geographical indications.

It should be clarified that there are many personal opinions representing neither official standpoint nor experts' views.The cases referred to are mostly cited from published literature,with some being obtained from speeches at forums or documents of seminars and professional meetings in addition to reports from official domestic media and personal experience.Some of the cases,due to the time of their occurrence, may have undergone changes or discrepancies with the current status. They only reflect the situations at that time.

In general, the GI system plays positive roles in achieving the SDGs.Nevertheless,we must be conscious of its limitations.Being favorable for promoting environmental protection, for relieving climate change and inheriting culture and history,the traditional techniques and low-density plantation and breeding encouraged by the GI system,for instance,may result in poor output and a lack of scale,failing to meet market demands.In addition,the positive roles the GI system plays in job creation and gender equality are generally confined to relevant rural population.In other words,the GI system is not a universal recipe. Even for the agricultural sector alone,it is mostly adapted to those geographical areas with special natural conditions where mass production is not viable.

It should be noted that despite references to plenty of literature, the analysis about the GI system and its relations with the SDGs is insufficient.Some of the opinions lack proven evidence.Comments and criticisms from readers are therefore highly appreciated.

目 录
CONTENTS

绪 论 ‖ 1

第一章 地理标志保护的基础条件与要素分析 ‖ 8

　第一节 客观划定产地范围 / 8

　　案例1：杜康酒产地之争 / 15

　　案例2：东阿阿胶产地之争 / 16

　第二节 维护地理标志名称的市场价值 / 20

　第三节 科学制定质量技术要求 / 30

　第四节 典型问题探讨 / 35

　第五节 制度实施中存在的缺陷与不足 / 43

第二章 地理标志与实现可持续发展目标 ‖ 51

　第一节 联合国可持续发展目标 / 52

　第二节 地理标志与可持续发展目标之间的关联性 / 56

第三章　地理标志制度助力消除全球贫困、维护生命健康 ‖ 59
第一节　地理标志保护促进减贫脱贫目标实现 / 59
目标1：无贫穷 / 59
目标2：零饥饿 / 74
第二节　地理标志保护促进健康事业发展 / 88
目标3：良好健康和福祉 / 88

第四章　地理标志制度促进经济增长和社会公平 ‖ 92
第一节　地理标志保护促进实现性别平等 / 92
目标5：性别平等 / 92
第二节　地理标志保护促进区域经济发展 / 96
目标8：体面工作和经济增长 / 96
第三节　地理标志保护促进减少不平等 / 103
目标10：减少不平等 / 103
第四节　地理标志保护促进可持续生产和消费 / 111
目标12：负责任的消费和生产 / 111

第五章　地理标志制度助力保护地球生态环境 ‖ 122
第一节　地理标志保护促进应对全球气候变化 / 122
目标13：气候行动 / 122
第二节　地理标志保护促进保护海洋渔业资源 / 135
目标14：水下生物 / 135
第三节　地理标志保护促进保护陆地资源环境 / 142
目标15：陆地生物 / 142

第六章　建立伙伴关系，促进地理标志保护国际合作 ‖ 151
目标17：促进目标实现的伙伴关系 / 151

结　语 ‖ 161

Contents

Introduction ‖ 165

Chapter 1 Conditions and factor analysis of the GI system ‖ 173
- Section 1 The demarcation of producing areas / 173
  - Case 1. The dispute over the origin of Dukang Liquor (Chinese Baijiu) / 181
  - Case 2. The dispute over the origin of Dong E Ejiao (donkey-hide gelatin) / 183
- Section 2 Maintaining the market value of GI names / 187
- Section 3 The specification / 198
- Section 4 Notable issues / 204
- Section 5 Flaws of the GI system / 213

Chapter 2 The GI system helps to achieve the SDGs ‖ 222
- Section 1 The Sustainable Development Goals (SDGs) / 223
- Section 2 Links between the GI System and the SDGs / 227

Chapter 3 The roles of the GI system in support of poverty eradication and wellbeing of mankind ‖ 230
- Section 1 The GI system helps to eradicate poverty / 230
  - Goal 1. No poverty / 230
  - Goal 2. Zero hunger / 249
- Section 2 The GI system benefits the health sector / 266
  - Goal 3. Good health and well-being / 266

Chapter 4 The GI system enhances economic growth and social equality ‖ 271
- Section 1 The GI system promotes gender equality / 271

　　　　Goal 5. Gender equality ／ 271
　　Section 2　The GI system promotes regional economy ／ 276
　　　　Goal 8. Decent job and economic growth ／ 276
　　Section 3　The GI system helps reduce inequalities ／ 284
　　　　Goal 10. Reduced inequality ／ 284
　　Section 4　The GI system benefits sustainable
　　　　　　　production and consumption ／ 293
　　　　Goal 12. Sustainable consumption and production ／ 293

**Chapter 5　The GI system helps to protect the ecosystem of
　　　　　　the earth　‖　307**
　　Section 1　The GI system helps combat climate
　　　　　　　change ／ 307
　　　　Goal 13. Climate action ／ 307
　　Section 2　The GI system helps protect marine
　　　　　　　resources ／ 322
　　　　Goal 14. Life below water ／ 322
　　Section 3　The GI system helps protect terrestrial
　　　　　　　resources ／ 331
　　　　Goal 15. Life on land ／ 331

**Chapter 6　Partnership promotes international cooperation
　　　　　　in geographical indications　‖　342**
　　　　Goal 17. Partnerships for the goals ／ 342

Postscript　‖　352

附　录　专有名词翻译　‖　356

绪 论

地理标志保护制度起源于 19 世纪,前身是法国针对葡萄酒等具有显著地域关联性产品所实施的原产地命名监控制度(Appellation d'origine Contrôlée,AOC)。其基本原理是,对于质量特色与产地自然因素和人文因素关联性较强的产品,清晰界定产地范围,通过法律手段保护以原产地地名所命名的产品名称(如香槟 Champagne、干邑 Cognac),非原产地的同类产品不得使用同一产地名称,包括与之近似的名称,以此来确立原产地产品的名称专有权,保护优质特色产品不被假冒侵犯。同时,通过制定严格的技术法规(质量技术要求),对产品的原料来源、生产工艺、质量特色、包装乃至销售等各环节予以限定,以保证特色产品质量特征的长久保持。

仅从字面理解,地理标志一词大体指"一个地方的标志性物产",当然这并非地理标志的确切含义,有关定义将在后续段落中讨论。"地理标志"为翻译名词,英语是"geographical indication"❶（GI）。其中的"indication"一词还可译为"标识""标示""表明""指示"等。因汉语"标志"还具有"标签""记号"等含义，所以"地理标志"这一名词往往使人联想到标签、符号或专用标记，但原文中其实并没有这样的含义。英文以"symbol""sign"或"logo""label"等词汇来表达上述含义。这从一个侧面解释了为什么国外地理标志产品包装上往往并未使用任何专用标志，而仅在商品标签上标注"受保护的原产地命名或受保护的地理标志"（Protected Designation of Origin /Protected Geographical Indication）字样。该标注行为已向消费者表明产品受地理标志保护的性质，而使用专用标志的目的之一是强调、凸显该性质。在我国，只有那些符合条件、经主管部门核准的生产企业才能使用地理标志保护产品专用标志。

地理标志和原产地命名概念的基础是"土地"或"风土"。"风土"（terroir）一词原文为法语。按照法国国家原产地和质量管理局（Institut National de l'origine et de la Qualité，INAO）给出的定义，所谓风土，"指的是某个特定的地理范围，在该地生产（产品）的独特性直接来源于产地特殊的自然条件。风土基于物理和生物环境之间的相互作用系统，以及某一空间内存在的一系列人为因素，这些人为因素由人类社会在历史上运用集体生产知识建立起来。所有这些因素构成了产品的独特性。"❷ 简而言之，它是与土地密切相关的各种自然和人文因素与产品质量特色间的相互作用和影响。

风土这一概念对于原产地命名监控制度以及发展到后来的地

---

❶ 法语、西班牙语、意大利语等其他西方语言普遍采用同一词根。
❷ 参见：https://www.inao.gouv.fr/eng/official-sign-identifying-quality-and-origin/PDO-AOC.

理标志保护制度产生了很大影响。它指出了土地、环境与产品质量之间的内在关联，有助于我们理解地理标志保护的基本原理和内涵。

1994年，历时8年的乌拉圭回合全球贸易谈判结束。在1994年4月举行的马拉喀什部长级会议上，各成员签署了《最后决议》（Final Act），发布了《马拉喀什宣言》（Marrakesh Declaration），并通过决议，成立世界贸易组织（World Trade Organization，WTO）。《与贸易有关的知识产权协定》（the Agreement on Trade-Related Aspects of Intellectual Property Rights，TRIPS）作为60个协议文件之一被列入其附件1C。[1] TRIPS第22条至第24条明确了地理标志的定义、对葡萄酒和烈酒地理标志的高水平保护以及例外条款。其中第22条第1款关于地理标志的定义为：

就本协定而言，"地理标志"指识别一货物来源于一成员领土或该领土内一地区或地方的标识，该货物的特定质量、声誉或其他特性主要归因于其地理来源。

TRIPS中关于地理标志的规定是WTO成员普遍遵循的主要法律依据。该协定也是迄今为止知识产权法律和制度上影响最大的国际公约。

地理标志具有明显的地域特征和排他性，将自身的质量特色归因于地理环境（土壤、气温、湿度、地势、海拔、降水量、水质、森林覆盖率等）的特殊性，以及特殊的生产工艺等人为传承因素。地理环境的特殊性无法复制，生产工艺等人为因素也与地理环境和历史传承密切相关，同样具有独特价值。即便有人提出

---

[1] 参见：世界贸易组织官网，https://www.wto.org/english/docs_e.htm。

某些地理标志产品在理论上可复制、可转移，也因地理环境条件的差异，尤其是缺乏历史、人文因素的支撑而难以成立。因此，地理标志强调的是排他性和专用权，将自身与同类产品区别开来，以此来凸显其特色质量和特有价值，并在市场上获得更高溢价。

"在许多国家，地理标志越来越被视为一个机会，其独特的外观和文化渊源可将产品转化为与众不同的东西。"❶ 很明显，这种将自身与同类产品区分开来的"特权"，只有经严格的标准认定和完善的法律制度保障才具有其合理性，也才有可能实现对它的有效保护。而一旦做到了这一点，地理标志产品就有可能发展成为当地的知名品牌和对外宣传名片，并带动当地人口参与生产就业，同时还可通过市场溢出效应，促进包装、物流、旅游、环保等相关产业的协同发展。

"地理标志具有高端品牌的许多特性，它们可对整个供应链，甚至对其他产品和服务产生影响，并以此推动商业聚集和农村融合。"❷ 地理标志产品浓厚的地域特征意味着它主要与农产品、食品和手工艺品相关，基本不涉及工业产品和服务类产品，❸ 后者的产品质量基本不受地理环境或人工技艺影响。地理标志农产

---

❶ 参见：国际贸易中心（ITC）的相关网站，http：//www.intracen.org/itc/market-info-tools/geographical-indications.

❷ 原文为：GIs possess many of the characteristics of an upmarket brand. They can have an impact on entire supply chains and even other products and services in a region and thereby foster business clustering and rural integration. Their differentiation from commodities can offer a valuable competitive advantage that is difficult to erode.
参见：国际贸易中心（ITC）的相关网站，http：//www.intracen.org/itc/market-info-tools/geographical-indications.

❸ 也有例外，如瑞士将手表以及服务等纳入地理标志保护范畴。参见：https：//www.ige.ch/en/protecting-your-ip/indications-of-source/protecting-geographical-indications/protection-in-switzerland.

品和食品的范围很广，粗略可分为种植（养殖）类初级产品和仅改变初级产品物理形态（如切片、去壳，宰杀、分割）的食品，或以初级产品为原料加工生产的食品（如干酪、葡萄酒、白酒、食醋、腐乳等）。国际上对于是否将手工艺品以及其他非农食产品纳入地理标志保护范围尚无统一做法。以商标法、反不正当竞争法或消费者权益保护法保护地理标志的国家或地区，往往未刻意限定受保护产品类别。而以制定专门法（*sui generis*）（包括法律、法令、条例等）保护地理标志的国家或地区里，有明确将非农食产品纳入的，如中国、印度、瑞士、泰国、老挝等；也有未纳入的，如欧洲联盟（European Union，EU，以下简称"欧盟"）。而欧盟内部又有 14 个成员国以商标法或反不正当竞争法保护非农食地理标志。❶

未将非农食产品纳入专门法保护范围的主要原因在于，这些产品的质量特色与产地自然环境的内在关联性难以清晰界定，而主要依赖于产地的历史和人文因素，即工艺上的历史文化传承。有观点认为，仅凭历史或人文因素来判定某一产品为地理标志产品缺乏科学依据，即，无法证明产品与产地环境的内在关联性以及产地的不可复制、不可转移性。而赞成保护工艺品等非农食产品的观点则认为，TRIPS 并未限定地理标志产品范围，第 22 条第 1 款关于地理标志的定义中"……该货物的特定质量、声誉或其他特性主要归因于其地理来源"中"质量""声誉""或"的含义是选择性的，也就是说，主要因声誉或人文因素而指向某个地理方位的产品，可以被视为地理标志产品。因此，享有市场声

---

❶ European Commission. Green Paper on the protection of geographical indications for non-agricultural products–Frequently Asked Questions [EB/OL]. (2014-07-15) [2022-03-21]. https：//ec. europa. eu/commission/presscorner/ detail/en/ MEMO_14_486.

誉、具有历史人文特征的工艺品（如云锦、湘绣）可以被纳入地理标志保护范围，无须考证其产品质量与产地自然环境的内在关联性。

近年来，越来越多的国家开始以专门法体系开展地理标志保护，[1]并且涵盖了非农食产品。欧盟内部也在研究，是否将保护范围扩大至食品和农产品以外的领域。欧盟甚至已经突破现有法律规定，在已签署的双边贸易协定中，对哥伦比亚和秘鲁两国的两种非农食产品在欧盟范围内实施了地理标志注册保护[2]。欧盟有关2014年进行的一项公共磋商的总结报告[3]中显示，欧盟内部有57.1%的人赞成扩大保护范围，反对者仅占5%，其他人无明确倾向。而且多数受访者倾向于弱化原料必须产自最终产品本地的要求，赞成更多地强调生产技艺等人文因素，而人文因素在地理标志保护传统观点里通常被视为"松散"的关联。

关于地理标志的概念和产品范围的不同认识可归纳出以下基本脉络：①地理标志是一个地方的特色产品和稀缺资源，与产地的自然因素和/或人文因素密切相关；②地理标志具有显著地域特征，应予以保护，使其免受假冒侵权；③地理标志受历史文化因素影响，传统工艺等人文因素应加以传承；④地理标志与环境因素密切相关，保护地理标志的同时应保护产地自然环境，只有这样，才能保证地理标志的质量特色不受损害，市场信誉得以维护。

鉴于地理标志保护在我国的发展历程仅有20多年，客观上

---

[1] 据欧盟统计，大约有80个国家以专门法体系开展地理标志保护。
[2] 来自哥伦比亚的Guacamayas（手工艺品）和来自秘鲁的Chulucans（陶器）。
[3] 参见：KOENIG M, et al. Summary of Results, Public Consultation on geographical indication protection for non-agricultural products in the EU.

仍属于一个发展中的新生事物。在讨论地理标志与实现可持续发展目标之间的关系之前，有必要围绕地理标志保护制度中与可持续发展理念密切相关的技术内涵进行分析，以增进读者对相关议题的认识和了解。这些技术层面的内容包括但不限于：划定产地范围、地理标志名称、质量技术要求等。需要说明的是，本书重点围绕以专门体系保护地理标志的做法展开讨论，其他法律体系（如商标法、反不正当竞争法）下的地理标志保护，因制度设计要求不同，不在本书讨论范围。

另外，鉴于本书着重探讨地理标志保护与实现可持续发展目标之间的内在联系和促进作用，有关地理标志保护在国内外的发展历史、法律制度对比以及知识产权执法实践等内容均不在本书的讨论范围。

CHAPTER 01 >> 第一章
地理标志保护的基础条件与要素分析

地理标志保护从发现具有地域特征的特色产品开始,通过产地申请、实地考察、史料查阅、市场反馈、检测分析等手段,深入了解潜在的地理标志产品,客观划定产地范围,精准制定质量技术要求,并以此建立地理标志保护的基础条件。

第一节 客观划定产地范围

客观划定产地范围是地理标志保护的先决条件,是产地主管部门对产品生产范围的官方认可。在我国,按照《地理标志产品保护规定》第9条的规定,地理标志产地划分由所在地县级以上(含县级)人民政府完成。

既然特色质量的产生与产地的自然环境和人文因素密切相关，那么首先应明确产地范围面积有多大，包括哪些村落、乡镇或县、市，具体覆盖哪些地块或水域。要完成这一任务，需调查了解产品的市场知名度、生产历史和现状，掌握产地自然环境和生产条件。实地考察可获得有关产地的第一手资料。产品名称的使用和生产历史可经由查阅史料、市场反馈和实地走访等形式完成。划定产地范围的目的，是将符合地理标志产品生产条件、使用地理标志产品名称、保留相关历史文化传承的地理范围界定出来；将达不到特色质量要求，或历史上未曾参与特定产品生产活动，未正当使用相关地理标志名称的地方排除在外，以此来保护地理标志名称，保证特色产品质量，传承生产技艺。因此，这一过程应秉持客观公正的态度，该划入保护范围的不可遗漏，该排除在保护范围以外的不应勉强，且应有充分依据。

地理标志保护十分关注产品的市场知名度。市场知名度是地理标志产品的价值体现，是消费者对带有地域特征产品的态度和回应，也是地理标志保护申请审核阶段所关注的核心内容之一。按照市场知名度和影响力，地理标志产品可被分为不同层级。层级最高的是享誉国内外市场、知名度很高的产品，如茅台、香槟、苏格兰威士忌、哥伦比亚咖啡等。层级最低的是那些市场影响力小，仅在产地及周边县域拥有某种知名度的产品。介于二者之间的，是在产地及周边地、市或本省（自治区、直辖市）范围内拥有一定知名度的产品。在我国，这类地理标志占较大比重。

能够享誉全国甚至国际市场的知名产品毕竟是少数。对于知名度不够高（如仅限于县域范围）、市场影响力小的产品，因涉及的区域和人口范围较窄，在划定产地范围时分歧或相对较少。

而对于市场知名度高、影响力较大的产品，客观划定产地范围可能面临一些困难和争议。这关系到知名产品质量特色的可持续发展，关系到产品市场信誉和消费者权益，关系到是否尊重历史和文化传承，也关系到有关生产者是否应该享受地理标志保护带来的收益。那么，如何客观划定地理标志产地范围？

首先，要尊重客观事实。地理标志既然是特定地理和人文环境下的产物，那么理应在严格遵循地理和人文环境的一致性、尊重产品名称使用和实际生产范围的基础上，客观界定产地范围。对初级产品而言，要综合考虑产地气候、土壤（或水体）、地形、地貌、海拔落差、林草覆盖率等因素；对加工产品而言，可考虑产地与初级产品产地的物理距离，或产地水质、气候（包括当地因地形、地貌造成的小气候）、环境、工艺的特殊性以及其他人文因素等产生的影响；对于一些质量特色与自然环境关联性较强，却又难以仅凭感官或环境条件判断的产品，划定产地范围时还应有实验室比对数据支持。

以"茅台酒（贵州茅台酒）"扩容为例。茅台酒于2001年3月29日获得原产地域产品保护（国家质量技术监督局公告2001年4号），界定了7.5平方公里的原产地域保护范围，即，贵州省仁怀市茅台镇内，南起茅台镇地辖的盐津河出水口的小河电站，北止茅台酒厂一车间的杨柳湾，并以杨柳湾羊叉街路上到茅遵公路段为界，东以茅遵公路至红砖厂到盐津河南端地段为界，西至赤水河以赤水河为界。之后，贵州省先后组织了政府、政协专家调研组到茅台镇多次调研、论证，确定保护以茅台酒原产地域保护区域（7.5平方公里）为主的核心生态保护区和4800多平方公里的茅台酒周边生态环境保护区规划，规划初步划定了茅台镇以南（上游）100公里，以北（下游）50公里，东西各20

公里的赤水河生态保护范围，提出了保护区域内的工业、农业发展指导方向，有效地保证了"贵州茅台酒"这一地理标志产品生产的健康发展。❶

2012年，贵州省人民政府向原国家质量监督检验检疫总局（以下简称"原国家质检总局"）提出申请，调整"茅台酒（贵州茅台酒）"地理标志保护产品名称及保护范围。从原有产地范围往南延伸，地处赤水河峡谷地带，东靠智动山、马福溪主峰，西接赤水河，南接太平村以堰塘沟界止，北接盐津河小河口与原范围相接，延伸面积约7.53平方公里，总面积共约15.03平方公里。❷ 需要说明的是，贵州茅台酒集团有限公司为做好此次调整申请工作，进行了大量研究、实验和比对工作，收集了有关产地环境和成品质量特色的原始数据，证明延伸出来的地理环境能够生产出相同品质的茅台酒（贵州茅台酒）。原国家质检总局也正是在综合上述前期工作的基础上，同意调整延伸其产地范围。

其次，要尊重历史。知名地理标志产品大都有着较为悠久的历史，历经时代和市场的检验，通过查阅史料记载，基本可获取史实依据。而关于如何判定一个产品属于历史悠久，以多长时间为准，国际上并无统一标准。欧盟法律要求，产品名称应在市场上使用30年以上。❸ 我国在《地理标志产品保护规定实施细则

---

❶ 参见：季克良2009年10月27日在地理标志产品保护实施十周年纪念会议上的发言。
❷ 参见：《质检总局关于批准调整茅台酒（贵州茅台酒）地理标志产品保护名称和保护范围的公告》（2013年第44号）。
❸ Regulation (EU) No 1151/2012 of the European Parliament and of the Council of 21 November 2012 on quality schemes for agricultural products and foodstuffs [EB/OL]. [2022-03-15]. https：//eur-lex.europa.eu/legal-content/EN/TXT/? uri=CELEX.%3A32012R1151&qid=1660293292963.

（暂行）》中未明确年限要求，仅规定"生产历史较长"（第19条）。在实际操作中，基本把握在30年以上历史，并结合生产规模和市场知名度综合考量。

最后，要妥善解决矛盾分歧。申请地理标志保护所产生的潜在经济利益，势必给产地和周边区域带来一定影响，促使有关各方争取纳入保护范围。在实践中，缺乏依据地扩大或缩小产地范围，或笼统地将某一行政区划全部纳入保护范围的情况依然存在。造成这种情况的原因包括：①地理标志申请人希望尽可能扩大产地范围，增加受益群体，提高规模效益；②邻近实际原产地的生产者有纳入保护范围的诉求，希望分享地理标志保护可能带来的收益；③划定产地范围时存在其他未尊重客观事实的问题。

关于产地范围的异议时有发生。异议通常出现在与划定的产地相邻的区域，争议的原因主要涉及三个方面：一是产地界线内外同类产品质量是否存在特色差异；二是界线之外的生产经营者也在使用同一产品名称，形成既定事实，是否应划入保护范围；三是对地理标志保护的申请人资格存在异议。无论是何种原因，举证责任均在提出异议的一方，应有事实依据佐证。异议往往涉及产品的历史渊源和时代沿革，情况可能颇为复杂，需要当事各方充分协调，审慎处理。划定产地范围的方式方法涉及一个国家或地区的行政管理模式，同时也与地理标志保护的制度设计有关。无论是国内外哪一种管理模式，划定产地范围都需要协调产地有关各方，包括生产者、经营者、行业组织、政府部门以及消费者在内的意见。必要时，还应协调与产地相邻的利益相关方意见。在欧洲，划定产地范围通常由地理标志主管部门授权委派的独立专家完成，如法国，是由法国国家原产地和质量管理局授权完成的。专家职责包括：

确定划分的客观指标（基于自然和人文因素）和原产地关联性的主要内容；

依社区或社区相关方划定地理范围或地块。

此项工作完全由专家和被指定机构完成，其间与保护组织和经营管理者保持协作关系。拟划定范围经过公开协商阶段后，向国家级专家技术委员会提交确定的原产地保护地理范围建议。

对于地理标志保护（IGP），由被指定机构分析研究产地范围计划。审核内容为：

（1）提交国家级专家技术委员会批准的产地范围是否考虑到各关联因素，是否合乎逻辑，产品与产地地理的关联性是否清晰阐述；

（2）向国家级专家技术委员会提交异议的动机。

对于原产地命名保护（AOP），产地范围划分工作完成后，由国家级专家技术委员会提名，由 INAO 指派独立专家。❶

作为欧盟成员国，法国执行欧盟统一的地理标志保护制度，将地理标志保护申请分为两大类，一类是地理标志保护，即 Protected Geographical Indication，PGI（英）/indication géographique protégée，IGP（法），这类产品不要求生产原料完全来自申请地理标志保护的原产地；另一类是原产地命名保护，即 Protected Designation of Origin，PDO（英）/appellation d'origine protégée，AOP（法），要求产品原料完全来自该产品产地，并且生产全过程，甚至包装、储存均须在该产地完成。因此，在处理产地划分时，法国根据申请保护的类别采取了不同做法。对于原产地命名保护（PDO/AOP）申请的产地划分要求更为严格，授权管理部

---

❶ INAO. Guide du demandeur d'une appellation d'origine protégée（AOP）ou d'une indication géographique protégée（IGP）. 参见：https：//www. inao. gouv. fr.

门层级更高。

在我国，申请地理标志保护的产地范围基本局限在市、县级行政区划以内，跨省、市行政区划的情形较少。《地理标志产品保护规定》第9条规定，申请保护的产品在县域范围内的，由县级人民政府提出产地范围的建议；跨县域范围的，由地市级人民政府提出产地范围的建议；跨地市范围的，由省级人民政府提出产地范围的建议。《地理标志产品保护工作细则》第10条第（二）项要求申请人提供"当地县级以上人民政府关于划定申报产品保护地域范围的公函，保护范围一般具体到乡镇一级；水产品养殖范围一般以自然水域界定"。如果出现产地划分方面的异议，《地理标志产品保护工作细则》第13条规定："……异议协调一般遵循属地原则。在异议期内如收到异议：（一）异议仅限于本省的，由国家质检总局授权有关省级质检机构进行处理，并及时反馈异议处理结果。必要时，国家质检总局可应省级质检机构的要求，听取专家意见并组织协调；（二）跨省的异议由国家质检总局负责组织协调。"按照这一规定的要求，解决产地异议问题的基本原则是交由产地所属上一级地方政府协调处理，即假如争议出现在临近的县，则应由相关的地（市）级人民政府协调解决，以此类推。这种做法鼓励有关地方政府通过协商解决意见分歧，地理标志主管部门不承担协调义务。如地方政府间无法达成一致，则该地理标志保护申请将被搁置。

涉及历史渊源和时代沿革的产地划分情况比较复杂。就我国而言，纵观历史，行政区划始终处于变化中，这给一些地理标志产品划定产地范围带来了一定困难。有两个案例可以说明。

案例1：杜康酒产地之争

相传杜康是中国古代的"酿酒始祖"，东汉《说文解字》"巾部"释："古者少康初作箕、帚、秫酒。少康，杜康也。"❶ 魏武帝曹操也曾有"何以解忧，唯有杜康"之说，说明杜康作为与酿酒相关的名称已有很长的历史。至于杜康酒的原产地，说法不一。"陕西省白水县康家卫村，传说是杜康的出生地；河南省汝阳县的杜康矶，传说是杜康酿酒处；河南省伊川县皇得地村的上皇古泉，传说是杜康汲水酿酒之地。"❷ 上述三地都宣称本地是杜康酒的原产地，其间不乏争议。而当今业界可以接受的观点是，杜康酒自20世纪70年代才重新开始恢复生产。伊川县杜康酒厂注册了"杜康"酒类商标，成为全国唯一持有"杜康"商标的酿酒企业。在之后的数十年时间里，围绕"杜康"商标的纷争可谓旷日持久，涉及河南伊川、河南汝阳和陕西白水三个产地的杜康酒企业。这期间，汝阳杜康酒厂于2001年向原国家质检总局提出"汝阳杜康酒"原产地标记（地理标志）注册申请，成为首个申请原产地标记（地理标志）注册的杜康酒企业。伊川杜康酒厂遂在公示异议期内提出异议，异议理由主要涉及所谓"杜康"商标侵权问题，认为汝阳杜康酒厂侵犯其"杜康"商标专用权。其他理由包括伊川杜康酒厂厂址就设在史料记载中杜康当年酿酒所在的古泉遗址上，伊川才是杜康酒真正的原产地，汝阳杜康酒无权申请原产地标记（地理标志）注册保护。

---

❶ 赖登燡，王久明，余乾伟，等. 白酒生产实用技术 [M]. 2版. 北京：化学工业出版社，2021：2.
❷ 张嘉涛，崔春玲，童忠东，等. 白酒生产工艺与技术 [M]. 北京：化学工业出版社，2014.

鉴于杜康酒历史久远，市场知名度较高，且"杜康"商标之争由来已久，相关部门在协调、处理异议的过程中十分慎重。通过翻阅历史资料，并与异议双方多次沟通，了解到"杜康"商标注册于20世纪80年代初，早于《中华人民共和国商标法》（以下简称《商标法》）颁布时间❶，围绕该商标注册使用的纠纷属历史遗留问题，并且"汝阳杜康"也已被注册为酒类商标。汝阳杜康酒原产地标记申请资料声称，汝阳县是古代杜康酒的原产地，所提供资料显示，汝阳杜康酒厂正是在"杜康村"改造民间酿酒作坊的基础上兴建的，且有一口古井为证。进一步了解发现，所谓汝阳杜康村和伊川古泉的地理位置均位于古代伊阳县境内，涉及现今河南省洛阳市下辖的汝阳县和伊川县。双方所提供的证明材料均有一定依据，但又过于强调自身的唯一性。因"汝阳杜康酒"申请原产地标记（地理标志）保护有事实依据，符合《原产地标记管理规定》的有关要求，其产地范围仅限于汝阳县境内。该原产地标记注册未形成对"杜康"商标专用权的侵权，故不支持伊川杜康酒厂提出的异议，批准"汝阳杜康酒"注册原产地标记（地理标志）。

案例2：东阿阿胶产地之争

这又是一个围绕地理标志产地划分的纠纷，同样发生于地理标志保护制度在我国实践之初。阿胶为著名滋补类中药，而东阿阿胶是中国知名度最高的阿胶产品。阿胶生产企业集中于山东省境内，其中规模最大、市场占有率最高的是山东东阿阿胶股份有

---

❶ 《中华人民共和国商标法》1982年8月23日第五届全国人民代表大会常务委员会第二十四次会议通过。

限公司生产的"东阿"牌东阿阿胶。❶ 东阿为地名,东阿阿胶有限公司的所在地位于山东省东阿县境内,为聊城市下辖。关于东阿阿胶原产地标记(地理标志)的纷争起源于 2001 年底。当时,位于山东省平阴县东阿镇的山东福胶集团公司率先向原国家质检总局提出"东阿阿胶"原产地标记(地理标志)注册申请。而东阿镇位于山东省平阴县,属济南市下辖。之后,山东东阿阿胶股份有限公司也提出了原产地标记(地理标志)注册申请。两个同样以"东阿"命名的县、镇,却分属于不同的上一级行政区划,这样的情形在国内并不多见。公示后不久,位于东阿县的东阿阿胶股份有限公司提出异议,认为东阿镇生产的阿胶申请"东阿阿胶"原产地标记(地理标志)注册申请侵犯了"东阿"商标专用权,且缺乏原产地事实依据。

  调查发现,东阿阿胶是具有显著地域特色的地理标志产品,生产历史距今已有上千年。但东阿镇与东阿县分属济南、聊城两个省辖市,二者不存在隶属关系,东阿镇与东阿县鱼山乡隔黄河相望。史料显示,二者历史上皆为阿胶产地。位于东阿镇的山东福胶集团还被认定为中国阿胶行业"中华老字号",其制作工艺收录在"非物质文化遗产保护名录"内。同一个特色产品,却产自不同的行政区划,而两个不同的县、镇又使用同一地名,这种情况十分罕见。进一步调查发现,历史上东阿一地的隶属关系曾发生过变化,这种变化或与流经该区域的黄河数次改道有关。而东阿县和东阿镇在历史长河中不断变迁的隶属关系,并未改变

---

❶ 《商标法》(2019 年第四次修正)第 10 条第 2 款规定:县级以上行政区划的地名或者公众知晓的外国地名,不得作为商标。但是,地名具有其他含义或者作为集体商标、证明商标组成部分的除外;已经注册的使用地名的商标继续有效。

当地劳动者使用驴皮加工生产阿胶的传统文化和工艺。这才造就了现今虽分属不同行政区划，但却生产同一特色产品的现象。原国家质检总局有关部门根据以上情况，认为上述两个产地均有权申请原产地标记（地理标志）注册，并分别批准"东阿县阿胶"和"东阿镇阿胶"注册原产地标记（地理标志）。

上述两个涉及产地纠纷的案例发生时间较早，提出异议一方均为商标持有人，争议重点也都是商标侵权问题，以及由此引发的知名产品产地纠纷。客观分析上述两个案例，它们均发生在中国加入 WTO 伊始，也是地理标志保护制度在我国具体实践的初始阶段，遵照执行的是原国家出入境检验检疫局 2001 年 3 月发布的《原产地标记管理规定》❶，其中的第 4 条第 3 款规定：

地理标志是指一个国家、地区或特定地方的地理名称，用于指示一项产品来源于该地，且该产品的质量特征完全或主要取决于该地的地理环境、自然条件、人文背景等因素。

这一定义参照了 TRIPS 第 22 条关于地理标志的定义，这也是我国首次在规范性文件中明确"地理标志"的概念。鉴于当时相关部门对地理标志的研究起步不久，《原产地标记管理规定》在诸如地理标志名称、申请人资格、产地划分等具体事项的规定上存在一定欠缺，主管部门对于地理标志与原产地命名、商标以及通用名称之间的关系也存在某种认识上的不足。尽管如此，相关部门在地理标志产地划分上采取了尊重历史和客观事实的态度，对地理标志与商标之间关系的把握符合地理标志保护制度的要求。

---

❶ 另一部有关地理标志的部门规章是原国家质量技术监督局 1999 年发布的《原产地域产品保护规定》，原国家质量监督检验检疫总局于 2005 年在原有两个部门规章的基础上制定发布了《地理标志产品保护规定》。

以申请人资格为例，由于白酒等加工产品生产模式的特殊性，上述两个案例均由单一生产企业提出，这对于地理标志保护申请而言应属于特例，而非一般情形。事实上，基于历史的原因，我国围绕加工食品产地的纠纷主要集中在商标专用权上，商标持有人往往以在先注册的含有地名的商标为由，试图独占某一地域范围的名称专用权。这在很多情况下有失公允，不符合客观实际。《地理标志产品保护规定》发布实施后，对申请人资格进行了修正，以产地地方政府和行业组织为主，特殊情况下允许企业申请。❶ 这一原则既符合我国实际，也与国外做法基本一致。例如，欧盟对单一企业申请地理标志保护的规定为：

单一生产者申请地理标志应满足一定条件。如果当地情况无法造就一批生产者，单一生产者不应受到牵连。但应明确说明，即使受保护的名称由单一生产者名称组成或包含其名称，其他生产者只要在划定的产地范围之内，并且符合产品的质量技术要求，均可使用受保护的地理标志名称。❷

以上两个案例说明，划定地理标志产地范围不仅仅需要确认生产环境条件和生产工艺，还要综合考虑当地历史、地理和产品的历史沿革。要充分尊重当地历史文化遗存，聚焦地理标志保护

---

❶ 《地理标志产品保护规定》第8条规定：地理标志产品保护申请，由当地县级以上人民政府指定的地理标志产品保护申请机构或人民政府认定的协会和企业（以下简称申请人）提出，并征求相关部门意见。

❷ Commission Delegated Regulation (EU) 2019/33 of 17 October 2018 supplementing-regulation (EU) No 1308/2013 of the European Parliament and of the Council as regardsapplications for protection of designations of origin, geographical indications and traditionalterms in the wine sector, the objection procedure, restrictions of use, amendments to product/specifications, cancellation of protection, and labelling and presentation [EB/OL]. (2019-01-14) [2022-01-05]. https://eur-lex.europa.eu/legal-content/EN/TXT/?uri=CELEX%3A02019RO033-20190114.

重点，梳理历史文化传承要素，合理利用当地自然禀赋，落实可持续发展理念。

第二节 维护地理标志名称的市场价值

我们知道，地理标志保护制度属知识产权保护范畴，所保护的首先是地理标志的名称，地理标志产地之外的任何人不得侵权使用受保护的地理标志名称。地理标志名称属于显著性标志（sign distinctive）。消费者看到地理标志产品时，自然将产品及产地与某一特色品质相关联，从而其消费意愿受到影响。从市场反应来看，拥有较高知名度、受到市场追捧的产品，在广受欢迎的同时，更有可能成为假冒侵权的对象。前文提到，相邻但分属不同行政区划的土地（水域）上可能生产出质量特色相同或相似的产品，且产品在市场上均以同一名称出现。在这种情况下，产地划分可打破行政区划的界限。正是产品已经建立起的市场美誉度决定了产品名称的趋同性，并且这种趋同性不会因行政区划的改变而发生变化。换句话讲，什么名称能叫得响，在市场上受欢迎，生产经营者便会主动使用，有人试图假冒的也一定是畅销品牌的名称而非其他。

既然地理标志名称的知名度是在市场上建立起来的，这种良好的声誉就一定是生产经营者和消费者口口相传，逐渐形成并广为传播的。产地地名成为特色产品的标志性符号，生产和经营者主动将产品和产地结合在一起，力图使消费者将产地与特色质量联系起来，提高其购买意愿。与注册商标等私权利的不同之处在于，地理标志产地生产者使用地名称谓完全是一种市场环境下的自发行为，并不需要事先注册登记。地理标志产品由产地符合条件的企业、组织或个人共同生产，使用同一个地理标志名称对外销售，地理标志的知名度由产地内不同属性的生产者共同分享。

从本质上讲，地理标志的知名度不是产地生产经营者策划和宣传出来的，而是在长期的市场交易过程中逐渐形成的。在某种程度上，一方面，产地生产者只是继承了前人的技艺，沿用了前人一直使用的产品名称，沿着前人走过的路走下去。另一方面，地理标志产地的自然环境往往不可复制、不可移动。无论时代如何变迁，只要产地环境不发生实质性改变，生产技艺延绵不断，地理标志产品就会"生于斯，长于斯"，是大自然和先辈赋予当地百姓的"厚礼"。所以，就地理标志产品生产而言，传承的成分或大于创新。

国际上对于地理标志与创新之间的关系存在一定争议。Stéphane Fournier 等（2016）引用 van Caenegem（2003）的观点，认为地理标志由于可能引发"创新上的刹车"，对生产系统的适应能力产生负面影响。按照 Bowen & De Master（2011）的说法，地理标志甚至可能导致"生产博物馆"现象。Stéphane Fournier 等（2016）同时引述了另一相反观点，认为地理标志保护实施中的创新过程具有积极影响，称"地理标志有时被特别用来引入和发展当地创新活动。"❶

---

❶ FOURNIER S, VANDECANDELAERE E, TEYSSIER C, et al. Geographical Indications: what institutional innovations for territorial construction of technical innovations? [EB/OL].（2016-12-31）[2021-10-10]. https://www.researchgate.net/publication/334315727_Geographical_Indications_what_institutional_innovations_for_territorial_construction_of_technical_innovations.

笔者认为，强调传承对于地理标志发展的重要性，并不意味着否认创新与变革。事实上，地理标志生产大都遵循了传承与创新相结合的道路，在尊重传统、传承延续的基础上，结合现代农业、食品工业等管理体系和创新技术要求，开展地理标志产品生产。在农业领域，一些地理标志产地积极采用先进农业技术和管理手段，淘汰过时的管理方法和技术要求。在食品加工领域，引入危害分析及关键控制点（HACCP）等国际通行的质量管理体系，在保证地理标志产品品质特色的前提下，结合实际调整技术手段。综合评价，地理标志的创新形式更多地体现在组织结构、质量管理体系和市场营销能力的提高上。成立合作组织、执行统一的生产标准、加强过程监管、提高对外议价能力等，都是地理标志在创新发展方面的体现。[1]

本节简述了地理标志名称的重要性，以及传承与发展之间的关系。下面围绕地理标志名称，再着重讨论以下几个问题。

1. 主观造名的问题

国内普遍存在这样一种现象，申请地理标志保护首先要为产品定个好名字。为此，产地政府部门和生产企业不厌其烦，反复研究申报产品的名称、叫法。而最后"研究"出来的名字，往往是以所在行政区划中层级较高的一个冠名，以为只有这样才能体现出是产自某省或某市的产品，才能使消费者将特色产品与产地联系在一起。殊不知，这样做其实犯了不尊重事实、不了解市

---

[1] FOURNIER S, VANDECANDELAERE E, TEYSSIER C, et al. Geographical Indications: what institutional innovations for territorial construction of technical innovations? [EB/OL]. (2016-12-31) [2021-10-10]. https://www.researchgate.net/publication/334315727_Geographical_Indications_what_institutional_innovations_for_territorial_construction_of_technical_innovations.

场、违背市场规律、扭曲地理标志含义的错误。地理标志名称，是市场上广为流传、消费者普遍认可的产物，不是专家学者或政府官员、企业家评议研究的结果。在时间上，先有地理标志名称的市场知名度，后有地理标志保护申请，切不可本末倒置。尽管许多地理标志的确以所在的县或市命名，但并不绝对，存在很多例外情况。总体来讲，名字好不好听，有没有包含所在省、市、县地名，与地理标志的市场美誉度没有必然联系。至于消费者是否能清楚地认知产地来源，也主要看产品的知名度和美誉度。地理标志产品之所以拥有知名度和美誉度，是因为在消费者心目中留下的长期印象和美好联想，是市场的力量和品牌的价值。任何不顾客观事实，主观起名字的行为都与地理标志保护制度背道而驰，也偏离了品牌建设的方向。

2. 地理标志名称使用与申请保护之间的关系

有人认为，只有经主管部门批准，才能使用地理标志名称。这是对地理标志的另一种误解。地理标志是一种客观存在，地理标志名称是长期在市场上积蓄起来的声誉和形象。而地理标志保护则是运用法律手段对地理标志实施的知识产权保护制度，属法律认定或行政确认的范畴。换言之，无论是否申请地理标志保护，地理标志产品都是一种客观存在，地理标志名称都可在市场上使用，无须得到官方批准。事实上，地理标志保护符合性审查的条件之一，是所申请的产品名称是否已在市场上广泛使用。生产经营者不主动使用地理标志名称，意味着该名称知名度较小，或者生产经营者缺乏品牌意识。而仅就产品名称使用来看，获得地理标志保护后的区别在于，产地需进一步规范地理标志名称的使用，并经主管部门核准，在产品上施加地理标志保护专用标志。

3. 名称"大"与名称"小"的问题

有人认为，要想地理标志产品叫得响，就应该起个"大一点"的名字，产品要以地、市甚至省（自治区、直辖市）名来冠名，只有这样才能体现出产品的代表性和包容性，村落、乡镇地名不宜作为地理标志产品名称。这同样是对地理标志保护制度的曲解。地理标志名称没有大小之分，只有知名度上的差异，没有"好"与"坏"的区别，只有市场受欢迎程度上的差距。

首先，产品名称里的地名"小"不等于产品知名度小。举例来讲，"龙井"仅是一村落名，但丝毫不影响"龙井茶"的美誉度，而龙井茶所代表的也并不仅仅是龙井村范围内生产的茶叶，而是经官方认可，包括了三个茶叶产区的地理标志产品名称。同样道理，茅台镇属贵州省遵义市仁怀县，但茅台早已成为享誉世界的中国第一白酒品牌，其名称背后所蕴含的恰恰是茅台酒（贵州茅台酒）产地独特的自然环境和历史人文因素，具有巨大的无形资产价值。可以预见的是，无论时代如何发展，茅台酒（贵州茅台酒）这一名称都不会改变。

其次，产品名称里的地名"大"也并不代表名下所包含的地理范围和名称所指向的地理范围完全一致。比如，"波尔多"（Bordeaux）酒地理标志保护范围并不是法国整个波尔多大区，而是波尔多大区内特定的地理范围。❶ 陕西苹果地理标志保护范围并非陕西全省，而以渭北黄土高原苹果优生区为主。之所以产生这种情况，归根结底还是市场的力量。上述产品名称的出现，

---

❶ 参见：《国家质量监督检验检疫总局关于受理"波尔多"（Bordeaux）附属产区申请地理标志保护的公告》（2015 年第 71 号）。

是在商品交易过程中约定俗成的现象，是市场上"喊出来"的结果。当然，在地理标志保护实践中，类似这种指向一省甚至一国的"大名称"有时也会给生产者和消费者造成一定困惑。例如，洛川县位于陕西苹果地理标志保护❶范围内，属于陕西苹果的核心产区。因知名度高，洛川当地人更愿意称自己的苹果为"洛川苹果"。再比如，宁夏枸杞地理标志保护❷范围为银川平原和卫宁灌区，这其中就包括了中宁县全境。中宁县是宁夏枸杞的核心产区，其产量约占宁夏枸杞总产量的1/4，质量最优。业界由此习惯于将中宁生产的枸杞称为"中宁枸杞"。中宁枸杞在宁夏知名度很高，在其他省、区、市也享有一定知名度。

以上两个事例是地理标志保护中存在的大产区与小产区（核心产区）的关系问题。农业生产受地理、气候等因素影响，当产地范围较大，覆盖多个市、县时，地理环境以及小气候的差异可能对产品质量产生一定影响。这一点很容易理解。但问题是，如果产品质量存在某种差异，是否就应该再细分为几个不同的地理标志产品，分别申请地理标志保护。回答这个问题，还是要回归到地理标志的知名度上来。到底是哪个名称在市场流通中普遍使用？普遍使用的名称是否能够涵盖产地全部同类产品？前文讨论过地理标志产品名称大小与指代不一致的现象，旨在强调不能违背市场规律，凭主观认识造名。陕西苹果和宁夏枸杞的情况与前文事例不尽相同。之所以"陕西苹果"和"宁夏枸杞"地理标志保护申请能够获得支持，主要由于陕西苹果在国内知名度较

---

❶ 关于陕西苹果地理标志产品保护公告参见：《国家质量监督检验检疫总局公告》（2003年第91号）。
❷ 关于宁夏枸杞地理标志产品保护公告参见：《国家质量监督检验检疫总局公告》（2004年第54号）。

高,"好枸杞出宁夏"也得到了消费者普遍认同的市场现象。洛川苹果与中宁枸杞的地位分别是陕西苹果和宁夏枸杞的核心产区,是陕西苹果和宁夏枸杞的上乘代表。二者相互依存,共同发展。任何关于地理标志名称的修订或改变都应得到产地生产者广泛认可,并与区域品牌战略协调一致。

客观分析,类似这种大产区中包含核心产区的情况并非罕见,在保护大产区名称的同时,核心产区生产经营者往往更倾向于使用其原有名称,这也符合一般市场规律。至于是否有必要再申请对核心产区的地理标志保护,应由产地生产经营者和管理部门决定。只要符合地理标志保护的规则要求,且经行业和主管部门协调同意,就可以提出相关保护申请。但应处理好二者之间的关系,实现大产区与核心产区之间的协调发展,共同维护和提高地理标志产品的质量特色和市场知名度。一是应制订覆盖大产区和核心产区的统一规划和管理措施;二是核心产区应制定更高标准的管理规范,突出其品质特色;三是应协调二者的营销策略,研究细分市场。

4. "一品多名"的情形

尊重历史和客观事实是地理标志保护的基本要求,这其中包括对产品名称使用历史的尊重。某些产品在历史沿革中形成了两个或两个以上的名称,即"一品多名"的现象。这样的例子很多,如茅台酒(贵州茅台酒)、大方豆干(大方手撕豆腐)、嘉黎牦牛(娘亚牦牛)、宝应荷藕(宝应莲藕)、黄山贡菊(徽州贡菊)、方城丹参(裕丹参)、凤县大红袍花椒(凤椒)等。"一品多名"现象一方面折射出市场流通过程中业者对于知名产品的习惯称谓,另一方面与当地民族语言或方言有关。例如,嘉黎牦牛又名娘亚牦牛,是西藏自治区嘉黎县的土生牦牛畜种,也是国家地理标志保护产品。"娘亚"是当地藏语方言称呼的汉语音译。因上述两个名称都具有一定的市场影响力，故两个名称都属于地理标志保护名称。

5. 名称含有方言俗语或传统译名的情形

有些特色产品在市场流通中所使用的名称并不是规范用语，或夹带了方言，或使用了十分口语化的说法，例如，狗不理包子。本着尊重地理标志历史、尊重市场知名度的原则，原则上应允许地理标志产品名称使用方言或含有方言词汇，但目前在我国的地理标志保护规定中尚未提及这方面内容。在国外做法中，法国INAO在《受保护的原产地命名和受保护的地理标志操作指南》中指出，只要能证明产品名称的使用具有一定历史，地理标志名称就可以使用方言，但应同时提供方言的规范法语翻译。❶

还有一种情况是，有些产品不仅历史悠久，而且海外市场开发较早，外销产品当初的译名或与产地方言发音有关，或使用了所处时代的拼音方式，如，茅台酒（贵州茅台酒）（Kweichow Moutai Chiew）、正山小种茶（Lapsang Souchong）。这些地理标志产品往往历经时代变迁而经久不衰，深得海内外市场拥簇。本着尊重历史、尊重消费者权益的原则，相关地理标志产品的译名应延续原有拼写方式，不作任何更改，以免给消费者造成误解，给产地生产者额外增加市场运行成本。

6. 通用名称问题

讨论地理标志保护，就有必要说明地理标志与通用名称之

---

❶ INAO. Guide du demandeur d'une appellation d'origine protégée（AOP）ou d'une indication géographique protégée（IGP）. 参见：https：//www.inao.gouv.fr/.

间的关系。地理标志与含有地名的通用名称都是含有地名或以地名命名的产品名称，区别在于，通用名称中所包含的地名已经失去了地理指向功能，而仅被作为一个动植物品种或特定工艺类型存在于市场。之所以沦为通用名称，是原本具有地理指向功能的产品或被列入国家动植物品种名录或药典，或被视为一种工艺类型，被迁移至原产地以外多个产地生产，导致名称中的地名逐渐失去了地理指向功能，成为一个品种或生产工艺的代名词。这样的事例很多，如藏红花、武昌鱼、约克夏猪等。藏红花，又名西红花（saffron），原产于西亚，后经青藏高原传入中原地区。虽然从中文名称上看与西藏有关，但现实中，藏红花这一名称已被列入《中华人民共和国药典》，成为中国药品通用名称（China Approved Drug Names，CADN），且近年来已在上海、浙江等多地栽培种植，使得"藏红花"这一名称在很大程度上丧失了产地指向的功能。因此，当西藏自治区行业组织申请藏红花地理标志保护时，不得不以"西藏藏红花"的名义申请，因为只有这样才能与"藏红花"这一通用产品名称区分开来。

地理标志与通用名称之间的矛盾和冲突在国际上由来已久，而且是世界贸易组织知识产权理事会（WTO/TRIPS Council）关于地理标志的多边谈判中涉及的主要争议之一，影响到国际贸易和相关国家利益。鉴于它与本书主题无甚关联，故不展开讨论。而就地理标志保护而言，一个基本原则是，通用名称不能申请地理标志保护。

7. 名称使用不规范的问题

按照正常逻辑，既然地理标志享有市场知名度，生产经营者会主动使用地理标志名称。但当我们走进市场，试图寻找货架上的地理标志产品时,时常发现一种奇怪现象。在一些带有地理标志保护产品标识的包装上,最醒目的不是地理标志名称,而是一些通用产品名称,如黑木耳、腐竹、金针菇等。

这种现象给消费者传递的信息十分模糊。除了表明包装内容物以外,产品名称没有指向任何产地,没有将产品与质量特色挂钩,消费者仅凭"打量"难以产生与产地和质量相关的联想,难以进行消费选择和判断。这种情况,说明存在以下几种可能:一是该地理标志产品知名度不高,生产经营者没有使用地理标志名称的意识;二是地理标志保护监管不到位,生产经营者没有规范使用地理标志名称;三是生产经营者对地理标志保护缺乏认识,没有意识到地理标志名称的重要性;四是生产和经营脱节,经营者不了解地理标志内涵,未正确标示地理标志名称。从问题表现来看,以上情况大都属于监管上的问题。但从主观认识上分析,第一种和第三种情况虽然表现相仿,原因却不尽相同。其中第一种现象可以被视作地理标志保护的"软肋",是对缺乏知名度、市场表现低迷的地理标志产品的变相否定。这一方面说明,要打开地理标志产品市场销路,生产经营者还有很多"功课"要做,任重而道远;另一方面,也反映出相关地理标志保护申请的基础条件较弱,尚不足以扛起地理标志这杆大旗;提醒地理标志主管部门有必要进一步严格地理标志保护审批尺度,并研究逐步建立地理标志保护的退出机制。

第三节　科学制定质量技术要求

具有地域特色的产品是一方水土的产物，当地生产者往往凭借多年的生产经验，综合气候、水土等自然条件，拥有一套传承下来的"管用"的生产技术（know-how）。只不过这种凭经验产生的方法，由于缺乏系统性的归纳梳理和制度设计，往往属于个人体验，缺乏协调和统一。即便是同一村落的百姓，也有各自的"绝招"，难以实现"共享"。如何实现经济效益最大化，用好有限的自然资源，发挥好特色工艺的作用，发展好特色产业，是地理标志保护制度关注和要解决的问题。

首先需要明确的是，第一节和第二节所讨论的内容均为质量技术要求的组成部分。除此之外，还应研究确立地理标志产品的生产条件，着手制订并实施地理标志产品的质量技术要求。

"质量技术要求"是我国的称谓，欧盟和瑞士使用 specifications（规范）一词，还有的国家使用 code of practice（CoP）（操作规程）或 code of conduct（CoC）（行业规则）。这些说法不一，但内容相仿，都是指导地理标志产地生产者规范开展生产活动的"行为指南"，是对地理标志产地条件和生产方法的梳理和归纳，是保证地理标志产品质量特色必不可少的工作环节。不仅于此，艾米丽·凡德肯德莱尔（Emilie Vandecandelaere）等（2018）认为："它是保证农民和生产者获得较好回报的关键工具，它明确了生产者在提供独特的自然和人工资源时各自的作用，使地理标志价值链向源头生产者倾斜，进而使生产者对地理标志产品拥有议价权和广泛的管理权。"[1]

制订质量技术要求是观察学习、分析研究、归纳总结、组织实施的过程。所谓"观察学习",就是要首先了解特色产品原产地的自然条件和生产过程,了解产地生产者的传统技艺和特殊做法,从中发现生产要素和特色手段。所谓"分析研究",是要在观察学习的基础上,研究产品的质量特色,以及特色产生的原因,分析到底是哪些因素对产品的特色质量产生了有利影响。所谓"归纳总结",就是在发现的基础上,充分吸纳当地的传统知识,梳理出产品质量特色,将生产工艺的关键要素固化下来,结合标准化生产和质量管理体系,上升为全体生产者必须遵循的生产技术规范。所谓"组织实施",目的在于把已制订完成的质量技术要求普及推广给产地全体生产者,并在操作过程中跟踪辅导,督促检查。

上述过程是实施地理标志保护的典型做法。值得一提的是,在地理标志保护实践中,产地生产者在质量技术要求制订完成后,还可能整理编写出一份手册。这种手册并不是一般意义上的标准或生产技术规程,而是以简明扼要、通俗易懂的形式,将质量技术要求的内容与执行标准或生产技术规程相结合,使之成为生产者人手一份的"操作指南"。它更接地气,也更容易被当地生产者所掌握。再辅以组织培训,有利于达到维护和提高特色产品质量的目的。

质量技术要求的制订过程必须建立在对产品生产和产地环境

---

[1] VANDECANDELAERE E, TEYSSIER C, BARJOLLE D, et al. Strengthening sustainable food systems through geographical indications: an analysis of economic impacts [M/OL]. Rome: FAO, 2018 [2021-09-08]. https://www.researchgate.net/publication/334191901.

充分了解的基础上，要在保证产品质量特色的同时，最大限度保护好产地环境这一生产条件。"包含地理标志的农产品和食品须满足质量技术要求中设定的条件，如旨在保护自然资源或产地环境或改善饲养动物生长条件的要求。"（欧盟条例第1151/2012号）

　　这与制定产品通用标准或生产技术规程存在一定区别。所谓"充分了解"，是指对产品质量特色、生产工艺、历史沿革、知名度、消费者认知等全方位的认识，从中抓取最具质量特色的特征性指标，分析影响产品质量特色形成的关键工艺，研究传承传统工艺的必要性和可行性。可想而知，这项工作需要投入大量时间和精力才能完成。

1. 如何描述地理标志产品的质量特色？

　　什么是地理标志产品的质量特色？地理标志产品属于消费品范畴，是人们日常生活中接触到的商品。地理标志产品的质量特色体现在其外观和内在品质上。关于描述一个地理标志产品，最普遍、最常用的方法是感官描述，也就是从外观、形状、尺寸、色泽、气味、口感、质地等看得见、摸得着、闻得见等方面进行描述。诚然，地理标志产品的质量特色还需通过理化分析得出量化指标，提供质量特色的科学依据。但从逻辑上讲，地理标志产品之所以能在市场上占有一席之地，主要依赖于消费者对产品特色质量的认同，是通过眼看、手摸、耳闻、品尝等方式得出的消费体验。普通消费者购买时并不会进行仪器检测，而主要凭消费经验和感官认知产生购买意愿。所以，感官描述才是展现地理标志产品的主要方法。实验室分析的目的是提供科学数据支撑，但现实中并不是所有特色指标都能够通过仪器分析得出明确结论依据。

　　关于如何描述一个地理标志产品，比较典型的例子是茶叶。

我们知道，不同类型的茶叶（绿茶、红茶、黑茶等）仅从外观便可分辨。以绿茶为例，再细分下去，市场知名度高、消费者耳熟能详的绿茶包括龙井茶、信阳毛尖、黄山毛峰、六安瓜片、太平猴魁、都匀毛尖、蒲江雀舌等。爱茶之人一眼便可看出其中的差异，原因在于以上几种绿茶特色鲜明、性状各异。当然，想要真正体验茶的滋味，鉴定茶的等级，还需亲口品鉴。以蒲江雀舌为例，其感官描述为：芽头匀整，外形扁平挺直，形似鸟雀之舌，色泽绿润；香气清香高长，汤色黄绿明亮，滋味醇厚鲜爽，叶底嫩绿匀整。❶ 其他茶叶品类的描述方法与此相近。再以六堡茶为例，其感官描述为：外形条索紧结、色泽黑褐，有光泽，汤色红浓明亮，香气纯陈，滋味浓醇甘爽，显槟榔香味，叶底红褐或黑褐色，简而言之具有"红、浓、醇、陈"等特点。❷ 可见，品茶、购茶的过程调动了口、眼、鼻等多个感官，对于说明如何正确描述地理标志产品具有一定代表性。

2. 如何描述产品的生产配方和工艺？

地理标志产品与产地环境存在的内在关联也体现在生产配方和工艺要求上。这方面根据产品的不同千差万别，不一而足。初级产品的生产不存在配方问题，生产工艺主要体现在动植物品种选育、种养殖密度、水肥管理、收获时间等生产技术规程管理的特殊方面。加工产品的情况比较复杂，但主要关注点都在于对原料的成分、来源地、动植物品种、规格等方面的特殊要求，以及有别于同类产品生产的特殊技术流程。所谓特殊技术规程，主要体现在是否全部或部分采用手工，是否沿用传统工具、机械、容

---

❶ 参见：《国家质量监督检验检疫总局公告》（2008 年第 119 号）。
❷ 参见：《国家质量监督检验检疫总局公告》（2011 年第 33 号）。

器，是否对生产时间、季节、时长、周期有限定性要求等。

艾米丽·凡德肯德莱尔等（2018）使用defensive（防守型）和offensive（进攻型）将地理标志产品的生产工艺划分为两类：一类是已经具有较高知名度的产品，这类产品的生产工艺描述遵循如实对现有生产工艺归纳总结的原则，强调传承和延续，目的是保护传统工艺，防止假冒侵权；另一类是知名度较低，甚至还没有知名度的产品，制订质量技术要求相当于规范、统一生产工艺，优化生产方式方法，提高产品总体质量和管理水平。❶

3. 质量技术要求与标准的关系

地理标志保护离不开质量技术要求，它是规定地理标志生产条件的核心。按照我国现有专门保护体系要求，对于获得地理标志保护的产品，产地还须制定和完善地理标志产品的标准体系，以完善地理标志保护体系建设，提高地理标志保护的执法效力。

根据《中华人民共和国标准化法》，标准的制修订分为五个层级，即国家标准、行业标准、地方标准、团体标准和企业标准。地理标志产品标准属于地方标准范畴，由省级标准化行政主管部门负责制定。地理标志产品申报单位可在获批后与本省（自治区、直辖市）地理标志主管部门商讨地方标准制修订事宜。对比国外地理标志保护情况，制定地方标准这一要求是我国地理标志产品保护的特点之一，目的是强化地理标志产地的质量监管，保证产品品质特色不发生改变。国外的做法不尽相同，欧盟以发

---

❶ VANDECANDELAERE E, TEYSSIER C, BARJOLLE D, et al. Strengthening sustainable food systems through geograhical indications：an analysis of economic impacts［M/OL］. Rome：FAO, 2018［2021-09-08］. https：//www.researchgate.net/publication/334191901.

布官方公告的形式发布地理标志注册保护的 specifications（质量技术要求），作为地理标志保护的技术法规，具有法律约束力。

第四节　典型问题探讨

以上讨论了涉及质量技术要求的注意事项。下面再结合地理标志保护申报，探讨几个相关问题。

1. 如何理解产品的历史沿革？

首先要消除一个误解。地理标志产品的历史沿革重点关注的并不是一个产品在产地生产的历史，而是地理标志名称的由来以及存在的时间跨度。关于这一点，乍听起来有些费解。产品的生产历史和产品名称使用的历史有什么区别？答案是，虽然所有产品都有开始生产的时间、地点，但生产出的东西原本和地名并无关联，而是与其通用名称（如茶叶、苹果、葡萄酒）相关联。其中，一些产品因为具有质量特色，有别于同类产品，在市场上获得好评后，才促使消费者将这一特色产品与产地联系在一起，也才使得生产者和商家主动使用包含特定产地的名称，以满足消费者的潜在需求，这便是地理标志名称的由来。因此，描述一个地理标志产品的历史沿革，需重点介绍地理标志名称的由来和演变过程，以此说明产品的市场美誉度和历史渊源。

2. 如何理解产品的知名度？

同样道理，地理标志的知名度指的是产品名称的知名度。地理标志保护的主要目的之一是防止假冒、侵权使用地理标志名称。因此，人们关注的是地理标志名称的市场表现和在消费者心目中的形象。所谓产品的知名度指的也正是地理标志名称所带来的美誉度。举例来说，海南美食有"三宝"：文昌鸡、加积鸭、和乐蟹。这三个带有地名的产品之所以在海南省家喻户晓，是长期存在于市场上的商业现象，是上述三个地方特殊的自然环境和人文因素成就了带有明显地域特征的产品，受到广大消费者欢迎。再深入解析，消费者不会将"文昌鸡"这一名称拆分为"文昌的鸡"或"文昌市的鸡"，"文昌鸡"这三个字在市场上、在消费者心目中已经密不可分，这就是地理标志名称的市场价值。再比如："太平猴魁"这四个字乍一看与地理标志并无关联，但在业界却是名茶。这一名称历史悠久，地理方位既指向安徽省太平县，也指向主产区——新明乡三门村的猴坑、猴岗，同时还包括茶的品质位于尖茶的魁首，以及首创人名叫魁成等多重含义。"太平猴魁"这一名称自清光绪年间至今从未改变，本身体现着厚重的传统文化底蕴，也见证了这一名茶历经起伏、至今仍广受好评的历史。实践中，判断一个地理标志名称是否知名，最简单的方法就是看其在市场上的习惯性称谓。被人们广泛使用、通常以地名命名或含有地名且与产品通用名称密不可分的便是有知名度的地理标志，如：茅台、龙井、信阳毛尖、苏绣、蜀锦等。反之，如果人们仍习惯于将地名与产品通用名称分开来说，如：××产的芒果、××的米酒，则说明该产品的知名度不够高，甚至没有知名度。

当然，在强调产品既有声誉重要性的同时，也应看到申请地理标志保护行为本身具有提高产品知名度的作用。有些地理标志虽然知名度小，但因具有一定质量特色且产地划分清晰，也基本符合地理标志保护的要求。艾米丽·凡德肯德莱尔等人通过实例证明，"那些缺少知名度的产品，通过地理标志注册可创造其知

名度"。❶

这方面也有一些成功案例。在我国的地理标志保护产品中,有一部分产品在组织申报时,知名度并不高,仅限于当地及周边县市,通过地理标志保护,提高了产品的市场知名度,取得较好的经济及社会效益。有关案例将在后续章节中有所反映。

3. 如何设定质量指标?

之所以提出该问题,在于确有产地技术人员在制订质量技术要求的过程中不够严谨,超出当地实际生产能力和条件设定产品的质量指标,追求所谓的"高质量"或同类产品之最。而按照地理标志保护制度的要求,产品质量指标一旦设定,不可随意变更,必须遵照执行。这也是监管部门针对地理标志保护产品质量特色的主要执法依据。因此,制订质量技术要求时切不可一味追求高指标,而应实事求是,重点突出特色指标。即使特色指标不够显著,也切忌盲目夸大,使得日后无法达到质量要求。

产生这一问题的主要原因是产地技术人员对地理标志保护制度理解不足,对产品的总体质量水平了解不够,或者简单地把申请地理标志保护混同于评优活动,以为只有选取最佳指标才能代表其产品质量水平。殊不知,这样做使得产地多数产品无法达到设定指标要求,相当于生产出的基本都是不合格产品。这既有损自身市场信誉,又侵犯消费者权益,给日后监管造成困难。

---

❶ VANDECANDELAERE E, TEYSSIER C, BARJOLLE D, et al. Strengthening sustainable food systems through geographical indications: an analysis of economic impacts [M/OL]. Rome:FAO, 2018 [2021-05-10]. https://www.researchgate.net/publication/334191901.

设定地理标志产品的质量指标相当于为地理标志设置"门槛",门槛过高会使得产地生产者难以达标,过低则会失去保护意义。因此,产地须组织专家和技术人员全面了解产品质量水平。由于地理标志产地往往涉及多个行政区划的各类生产经营者(利益相关方),参与制订质量技术要求的技术人员应体现出一定代表性,而且不应是少数专家意见,不可仅凭"拍脑门"式的一言堂来简单归纳产品的质量特色及指标参数。这就意味着,设定质量指标绝不是一朝一夕的功夫,需花费大量时间和精力,对照相关区域内检测结果反复讨论,得出具有代表性、能够涵盖受保护范围内所有地理标志产品的指标数据。

4. 哪些产品不宜申请地理标志保护?

这里谈的是地理标志保护制度的适用性问题。前文用较大篇幅分析了地理标志名称的知名度,目的是强调产品知名度的重要性。而那些知名度不高,比如仅在乡镇范围内为人所知的产品,原则上不具备地理标志保护的条件。因为这类产品即使符合地理标志保护关于质量特色的要求,但后续宣传成本高,综合投入大,很难以地理标志保护在较短时间内提高市场知名度和占有率,难以获得地理标志保护可能带来的收益。另外一个需考虑的因素是生产规模,规模过小,仅限于作坊式生产经营的产品不宜申请地理标志保护。地理标志保护制度虽然能有效提升产品的质量效益,但前提是应具备一定的基础条件,具有一定的生产规模,产地范围内的生产者有较广泛的生产经验,而且具备支持后续监管和市场营销的政策和手段。尽管前文提及,缺乏知名度的产品可以通过地理标志保护提高知名度,但"投资和财力同样也是一个地理标志经济发展的关键因素"。❶ 规模过小、缺少政策和资金支持的产品,往往难以达到地理标志保护的预期目的。这类产品可归入"培育"范畴,待条件成熟后再进行申报。

5. 地理标志与非物质文化遗产之间的关系

联合国教育、科学及文化组织(以下简称"联合国教科文组织",UNESCO)于2003年10月通过了《保护非物质文化遗产公约》,该公约第2条第1款对非物质文化遗产的定义是:"被各群体、团体、有时为个人视为其文化遗产的各种实践、表演、表现形式、知识和技能及其有关的工具、实物、工艺品和文化场所。各个群体和团体随着其所处环境、与自然界的相互关系和历史条件的变化不断使这种代代相传的非物质文化遗产得到创新,同时使他们自己具有一种认同感和历史感,从而促进了文化多样性和人类的创造力。"该公约第2条第2款进一步明确了非物质文化遗产的具体范围,即:

(a)口头传说和表述,包括作为非物质文化遗产媒介的语言;

(b)表演艺术;

(c)社会风俗、礼仪和节庆;

(d)有关自然界和宇宙的知识和实践;

(e)传统的手工艺技能。

定义中虽然提到器具、物品和手工艺品,但强调的是与技能

---

❶ VANDECANDELAERE E, TEYSSIER C, BARJOLLE D, et al. Strengthening sustainable food systems through geographical indications: an analysis of economic impacts [M/OL]. Rome: FAO, 2018 [2021-05-10]. https://www.researchgate.net/publication/334191901.

等因素相关联。第 2 条第 2 款进一步明确了保护范围,不涉及任何实物。由此可见,非物质文化遗产强调的是对传统技艺和文化活动等无形资产的保护,这与地理标志保护的内涵既有关联,又有显著区别。从逻辑关系上讲,非物质文化遗产所代表的传统技艺和文化内涵是成就许多地理标志产品的关键人文因素,地理标志产品则是这些非物质文化遗产的物质成果体现。从保护对象上讲,地理标志保护的着眼点是"产品",是市场上流通的商品以及与之相关的产地、技艺、历史、文化等一系列综合因素。而非物质文化遗产保护则侧重于传统技艺和人文活动的传承与发展。从保护对象上讲,非物质文化遗产涉及面更宽,传统技艺只是非物质文化遗产涵盖的内容之一,还有大量的非物质文化遗产与各民族语言文化和宗教、艺术形态等相关。因此,地理标志保护与非物质文化遗产保护相互关联而又有所不同。客观上,二者都为人类文明的传承延续和健康发展作出重要贡献。

截至 2019 年 12 月 31 日,我国入选联合国教科文组织非物质文化遗产名录的项目共 40 个,列入国家级非物质文化遗产代表性项目名录的有 1372 个,共计 3145 个子项,涉及民间文学(230),传统音乐(401),传统舞蹈(324),传统戏剧(445),曲艺(193),传统体育、游艺与杂技(124),传统美术(359),传统医药(137),传统技艺(506),民俗(426)等十大门类。[1] 这十大门类中,与地理标志相关的只有传统技艺、传统美术和传统医药等 3 类。关于传统技艺,前文已有讨论,涉及传统美术的地理标志产品主要是一些传统手工艺品,如剪纸、刺绣、石雕、木雕、泥塑、竹编、香包等。涉及传统医药的地理标志产

---

[1] 参见:http://www.ihchina.cn.

品主要是中药材。

6. 地理标志与含有地名的字号、商号、地方美食之间的关系

含有地名的字号、商号、地方美食在我国十分常见，如，兰州拉面、沙县小吃、岐山臊子面、柳州螺蛳粉等。从名称上看，字号、商号、地方美食泛指制作经营字面含义商品的商户。从商品本身上讲，这类商品（主要涉及地方美食）明确指向某一地理方位，是当地特产，并时常因其美誉度而扩展到原产地之外制作经营。问题是：它们能否被视为地理标志产品并获得地理标志保护。笔者认为，答案是否定的。虽然这类特色食品的经营商户主打的是地方特色，具有地域关联性，相应制作手法也基本遵循当地传统工艺，但往往只是对有关技艺的学习和模仿，同一名号下的食品质量特色可能存在明显差异。一方面，原料、水质、气候等可能对饮食特色产生影响的因素，若离开当地则很难完整复现，从本质上讲，这是一种非物质文化遗产，也就是制作技艺的传承和发扬。另一方面，这类美食即便在原产地，即便在同一行业组织成员内部也可能缺少统一标准，或者说，正是由于特色不统一，才成就了当地百家百味的细分市场，满足了消费者的差异化需求。

对照地理标志的定义，这类产品虽然含有地名，具有地理指向意义，但只是与当地历史人文相关的传统特色饮食。欧盟将类似产品划归"传统特色保证"（Traditional Specialty Guaranteed，TSG）范畴，它保护的是特定传统工艺和配料等，不限定产地范围。[1] 该机制与地理标志保护体系相互独立运行，有自己的专用

---

[1] 参见：https://ec.europa.eu/info/food-farming-fisheries/food-safety-and-quality/certification/quality-labels/quality-schemes-explained_en.

标志。我国尚未对这类商品进行专门规范。《商标法》第3条第2款和第3款明确了集体商标和证明商标的定义：

本法所称集体商标，是指以团体、协会或者其他组织名义注册，供该组织成员在商事活动中使用，以表明使用者在该组织中的成员资格的标志。

本法所称证明商标，是指由对某种商品或者服务具有监督能力的组织所控制，而由该组织以外的单位或者个人使用于其商品或者服务，用以证明该商品或者服务的原产地、原料、制造方法、质量或者其他特定品质的标志。

《商标法》第10条允许地名作为集体商标、证明商标的组成部分。此外，《商标法实施条例》第4条第2款对地理标志注册为集体商标、证明商标作出了规定：

以地理标志作为证明商标注册的，其商品符合使用该地理标志条件的自然人、法人或者其他组织可以要求使用该证明商标，控制该证明商标的组织应当允许。以地理标志作为集体商标注册的，其商品符合使用该地理标志条件的自然人、法人或者其他组织，可以要求参加以该地理标志作为集体商标注册的团体、协会或者其他组织，该团体、协会或者其他组织应当依据其章程接纳为会员；不要求参加以该地理标志作为集体商标注册的团体、协会或者其他组织的，也可以正当使用该地理标志，该团体、协会或者其他组织无权禁止。

随着全社会知识产权保护意识的不断增强，一些地方的行业组织为这类商品或字号、商号申请注册了普通商标或集体商标。但对照上述规定不难看出，即使出现未经允许使用已注册含有地名商标的情形，商标持有人也无权禁止。最高人民法院民事审判三庭负责人2021年12月在就地理标志司法保护问题答记者问时指出,根据《商标法》规定,即便取得注册商标专用权,权利人亦无权禁止他人正当使用注册商标中包含的地名。权利人提起相关诉讼的,人民法院依法不予支持。❶

笔者认为,这种情况与通用名称问题虽然性质不同,结果却有相似之处。对于已经散落在全国各地甚至海外的含有我国地名的字号、商号及地方美食,名称早已被通用化,成为某一种特色饮食的代名词。在这种情况下,使用含地名字号、商号的商户只要不附加他人已注册的品牌及图形、符号等,便不应被视为侵权。

第五节 制度实施中存在的缺陷与不足

多国实践证明,地理标志保护制度对于促进农业及其他领域特色产业的可持续发展、维护和提高特色产品质量、传承历史文化传统、保护地理标志知识产权具有重要意义。与此同时,也有必要客观分析该制度现存的一些缺陷和不足,以便更好地发挥地理标志保护的制度优势。笔者认为,我国在实施地理标志产品保护的过程中存在以下几方面缺陷与不足。

1. 申请程序烦琐、成本高的问题

地理标志保护在国际上存在几种不同的法律体系,本书重点关注的是以专门立法或制定条例、部门规章等方式保护地理标志

---

❶ 最高法回应"潼关肉夹馍"事件:严厉惩治恶意诉讼 [EB/OL]. (2021-12-12) [2021-12-12]. https://news.china.com/social/1007/20211212/40499519.html.

的申请程序问题。所谓专门法（sui generis），是针对特定对象而制定的法律规范。国际上以专门法保护地理标志的国家和地区主要包括欧盟、印度、日本以及其他一些亚洲、非洲和美洲国家。我国在国家层面尚未制定出台地理标志保护专门法。原国家质量技术监督局制定发布的《原产地域产品保护规定》和原国家质检总局制定发布的《地理标志产品保护规定》均为部门规章，其制度设计遵循了专门法的基本原则。而从我国实践和对欧盟等经济体的实施观察来看，无论法律层级如何，依照专门法原则开展地理标志保护的申请程序普遍较为烦琐。

以我国为例，根据《地理标志产品保护工作细则》第9条规定可知，申请人应为地方政府、地方政府指定的机构，或协会、企业等。第10条规定：

申请人应填写《地理标志产品保护申请书》（附件2），并提供以下资料：

（一）当地县级以上人民政府关于成立申报机构或指定协会、企业作为申请人的文件；

（二）当地县级以上人民政府关于划定申报产品保护地域范围的公函，保护范围一般具体到乡镇一级；水产品养殖范围一般以自然水域界定；

（三）所申报产品现行有效的专用标准或管理规范；

（四）证明产品特性的材料，包括：

1. 能够说明产品名称、产地范围及地理特征的；

2. 能够说明产品的历史渊源、知名度和产品生产、销售情况的；

3. 能够说明产品的理化、感官指标等质量特色及其与产地自然因素和人文因素之间关联性的；

4. 规定产品生产技术的，包括生产所用原材料、生产工艺、流程、安全卫生要求、主要质量特性、加工设备技术要求等；

5. 其他证明资料，如地方志、获奖证明、检测报告等。

上述材料备齐后，首先须提交省级主管部门进行初审，初审合格的再报送至国家局，由其进行形式审查后发布受理公告，设为期2个月的异议期。2个月无异议，或有异议但已解决的，再由国家局组织召开专家评审会。申请人还需准备相关参评文件，即陈述报告和质量技术要求等。通过专家评审的申请，还需按照专家意见修改完善申报材料，报国家局复核，并发布批准公告。而发布批准公告并不等于申报完成，申请人还需完善地方标准和检测体系建设，只有这样，才有资格申请使用地理标志专用标志。

上述申请程序经梳理归纳，基本流程为：指定申请人 → 划定产地范围 → 地方政府行文 → 制订质量技术要求 → 撰写申请材料 → 提供佐证材料 → 报送省级主管部门初审 → 上报国家主管部门形式审查 → 发布受理公告→2个月异议期 → 准备专家评审文件 → 专家评审会 → 材料整改 → 报国家主管部门 → 发布批准公告 → 完善标准和检测体系 → 申请专用标志使用→国家主管部门审核 → 发布专用标志使用核准公告。

上述每一个工作环节都需要相应的人力物力投入。其中一些环节，如撰写申请材料、完善标准和检测体系等，对于地理标志产地基层单位而言，可能存在一定困难，而对于偏远落后地区的基层单位来说，难度更大。由于不得要领，或者受文化水平等因素制约，仅凭当地力量很难达到申报相关要求。遇到这种情况，申请单位或委托中介机构协助组织材料，而这又进一步增加了申请成本。并且，中介机构由于缺乏对产品、产地的深入认识和了解，所组织的材料同样未必能达到申报要求。这在客观上影响到地理标志产地申请人的积极性，也对地理标志保护整体形象产生一定消极影响。

根据欧盟2014年组织的关于是否扩大地理标志保护范围的公共磋商结果，80%的中小企业认为值得为地理标志保护增加投入，20%的生产者认为申请地理标志保护将导致成本上升。有消费者认为，额外的规定和标识或给消费者造成混淆并推高商品价格。还有人认为，地理标志保护存在贸易中的保护主义倾向，有碍自由市场竞争。❶

2. 申请周期长、时效性差的问题

该问题与问题一相关。据统计，欧盟地理标志的申请周期大约为2年。在我国，从提交地理标志保护申请，到发布地理标志产品保护批准公告，粗略计算需要1年以上时间。另外，即便是已获得批准的地理标志产品，还需申请专用标志使用。一些申请人因各种原因（包括能力不足或无力支付检测费用等），达不到专用标志使用的核准要求，长期无法使用地理标志保护专用标志，造成事实上的申报工作半途而废。申请周期长、程序复杂，直接影响到产地申请人的积极性，也有损于地理标志保护的时效性。

---

❶ European Commission. Geographical indications for non‐agricultural products［EB/OL］.［2021-12-12］. https：//ec. europa. eu/growth/industry/strategy/intellectual-property/geographical-indications-non-agricultural-products_en.

3. 运行成本高、管理难的问题

地理标志保护是一项系统工程，涉及面广、管理要求高，在一些地方存在落实上的困难。在获得地理标志保护后，产地需完善质量保证体系、标准体系和检测体系建设。在管理上，要组织建立规模不一的合作组织和行业协会，宣传落实地理标志质量技术要求，申请、监督专用标志使用，开展对外宣传，协调议价、仓储、物流、市场等多个营销环节。地理标志以农产品和特色食品、工艺品居多，产地往往远离中心城市，普遍缺乏技术和管理人才。在我国，当地政府部门在牵头组织申报阶段发挥主要作用。但申报完成后，往往力不从心，无暇顾及地理标志的综合管理和品牌建设，易形成管理上的真空和纰漏。地理标志保护客观上要求产地各利益关系方协调合作，共同参与生产经营和管理。同时，还要求产地各有关方面在管理和对外宣传上持续投入。只有这样，才能维持地理标志价值链的良性循环，维护和提高地理标志品牌价值。

除了产地生产者和行业组织自身管理之外，监管部门加强对地理标志保护的监督管理也十分重要，需要配备必要的人力资源和经费保障，这方面同样也会增加地理标志保护的成本。因此，欧盟成员国甚至有人认为，地理标志保护造成的成本增加或超出其实际收益。[1]

4. 初级农产品的品种退化问题

初级农产品一直在我国地理标志保护产品中占比较大，这与初级农产品的品质特色较为显著、易于感官体验、与产地的内在

---

[1] Study on geographical indications protection for non-agricultural products in the internal market: Final report [EB/OL]. (2013-02-18) [2020-04-30]. https://ec.europa.eu/docsroom/documents/14897.

关联性更直接有着密切关系。但应该看到，果蔬类农产品经常面临品种退化的问题，需不断调整、改良品种，这在某种程度上或造成产品的品质特色缺乏稳定性，直接影响消费者的消费体验和地理标志品牌的市场声誉。

5. 初级农产品占比高、附加值低的问题

初级农产品不仅面临着品种退化的问题，而且还面临市场波动大、附加值低、农民利益难以维护等地理标志产业需要解决的发展难题。初级农产品的市场行情受气候、时间、年景、产量等因素影响，易产生价格波动。而即使在产销两旺的好年景，作为初级农产品的生产者，农民所得到的收入与供应链下游、价值链上游相比仍然偏低。地理标志保护的目的之一是提高特色产品的附加值，地理标志初级农产品的价格可在一定幅度内高于同类产品，但溢价能力受同类产品价格影响较大，附加值表现稳定性差。笔者认为，提高地理标志产品附加值的根本出路之一，在于适时转变主要以初级农产品申请地理标志保护的做法，逐步向农产品深加工领域发展。

对比欧盟地理标志保护名录不难发现，初级农产品占欧盟地理标志保护产品的比例较小，绝大多数受保护产品是葡萄酒、烈酒、橄榄油、干酪、火腿等以初级农产品为原料的加工食品，其附加值远高于初级农产品。而反观日本、韩国以及一些东南亚国家的地理标志产品名录，产品类别与我国相仿，初级农产品占较大比重。这说明，在地理标志保护制度发育较早的欧洲国家，地理标志产业重心已基本脱离了初级产品的范畴，而更多地转向初级产品深加工领域。而在开展地理标志保护初始阶段，由于初级产品的品质特色与自然环境的内在关联更为直接，各国普遍会从初级产品入手，发现并保护一批地域特色鲜明的地理标志食品和农产品。因此，随着地理标志保护制度引向深入，各国可更多地借鉴欧盟的经验，将保护对象向深加工领域延伸，挖掘那些存在地域关联性的加工食品。地理标志初级产品只有经过深加工才有可能实现较大幅度的价值提升，同时也有利于从根本上解决初级农产品市场波动大、农民收入不稳定的问题。与此同时，这也是区域经济发展转型升级的现实要求，有助于延长地理标志产业链，带动上下游企业与地理标志产业协同发展壮大。

关于加工食品溯源难的问题，有观点认为，许多初级产品一旦经过深加工（如咖啡豆、板栗研磨成粉后），将很难判定其原料真实来源，无法实施地理标志保护。因此，我国的地理标志农产品大多只保护其原果或仅经过诸如去壳、切片等简单加工的产品形态。其实，解决这一问题的关键还是在于管理和诚信体系建设。笔者认为，只要企业诚信守法，内部管理措施到位，辅以外部有效监管，深加工农产品、加工食品也可以获得地理标志保护，为产地带来更为丰厚的回馈。

关于加工食品与产地自然和人文因素的内在关联，欧洲国家的加工食品类地理标志集中在葡萄酒、烈酒、橄榄油、干酪、火腿等产品上，而生鲜类食品和农产品仅占已注册总数约20%[1]。造成这种情况的原因：一是上述几类加工食品原料和加工工艺地域特色鲜明；二是其与欧洲饮食习惯密切相关，居民日常消费不可或缺，市场需求大。而把这些产品拿到我国以及其他亚洲市场来分析，由于东西方饮食习惯不同，亚洲国家发展加工食品类地理标志不可能重复欧洲的老路，而应紧密结合本国实际，发现、

---

[1] 参见：欧盟官网截至 2019 年 12 月 21 日的数据，https：//ec. europa. eu/info/food-farming-fisheries/food-safety-and-quality/certification/quality-labels/quality-products-registers_en.

保护那些具备地理标志潜质的加工食品。以豆制品为例，它是我国餐桌上不可或缺的菜肴原料，老少咸宜。豆制品加工工艺历史悠久，产地遍布全国各地，且种类繁多。粗略来计，就有豆腐、豆腐皮、豆腐干、腐竹、豆浆、腐乳、豆豉、豆瓣酱等，仅豆腐一项又可分为南豆腐、北豆腐、内酯豆腐等。其中相当一部分采用的是发酵工艺，与西方的奶酪生产具有异曲同工之处，其品质特色同样与产地自然因素（水质、气温、空气湿度等）和人文因素关联度较强，产品在我国甚至海外都拥有稳定的消费市场，可作为地理标志保护的重要产品类别，得到更多支持和关注。此外，黄酒、酒酿、泡菜、酱油、食醋等都是东方特有的发酵食品，符合条件的均可纳入地理标志保护范畴。但与此同时，也应该看到，腐乳、豆豉、豆瓣酱等发酵食品普遍存在钠含量较高等问题，值得科研人员进一步研究改进方法，不断提高其食品安全健康水平。

以上围绕几项与可持续发展密切相关的地理标志内涵进行了讨论。下面分别论述地理标志与实现可持续发展目标之间的内在关系和促进作用。

CHAPTER 02 >>　第二章
地理标志与实现可持续发展目标

　　保护产地环境，合理利用产地资源是维护地理标志产品质量特色的客观需要；过度利用产地资源直接影响产品质量，威胁地理标志的生存和发展。以初级农产品为例，产品质量在一定程度上取决于种植或养殖密度，密度过大意味着营养分配失衡，产品质量下降。因此，合理制定种植或养殖密度是地理标志产品的生产要素之一，需要在生产标准或质量技术要求中予以明确并严格执行。

　　地理标志的作用不仅仅局限于对资源的合理利用。对照联合国可持续发展目标（Sustainable Development Goals，SDGs）不难发现，实施地理标志保护制度与该发展目标存在密切关联。

第一节　联合国可持续发展目标

可持续发展的概念首先出现在1980年《世界自然资源保护大纲》中。关于可持续发展的定义，1987年世界环境与发展委员会在发布的报告中将其表述为："既满足当代人需求，又不对后代满足需求的能力构成危害。"联合国于2015年通过了《2030年可持续发展议程》(The 2030 Agenda for Sustainable Development)，该议程认为"它为全人类和我们所在星球的和平与繁荣提供了共享蓝本。其核心内容为17项可持续发展目标，迫切要求世界各国，包括发达国家和发展中国家以及最不发达国家，作为全球伙伴采取行动。将消除贫困与改善健康和教育结合起来，减少不平衡现象，激发经济增长，同时还要应对气候变化，保护海洋和森林资源。"[1]

可持续发展目标共有17项内容，分别是：

目标1：无贫困

在全世界消除一切形式的贫困。

目标2：零饥饿

消除饥饿，实现粮食安全，改善营养状况和促进可持续农业。

目标3：良好健康和福祉

确保健康的生活方式，促进各年龄段人群的福祉。

---

[1] Knowledge Platform [EB/OL]. [2020-07-24]. https://sustainabledevelopment.un.org.

目标 4：优质教育

确保包容和公平的优质教育，让全民终身享有学习机会。

目标 5：性别平等

实现性别平等，增强所有妇女和女童的权能。

目标 6：清洁饮水和卫生设施

为所有人提供水和环境卫生并对其进行可持续管理。

目标 7：经济适用的清洁能源

确保人人获得负担得起的、可靠和可持续的现代能源。

目标 8：体面工作和经济增长

促进持久、包容、可持续的经济增长，促进充分的生产性就业和人人获得体面工作。

目标 9：产业、创新和基础设施

建造具备抵御灾害能力的基础设施，促进具有包容性的可持续工业化，推动创新。

目标 10：减少不平等

减少国家内部和国家之间的不平等。

目标 11：可持续城市和社区

建设包容、安全、有抵御灾害能力和可持续的城市和人类社区。

目标 12：负责任的消费和生产

采用可持续的消费和生产方式。

目标 13：气候行动

采取紧急行动应对气候变化及其影响。

目标 14：水下生物

可持续利用海洋和海洋资源以促进可持续发展。

目标 15：陆地生物

保护、恢复和促进可持续利用陆地生态系统，可持续管理森林，防治沙漠化，制止和扭转土地退化，遏制生物多样性的丧失。

目标 16：和平、正义与强大机构

创建和平、包容的社会以促进可持续发展，让所有人都能诉诸司法，在各级建立有效、负责、包容的机构。

目标 17：促进目标实现的伙伴关系

加强执行手段，重振可持续发展全球伙伴关系。

上述 17 个可持续发展目标几乎涵盖人类社会所有领域，从减贫脱贫到提高全民受教育水平，从保障卫生健康到实现性别平等，从增加就业到经济增长，从应对气候变化、使用清洁能源、保护生态环境到完善基础设施、实现可持续工业化，再到负责任的生产和消费、建设包容性社会、实现公正司法等。可以说，这 17 个可持续发展目标为未来人类社会发展指明了方向，但同时也对国家治理能力提出了更高要求，形成严峻挑战。世界各国只有团结一致，共同发力，才有可能如期实现上述发展目标。任何一方的不作为都将危及人类社会的健康发展和赖以生存的地球环境生态。

总体上看，17 个可持续发展目标涉及人类社会和自然生态两大范畴，但归根结底是人类社会的可持续发展问题，根子在人。只有世界各国形成广泛共识，充分认识到有关问题的严重性和落实可持续发展理念的迫切性，进而采取具体措施加以解决，才能如期实现发展目标。客观分析，由于各国发展水平存在明显差异，发展中国家和发达国家处于不同的发展阶段，实现可持续发展目标理应采取共同但有区别的方针，在保证各国人民享有充分发展权利的前提下，最大限度地减少资源消耗和对地球生态环境的负面影响，实现平衡和可持续的发展。

在将各国发展路径统一到联合国可持续发展目标上，有关国家在其中一些目标的实施过程中存在分歧，主要表现在发达国家和主要发展中国家之间就减少温室气体排放问题的矛盾。一些发达国家强调，主要发展中国家，如中国、印度等国目前的温室气体排放量位居全球前列，应与美国等主要发达国家一样，承担主要减排义务，大幅削减温室气体排放。而主要发展中国家则认为，发达国家的要求超出它们本国实际承受能力，将发展中国家与发达国家不加区别地等同看待既不合理，也无可操作性。发展中国家理应享有平等发展的权利。实现可持续发展目标应充分考虑发展中国家的实际情况，不应提出过高要求。客观分析，这样的主张具有合理性，发达国家经历了工业化初期造成的严重污染，而发展中国家工业化起步基本上在20世纪中后期，目前正处于重要上升阶段，因此，脱离实际的要求和做法并不可取。

围绕实现可持续发展目标过程中各国权利与义务的争论仍在继续。值得欣慰的是，世界主要发达国家和发展中国家在一些重要领域取得了广泛共识，包括中国在内的主要发展中国家主动提出了减少本国温室气体排放的中长期目标。2020年9月，习近平主席在第75届联合国大会一般性辩论中庄严承诺，中国将在2030年前实现碳达峰，2060年前实现碳中和。❶

---

❶ HAN B Y. Experts hail president's speech at general debate [EB/OL]. (2020-09-24) [2022-03-21]. https：//www.chinadaily.com.cn/a/202009/24/WS5f6bd5f3a31024ad0ba7b5b4.html.

第二节 地理标志与可持续发展目标之间的关联性

鉴于联合国可持续发展目标几乎涵盖人类社会发展各领域，探讨地理标志保护与实现可持续发展目标之间的关系，首先应结合地理标志保护的自身特点和适用范围，对照上述17个发展目标具体分析。不难发现，其中一些目标，如：目标4（优质教育）、目标6（清洁饮水和卫生设施）、目标7（经济适用的清洁能源）、目标9（产业、创新和基础设施）、目标11（可持续城市和社区）以及目标16（和平、正义与强大机构）等6项目标内容与地理标志保护体系关联性不强。地理标志保护体系难以对实现上述目标发挥有效作用。而反观其他11项发展目标，无论是对于消除贫困还是促进经济增长，或应对气候变化等，地理标志保护制度均可在一定程度上发挥积极作用，在有些方面甚至具有重要意义。因此，笔者认为，与地理标志保护存在直接关联的是其中11项发展目标，即：

目标1：无贫穷

目标2：零饥饿

目标3：良好健康和福祉

目标5：性别平等

目标8：体面工作和经济增长

目标10：减少不平等

目标12：负责任的消费和生产

目标 13：气候行动

目标 14：水下生物

目标 15：陆地生物

目标 17：促进目标实现的伙伴关系

以上 11 个目标依照其内涵又可大致划分为四个方面，即：

(1) 减贫脱贫与粮食安全（目标 1、2、3）；

(2) 实现经济增长与社会公平（目标 5、8、10、12）；

(3) 保护生态环境，应对全球气候变化（目标 13、14、15）；

(4) 开展国际合作（目标 17）。

当然，这一分类只是笔者为便于解析而为，并无权威依据。只不过上述各个方面所涉及的内容的确密切关联，并且在某种程度上互为因果。按照联合国官方解释，17 个可持续发展目标的核心是消除贫困、减少不平等和保护地球生态环境。目标 1、2、3 首先要解决的是人类生存问题，即保障基本人权。目标 5、8、10、12 是在上述基础上，赋予人与人之间平等发展的权利和各国之间、各国内部经济社会平等发展的机会。而目标 13、14、15 则强调人类社会的发展不应以牺牲地球生态系统为代价，世界各国应采取实际行动，保护生态环境，保护我们共同的家园。最后，目标 17 要求世界各国携起手来，加强合作，共同解决可持续发展实践中出现的问题，取长补短，化解分歧。

如前文所述，地理标志主要涉及食品、农产品和手工艺品，与农业、食品工业和文化等产业正相关。地理标志保护制度所倡导的传承历史、有限开发、就地保护等基本原则与可持续发展理念高度吻合，也与实现上述 11 个可持续发展目标密切相关。发展地理标志产业，遵循地理标志制度所要求的生产方式,将最大限度保护自然资源禀赋,传承和发展区域特色产业,有效促进实现消除贫困、平等发展、保护环境等重要领域的可持续发展目标。本书以下章节将依照有关可持续发展目标顺次展开讨论。

第三章
地理标志制度助力消除全球贫困、维护生命健康

第一节　地理标志保护促进减贫脱贫目标实现

目标1：无贫穷

无贫穷是可持续发展目标之首，是世界各国尤其是发展中国家的共同奋斗目标。根据世界银行统计，截至2019年12月，以每人每天1.9美元支出的极端贫困标准计算，世界上现有极端贫困人口超过7.34亿，约占全球总人口的10%。

世界银行统计显示，"由于新型冠状病毒肺炎（COVID-19）疫情危机以及油价下跌的影响，贫困人口逐年下降的趋势在2020年将出现

反转。由于失业、无收入来源、物价上涨、教育和医疗缺失等因素，新型冠状病毒肺炎疫情将对贫困人口造成更大影响。全球贫困发生率将由于全球经济衰退自1998年以来首次升高。据估算，2020年极端贫困人口（低于1.9美元/天）将增加4000万至6000万人，全球极端贫困率将上升0.3～0.7个百分点。亚太地区、南亚和撒哈拉以南非洲地区的贫困人口占到全球贫困人口的95%。全球多数穷人生活在农村，受教育程度低，以务农为生，年龄在18周岁以下。"❶

人口致贫的原因很多，既有长期战乱或自然灾害所造成的社会危机，也有因自然环境恶劣、地处偏远而不具备基本生存条件的现实情况，如我国的"三区三州"地区❷。还有因残疾或医疗保障不足所造成的因病致贫、因病返贫等。习近平总书记2020年6月在《求是》杂志发表的文章《关于全面建成小康社会补短板问题》中指出，我国目前的农村贫困人口中，因病因残致贫分别占40.7%、20.2%。

关于贫困的原因，胡联（2017）认为，经济因素、个体因素、社会因素、地理环境因素和脆弱性因素将会直接导致贫困的形成，制度因素和文化因素通过直接因素的作用间接导致贫困的形成。他认为，单纯的经济增长和普惠性政策措施并不能解决所有贫困问题。❸

贫困问题是世界性难题。致贫因素虽然很多，但其中有一种

---

❶ Poverty [EB/OL].（2020-04-16）[2020-04-20]. http：//www.worldbank.org/en/topic/poverty/overview.
❷ "三区"指西藏、青海、四川、甘肃、云南四省藏区以及南疆的和田地区、阿克苏地区、喀什地区、克孜勒苏柯尔克孜自治州四地区；"三州"指四川凉山州、云南怒江州、甘肃临夏州。"三区三州"曾是国家级深度贫困地区。
❸ 胡联. 中国产业发展的减贫效应研究 [M]. 北京：经济科学出版社，2017：51.

值得我们特别关注，即贫困发生地虽然拥有一定资源，但因总体发展水平落后而未能充分加以利用，贫困状况长期得不到实质性改变。有的地方农作物产量不小，但却"卖不上价"；有的农产品虽有一定特色，但因缺乏规范管理和有效经营，质量参差不齐，经济收益差，同样达不到脱贫增收的目的。

优化资源配置，改进生产方式，提高有限资源的收益是地理标志保护制度的目的和优势之一。地理标志保护制度"是对生产出多种多样优质产品的回报，有利于农村经济发展。尤其对于山区和偏远落后地区来说，在农业生产占经济主体、生产成本较高的情况下，（地理标志制度）可为农村发展做贡献……"❶

首先，地理标志保护制度最大限度优化资源配置，保证特色产品质量。前文谈到，有的地方自然环境恶劣、地处偏远，不具备基本生存条件；还有的地方虽然拥有一定自然资源，但却仍未摆脱贫困。实际上，某些贫瘠的环境里有时可能隐藏着不为人知的特殊自然条件，适合特定产品的生产，这种现象本书将在后文中举例说明。从这个角度来讲，自然条件差或只是造成贫困的必要条件。解决贫困问题，不妨从转变发展思路入手，深入挖掘和发现当地潜在的自然禀赋，寻找适合本地发展需求的机制和手段，推动特色产业发展和提高。而地理标志保护制度就是其中一个被证明行之有效的机制和手段。

地理标志保护制度在助力减贫脱贫上可以发挥重要作用，主要体现在以下几个方面。

---

❶ Regulation（EU）No 1151/2012 of the European Parliament and of the Council of 21 November 2012 on quality schemes for agricultural products and foodstuffs［EB/OL］.（2012-12-14）［2022-04-11］. https：//eur-lex. europa. eu/legal-content/EN/TXT/? uri=CELEX%3A32012R1151&qid=1660293292963.

1. 调动集体力量，扩大脱贫覆盖面

地理标志保护是面向产地全体生产者的制度，鼓励产地所有利益相关方积极参与到地理标志产品的生产和经营中，并由此获得劳动报酬和经济收益。与此同时，地理标志的集体属性意味着，它不是某家企业的私有品牌，也不是一家一户的宣传招牌。产地每个农户、每个家庭、每家作坊和企业，只要参与了地理标志产品的生产经营，都可分享地理标志保护的收益，共同为打造地理标志品牌作贡献。不仅如此，地理标志产品的市场声誉依靠全体生产者维护，保证地理标志的特色质量既是管理上的要求，也符合生产者个人利益。"全体从业者之间存在一荣俱荣、一损俱损的经济利益关系，不仅使生产的组织化程度得到明显提高，而且也提高了村民参与农村政治生活和社区治理的积极性，提升了共同参与的水平和深度。"[1] 广泛参与，利益共享，风险同担是地理标志保护的显著优势，也是有别于其他减贫脱贫手段的突出特点。

2. 降低品牌建设成本，提高市场营销成效

地理标志的知名度来自产地悠久的生产历史和已建立起的市场信誉。地理标志保护制度的主要作用是确权、规范、保护和发展。首先通过严格程序认定或确认地理标志的知识产权，任何人不得侵权使用地理标志名称。其次以规范化管理保证地理标志产品的质量特色，以绿色、环保、守信等先进理念促进地理标志产品的可持续发展。地理标志保护的确权过程是对产品已有知名度的确认，这意味着，在申请地理标志保护之前，产品已具有一定

---

[1] 王笑冰. 经济发展方式转变视角下的地理标志保护 [M]. 北京：中国社会科学出版社，2019：52.

知名度和市场美誉度。地理标志产地生产者无须注册商标，便有了属于自己的市场品牌。这与注册商标等行为下的产品营销有着显著区别，地理标志产品具有明显的"先天优势"。因此，地理标志在欧洲也被誉为"穷人的商标"。

3. 发挥合作组织作用，提高质量效益

这也是地理标志生产和经营的特别之处。地理标志的集体属性决定其生产经营通常不可由一家或几家企业垄断，而应由产地全体生产者共同参与。在极个别情况下，产地或仅有一家一户掌握某一地理标志产品生产技能，这时可允许其作为申请人独立申报。艾米丽·凡德肯德莱尔等（2020）指出，拥有独特的自然资源、特殊技艺以及采取集体行动的意愿是地理标志的主要支柱。[1] 从地理标志产品生产的角度分析，产地内所有符合条件的生产者均可参与地理标志产品生产。这其中可能有大企业、中小企业，也可能有小作坊，更多的则是个体农民或手工艺者。个体农民是弱势群体，处于供应链上游、价值链底端，缺乏对外议价和获取公平收益的能力。实施地理标志保护后，为规范管理，提高集约化水平，个体农户可组成大小不一的专业合作社，甚至组建覆盖全体产地生产者的产业协会。专业合作组织，使分散的各种生产要素在较大范围内实现优化配置和重新组合；对内制定统一的生产技术标准，统一管理，保证产品质量，设定最低收购价格，最大限度保护农民利益；对外统一定价销售，维护产地集体权益。合作组织在不改变生产者属性的前提下，实现集约化生产

---

[1] VANDECANDELAERE E, TEYSSIER C, BARJOLLE D, et al. Strengthening sustainable food systems through geographical indications: evidence from 9 worldwide case studies [J/OL]. Journal of sustainable research, 2020, 2 (4): 18 [2020-11-18]. https: //doi. org/10. 20900/jsr20200031.

经营，强化了产地在地理标志产品供应链上的声音，既有利于保证产品的特色质量，也有利于使生产者获得更高回报。实施地理标志保护能够给贫困地区生产者带来更可靠的收益，这对于长期从事农业生产、靠天吃饭、无所依靠的农民来说是十分重要的收入保障。

例如，贵州省贞丰县北盘江镇顶坛区域，是中国石漠化最严重的地区之一，其中极强度石漠化占总面积的80%以上，95%的面积是"石旮旯"。恶劣的环境、贫瘠的土地、严重短缺的水资源，使得农民只能在石缝中进行原始耕作。其被很多专家认定为"不具备人类生存条件的地方"。但与此同时，顶坛区域属北亚热带高原季风气候，当地花椒树长期生长于怪石立林，热辐射较强、干旱少土的特殊气候环境，使得花椒质量上乘。

研究表明，花椒很适合贵州喀斯特干热河谷区的自然气候环境。贞丰县委县政府通过深入调研，反复论证，制定了"因时因地制宜，改善生态环境，种植花椒致富"的政策。贞丰县把推行地理标志产品保护制度作为一项实实在在的"三农"工程，将地理标志产品保护工作列入当地经济发展规划，做到有计划、有安排，成立了地理标志产品保护申报工作领导小组，划定了顶坛花椒地理标志产地范围，做到专项工作有人管、具体事情有人做。同时，各级政府还从财力上给予了大力支持，为顺利开展地理标志产品保护的申报工作提供了有力的保障。此外，还充分利用新闻媒体和各类信息平台，广泛深入地进行宣传，提高企业和群众对地理标志保护工作的认识；把地理标志保护与农业标准化、品牌建设等工作有机结合起来，大力宣传地理标志产品保护工作对提升地方特色产品知名度、提高市场竞争力的重要作用，动员企业立足长远，主动参与，积极支持和配合地理标志产品保护工作。

顶坛花椒在 2008 年获得地理标志保护后发展成效显著。以贞丰县顶罈椒业有限公司为例，其主产的花椒油、花椒粉、干花椒、调味麻辣椒等花椒制品年加工量达 2300 吨，产值 3200 万元，正向"产、供、销一条龙"的方向发展，并解决了部分剩余劳动力的转化问题。同时，工厂规模的扩大带动了玻璃制品、纸箱、运输等相关产业的发展。随着关兴公路建成通车，依托北盘江大峡谷的旅游开发，顶坛进一步建设了以花椒为主的特色观光农业。至 2008 年，中央、省、州、县先后投入资金累计近千万元，已建成花椒种植面积达 15.3 万亩、产量 1.1 万吨、产值 1.2 亿元的绿色生态示范区。顶坛花椒已成为省内外知名品牌，创建了喀斯特石漠化治理与农村经济建设协调发展的"顶坛模式"。"顶坛模式"已成为石漠化治理的样板之一。[1]

同样是花椒，汉源花椒 2005 年获得地理标志产品保护后，四川省汉源县持续在"汉源花椒"品牌创建和保护方面下功夫。2012~2021 年，汉源花椒单价从 30 元/斤上涨到 85 元/斤，涨幅达 183%。根据汉源县政府提供的信息，截至 2021 年 12 月，全县年产干花椒 5000 吨，产值达 6.86 亿元，种植区农户人均栽种花椒面积 2 亩，收益超过 10000 元，有力地支撑了农民收入增长和脱贫攻坚。2020 年，全县近 7000 名贫困群众通过花椒产业脱贫，花椒产业成为汉源县中高山贫困地区脱贫致富、乡村振兴的有效途径之一。

再比如，甘肃省礼县位于甘肃省东南部，距离省会兰州市 345 公里，沟壑纵横，交通不便，经济发展长期落后，曾一直是国家级贫困县。但对礼县有所了解的人都知道，礼县是古代秦文

---

[1] 参见：贵州省黔西南州贞丰县质监局地理标志产品保护交流材料。

化的发祥地，历史悠久，而且在长期的农耕文明中有种植草药的传统，其中中药材大黄的种植历史可上溯至汉代，是全国著名的大黄产地，大黄质量上乘。礼县所在的陇南市"素有'天然药库'、'千年药乡'的美誉，《本草纲目》中的党参、当归、红芪、大黄、甘草等五大药材中，四种产于陇南，而且以量大质优闻名于国内外"。❶ 尽管如此，礼县大黄却曾长期停留在靠天吃饭、停滞不前的状态。

为保护礼县大黄的质量信誉，进一步提高市场知名度，礼县于 2004 年启动了礼县大黄地理标志保护工作，礼县大黄于 2005 年被原国家质检总局批准为地理标志保护产品。获批后，礼县人民政府加强生产管理，普及地理标志知识。经过大力宣传和引导，礼县大黄走上规模化、标准化发展的道路，地理标志产品的质量特色得到保证，市场销路不断拓展，综合效益显著提高，礼县大黄种植户终于品尝到了大黄带来的"甜头"——2018 年礼县大黄产量达 944 吨。在礼县大黄地理标志保护成功的基础上，礼县又将地理标志保护扩大至礼县苹果、礼县花椒等林果类产品，大力推进产业扶贫，林果、中药材成为当地农民增收的支柱产业，2017 年礼县苹果产量达 9.66 万吨，礼县荣获 2017 中国果业扶贫突出贡献奖，2018 年农业特色产业人均增收 3100 元。2018 年，礼县农村居民人均可支配收入达到 6529 元，较 2015 年增加近 30%。❷

生产出好的地理标志产品只是脱贫的第一步，要想将老百姓

---

❶❷《甘肃发展年鉴》编委会. 甘肃发展年鉴 2018 [M/OL]. 北京：中国统计出版社，2018 [2021-09-13]. http://tjj.gansu.gov.cn/tjnj/2018/indexce.htm.

手中的特色产品转化为实实在在的"真金白银",就还需要有好的营销。营销是个大课题,本书不展开讨论,仅以几个产品的营销案例作为参考。

(1) 如何破解交通物流制约

贫困发生率较高的地方往往交通不便,山高路远。交通是制约发展的大问题。"要想富,先修路",有了路,货物才出得去。接下来,即便路修好了,也还有个距离问题,长途运输造成的销售困难同样值得关注。山高路远仍然是脱贫的难点和痛点。即使是再好的产品,"藏在闺中人未知"的情况依然存在。要改变这一状况,除了打通物理上的道路,还要打通销售渠道,创新销售手段,充分利用现代科技带来的便利,拓展销售空间。西藏阿里地区措勤县地处羌塘草原腹地,距离拉萨880公里,距离阿里地区行署所在地狮泉河镇746公里,平均海拔4700米以上,自然条件恶劣,交通极为不便,是阿里地区最为偏僻的一个县。但措勤县畜产品资源丰富,紫绒山羊产绒量高、肉质细嫩、抗寒性强,是西藏特色优势畜种。近年来,措勤县大力发展紫绒山羊产业,优化草场使用,着手申请地理标志保护。同时,措勤县人民政府主动与淘宝、京东等知名电商企业接洽,利用电商平台的渠道优势,推介宣传措勤县特产,畅通市场销路。产自"地球第三极"青藏高原的纯天然产品对广大消费者具有强烈的吸引力。措勤紫绒山羊绒生产者在较短时间内获得了来自全国多个省、区、市的订单。

物流成本高是制约偏远地区产品外销的又一瓶颈。西藏、新疆的消费者都知道,网购不包邮是惯例,有时邮费甚至超过商品价格,有的甚至不对偏远地区发货。所有这些问题都指向物流运输成本。偏远地区物流主要依靠汽运,相对于铁路和航空,汽运的优势在于机动性强，不受铁路车皮配载周期长和航空运费高的影响，运输成本介于二者之间。而对于措勤县这样一个异常偏远的行政区而言，长期以来不仅只能依靠汽运，而且仅有"中国邮政"这个唯一的物流企业的定期班线可供利用。事实上，西藏大部分县、乡的物流运输主要依靠邮政的定期班线。但就靠这条仅有的运输线，措勤县把紫绒山羊绒卖到了北京、上海、西安等城市，脱贫效果明显。措勤县也一跃成为2017年西藏网络销量第一县。

"截至2019年底，通过电子商务平台、线下体验店、展销会等，措勤县实现销售额3100余万元，其中，畜产品销售高达2500余万元，特色产品销售金紫绒羊绒制品、藏雪鸡护肤品、扎日南木错藏香、手工艺品等达600余万元。同时，配合阿里地区打造门东电子商务第一村，打通措勤特色商品的市场销路，为农牧民群众带来丰富的经济效益。

"在推进电子商务进农村过程中，措勤县建立县级公共服务中心和电子商务特色产品网下体验馆、金紫绒网下体验馆，打造了'藏货通天下——措勤频道'并成功上线运营，建立基本覆盖全县12个电子商务进农村村级服务站，开展电子商务专项培训34期，为农牧民群众发放藏汉双语宣传材料2500余份等，不断提升群众对电子商务的认识和应用意识，极大方便了牧民日常生活。

"同时，根据本地特色产品情况，措勤县为西藏金紫绒工贸有限公司、扎日南木错藏香厂、舞凤责任有限公司等企业，统一产品打造和溯源体系建设等，依托藏货通天下、淘宝等各大平台推广，先后在内地相关博览会和西藏藏博会等展销会上大放异彩，成功走出西藏。

"此外，措勤县与中国邮政阿里分局成功签订合作协议，在日喀则萨嘎县22道班新建物流转运中心，实现县里所有邮政快递及电商商品1到2天内就能直达拉萨及其他物流公司转寄邮政到措勤县的物流方式。"❶

（2）如何宣传推广地理标志产品

宣传推广是市场营销的重要内容。地理标志产品的特殊性在于，它不仅仅是某一家企业生产的产品，而是产地范围内所有符合条件的生产者共同生产、利益分享的产物。在权利归属上，它具有集体属性。在组织成分上，生产者不仅包含农户或作坊，还有企业，甚至是规模较大的龙头企业。所以，地理标志产品的宣传推广不是一家一户的事，涉及产地所有生产经营者的利益。那么，该怎样有效地开展地理标志产品的宣传推广和市场营销呢？

理论上，地理标志产品的营销包含了两个层面：一方面可由地理标志合作组织（如协会、合作社）代表生产者集体利益，承担统一对外营销的任务；另一方面，产地内生产者个体（企业或个人）也可自行销售地理标志产品。在我国，获得地理标志保护后，由于产品销售需满足包装、标识等一系列规范性要求，个体独立完成成本较高，有一定困难，因此个体生产者普遍交由合作组织统一进行，这也是成立地理标志合作组织的初衷之一。而产地内具有一定规模的生产企业既可在符合地理标志统一要求的前提下自行开展营销活动，也可交由合作组织统一对外销售。对于地理标志产品，地理标志合作组织既负责地理标志产品管理措施的组织实施、监督落实，协调生产者关系，也负责对外开展营销谈判、协调交流和推广宣传，同时还肩负责任，使地理标志保

---

❶ 参见：http://www.xzcq.gov.cn/cgjj_1555/202005/t2020 0519_3068728.html.

护朝着有利于经济社会和环境可持续的方向发展。❶ 因此，建好地理标志产品合作组织是实施地理标志保护的关键一环。

关于如何进行宣传推广，以下几个国内外案例可以作为参考。

（1）Turrialba 干酪（哥斯达黎加）

2006 年，哥斯达黎加针对 Turrialba 干酪开展了一系列研究，以确定其质量特色与产地的关联性，并分析市场潜力和消费者需求。研究具体形式包括：走访农户和乳制品加工者，进行产品理化、微生物以及感官分析等。其中，有关消费者印象的调查，在零售场所问询了 201 位消费者，以帮助确认该奶酪的特色优点和声誉，同时了解到消费者特点和消费意愿。调查采用开放式问卷方法，以便消费者充分表达对产品的认识。调查提供了以下信息：

①确认了奶酪的传统形象、特殊风味和机理；

②识别出消费者购买该产品的主要场所；

③消费者对产品声誉的认知及其证据，如，81.6% 的消费者认为"Queso Turrialba"这一名称具有较高知名度。

以此为基础，产地生产者制订了营销计划，根据消费者类型和居住地点确定了分销渠道：

①通过中间商在郊外购物中心销售；

②通过本地商户在当地村镇和城市周边销售；

③通过节庆活动（尤其是产地生产者一年一度组织的活动）直销给消费者，也可在农场上利用旅游活动开展销售。❷

---

❶ VANDECANDELAERE E, ARFINI F, BELLETTI G, et al. Linking people, places and products-a guide for promoting quality linked to geographical origin and sustainable geographical indications [M]. Rome：FAO, 2009：97.

❷ VANDECANDELAERE E, ARFINI F, BELLETTI G, et al. Linking people, places and products-a guide for promoting quality linked to geographical origin and sustainable geographical indications [M]. Rome：FAO, 2009：107.

（2）哥斯达黎加香蕉（Banano de Costa Rica）

哥斯达黎加全国香蕉行业协会（CORBANA）成立于1971年。该协会为一公共实体，由蕉农、政府、国有银行等利益相关方共同所有和管理，其主要职责之一是通过产品推广活动，为国内香蕉生产者开拓营销渠道。

从2008年开始，CORBANA联合相关政府部门和研究机构进行了为期3年的研究，并最终于2010年使"Banano de Costa Rica"注册成为哥斯达黎加首个香蕉地理标志，也是中南美洲国家第一个香蕉类地理标志。

注册成功后，CORBANA使用"Banano de Costa Rica"地理标志名称和标识，通过制定香蕉营销战略，采取新的品牌营销方法开拓国际市场。哥斯达黎加政府运用地理标志这一知识产权工具，通过实施国际认可的质量安全标准，为本国农民创造竞争优势。在营销管理上，CORBANA采取了以下做法：

①透过大型活动开展产品推广和广告宣传，例如，为2008年奥斯陆马拉松赛提供官方赞助，发放香蕉和宣传品。

②在哥斯达黎加国家少儿博物馆搭建设施，通过模拟让少儿体验香蕉生产全过程，寓教于乐。同时，还结合环境保护和病虫害防护，不仅使青少年了解到香蕉产业，还有助于培育儿童这一未来的香蕉消费主力。❶

（3）孔泰奶酪（Comté）

孔泰奶酪是法国及欧盟著名地理标志（AOC/PDO），也是中欧10+10地理标志互认试点产品之一。孔泰和格吕耶（奶酪）

---

❶ WIPO GIs and rural development：a case of bananas［EB/OL］.［2022-01-05］, https：//www.wipo.int/ipadvantage/en/details.jsp?id=3111.

行业委员会成立于1963年,它既是供应链上的代表,也是行政、经营和行业合作伙伴,负责推广孔泰奶酪,保护行业利益,组织文化活动,开展产品研究。日常活动包括营销管理、落实地理标志保护各项规定、协调交流、广告宣传以及内部协商合作。❶

(4) 汉源花椒

汉源花椒在2005年获得地理标志保护后,产地积极组织开展各类营销活动,扩大市场知名度。

①参加全国各类博览会,广泛开展汉源花椒宣传推介活动。

②依托花椒产业及旅游发展优势,连续举办花椒节、花椒产业论坛、花椒采摘体验、花椒美食节等系列活动,助力提升市场影响力。

③在拓展营销渠道上,构建"农超对接""农贸对接""农商对接新"模式,推动花椒加工企业进入成都红旗连锁、家乐福、伊藤洋华堂等多家超市及农贸市场。推出的高端花椒产品成功入驻成都双流国际机场、秦皇岛北戴河国际机场、重庆川北国际机场、杭州萧山国际机场以及四川全省5A风景区,高端产品销售额占全年营业额的25%。

④参与品牌评价活动,提升品牌价值。根据汉源县人民政府提供的数据,在中国品牌建设促进会组织的2020年品牌价值评价中,"汉源花椒"品牌价值以三年翻六倍的增长速度,从2016年评估的7.04亿元,跃升到49.65亿元,实现了品牌形象和品牌价值的腾飞。

---

❶ VANDECANDELAERE E, ARFINI F, BELLETTI G, et al. Linking people, places and products-a guide for promoting quality linked to geographical origin and sustainable geographical indications [M]. Rome: FAO, 2009: 99.

（5）礼县苹果

礼县苹果于 2008 年获得地理标志产品保护。近年来，受益于政府部门的支持引导和电商企业的大力扶持，礼县苹果的网络营销成为新亮点。具体做法是：

①通过加入"2019 天猫双 11 狂欢夜"，搭建起产销对接的快速通道，网络主播、政府官员、明星艺人一同为礼县苹果推介代言。

②在优酷平台宣传推介"礼县苹果"品牌，通过公益助力消费扶贫。

③2019 年 9 月 17 日，阿里巴巴在北京举办公益直播活动，短短 3 个小时礼县苹果销售 1.5 万件（约 15 万斤），销售额超 50 万元。❶

礼县苹果的事例具有一定代表性。互联网时代打破了传统营销手段造成的"产、供、销脱节，中间商唱主角"的局面。在直播、短视频等营销手段成为电商发展重要突破口的当下，直播往往比其他销售推广效果更好、更直接。最近兴起的直播带货等经销方式更无限拉近了产地生产者与消费者之间的距离，使消费者能够直接面对产品、产地，获得更多商品信息，进而激发购买意向。直播带货这种方式非常适合农产品销售，尤其对于偏远地区百姓而言，给地理标志产品带来新的商机，值得宣传推广。当然，直播带货作为一种新的经销方式，也产生了诸如虚假宣传、信用缺失等问题，同样不容忽视，应加强规范和管理。

---

❶ 甘肃礼县：直播带货连接消费扶贫 激发脱贫攻坚新动力［EB/OL］.（2020-07-08）［2021-03-02］. http：//www.chinaxiaokang.com/xianyu/yaowen/2020/0708/998715.1.html.

目标2：零饥饿

该目标旨在消除饥饿，实现粮食安全，改善营养状况和促进可持续农业和食品工业发展。联合国2021年11月30日发布的一项最新研究报告指出，拉美国家仅2020年一年就增加了1380万饥饿人口，使饥饿人口总数达到5970万人。该报告援引联合国粮食及农业组织（以下简称"联合国粮农组织"，FAO）代表的观点，认为拉美及加勒比地区正面临严峻的食品安全问题，2014~2020年饥饿人口激增了79%，达到人口总数的9.1%，为过去15年新高。而全世界饥饿平均水平更是高达人口总数的9.9%。❶

食品安全的重要性不言而喻。与食品安全直接相关的是农业和食品加工业，源头是农业。这二者也正是国际上地理标志保护的主要产品类别。地理标志保护起源于对葡萄酒原产地名称的特殊保护，并由此发展成为对奶酪、火腿、咖啡、茶叶、水果、蔬菜、谷物、坚果等众多加工食品和农产品的地理标志保护制度。

"保护原产地命名和地理标志的目的是确保将某一优质特色产品或其生产方式带来的收益公平地回报给农民和生产者，同时在产品上标明产品特色与产地的特定关联，使消费者在作出消费

---

❶ New UN report：Hunger in Latin America and the Caribbean rose by 13. 8 million people in just one year［EB/OL］. （2021-11-30）［2021-01-10］. https：//www. fao. org/newsroom/detail/new-un-report-hunger-in-latin-america-and-the-caribbean-rose-by-13. 8-million-people-in-just-one-year/en.

选择时获得更多信息。"❶

地理标志保护制度通过执行严格的质量管理体系，实现对食品和农产品生产的过程管理，并作为对国际通行的质量管理体系的有效补充，使特色产品的特色质量得以保持和发扬，在更高层次上保证了食品安全。具体来讲，地理标志保护制度对于保证农产品和食品安全具有以下优点。

1. 把关从品种选育开始

农产品质量安全与品种选育关系密切，食品加工同样离不开优质农产品原料。因此，品种选育是生产出优质农产品和食品的前提条件之一。地理标志保护制度十分注重品种选育，选取植物品种或畜禽种苗是地理标志保护的基本要求，须在质量技术要求中予以明确。品种一旦确定下来，生产者须严格执行，不得随意变更。由于地理标志产品质量与当地自然条件密切相关，因此，在品种选择上优先考虑的往往是当地土生品种，或选取已在当地经过生产实验、反映良好、可以充分体现地理标志产品质量特色的优良品种。

关于品种，有以下几个方面值得关注。

一是处理好动植物品种与地理标志的关系。对此，各国做法不尽相同，但遵循的基本原则都是不可误导消费者。例如，法国规定，含有或以动植物品种命名的产品不得误导消费者，使消费者产生错误联想，误以为该产品产自品种名称所指向的地理方

---

❶ Regulation（EU）No 1151/2012 of the European Parliament and of the Council of 21 November 2012 on quality schemes for agricultural products and foodstuffs［EB/OL］.［2022-04-11］. https：/feur-iex. europa. e/legal-content/ENTXT/？uri=CELEX%3A32012R1151&qid=1660293292963.

位。❶ 欧盟规定，当申请的地理标志名称与动植物品种名相冲突，使消费者误以为该产品来源于品种所含的地名时，不予注册。(欧盟条例 1151/2012 第 6 条)

瑞士法律在规定动植物品种名不予注册的前提下增加了一款，即：

当地理标志与当地动植物品种名相同，但该产品的生产尚未离开原产地，或者在动植物品种名称可更改的前提下，申请地理标志保护不构成对消费者的误导。❷

我国在地理标志保护实践中，对于以动植物品种名命名的地理标志所采取的基本原则与瑞士的做法相仿。《中华人民共和国植物新品种保护条例》第 18 条规定，名称经注册登记后即为该植物新品种的通用名称。根据该条例，我国先后分批制定了《中华人民共和国农业植物新品种保护名录》，列入该保护目录的均为植物的属或种名以及学名，且均为产品的通用名称，如水稻、玉米、马铃薯等。在畜禽品种方面，2021 年 1 月，国家畜禽遗传资源委员会公布了《国家畜禽遗传资源品种名录（2021 年版）》，收录畜禽地方品种、培育品种、引入品种及配套系 948 个。❸ 该目录收录的地方品种中含有较多以地名命名的畜禽，如金华猪、延边牛、阿勒泰羊等。这类地方品种，或称为原始品

---

❶ 参见：INAO. Guide du demandeur d'une appellation d'origine protégée (AOP) ou d'une indication géographique protégée (IGP). https：//www. inao. gouv. fr/.

❷ 参见：Ordinance on the Protection of Designations of Origin and Geographical Indications for Agricultural Products, Processed Agricultural Products, Forestry Products and Processed Forestry Products (PDO/PGI Ordinance) of 28 May 1997 (Status as of 1 February 2019.

❸ 参见：http：//www. chinafarming. com/axfwnh/2021/01/26/3307297899. shtml.

种、土种，多与当地生态条件高度适应。

含有地名的品种被推广到其他地区种养殖，一方面可扩大优良品种的推广范围，或有利于各地品种改良，增产增收，但另一方面易造成地方品种逐渐失去地理指向功能，沦为产品的通用名称。因此，对于含有地名的品种申请地理标志保护，如一概不予受理，不仅不利于动植物品种的保护和质量提升，反而可能因本地品种持续外传，生长环境不断变化，造成种质资源退化，质量特色稀释。视情形允许含有地名的品种申请地理标志保护，符合保护动植物种质资源的目的要求。

王清印等（2005）认为："优良品种都是依靠丰富的基因材料育成的，无论是原始的、引进的，还是新培养的优良品种或品系，一旦因近亲交配或杂交等原因丧失了它们的基因库中原有的基因，就难以重新恢复。""保护种质资源的目的，就是尽最大可能维持物种的遗传多样性，维持种内遗传变异的水平，维持物种和种群的自然繁殖能力，维持物种的进化潜能，实现生物资源的可持续利用。"❶

在地理标志保护实践中，特色产品名称为本地土生种群（未列入国家动植物品种名录）的，可以申请地理标志保护，并在质量技术要求中予以明确。对已列入国家动植物品种名录，但生产繁育尚未扩散推广至外地的，也可申请地理标志保护。专家和地理标志主管部门或建议申请人主动向动植物品种管理部门申请修改品种名称，或要求原产地有关部门对该品种采取保护措施，避免品种外流和扩散。

这种做法与种质资源保护中鼓励的"就地保护"（in situ

---

❶ 王清印. 海水生态养殖理论与技术 [M]. 北京：海洋出版社，2005：7.

conservation）的理念相一致。所谓就地保护"是在物种（种群）发生或栖息的地方，在天然或人造的生态系统中，对种质资源进行保护。这是群体水平的遗传保护，也是一种生态保护。""就地保护是保护种质资源的最有效方式，它优于迁地保护。"❶

对已列入国家动植物品种名录，且已在异地较大范围推广生产，沦为通用名称的产品，地理标志保护申请原则上不予受理。推广扩散后的品种之所以不予受理，在于无法实施有效的地理标志保护监管，无法切实保护地理标志名称的知识产权，失去了地理标志保护的实际意义。以武昌鱼为例，湖北省鄂州市曾申请"武昌鱼"地理标志产品保护，但未被主管部门受理。原因是，武昌鱼原产地虽在鄂州市境内，但这一品种（学名"团头鲂"）已广泛推广至我国多地养殖生产，且均以武昌鱼命名，在全国各地市场上销售。走进各地水产市场和餐馆，很容易发现武昌鱼的招牌。这说明该品种养殖已广泛扩散，成为产品的通用名称。"武昌鱼"已失去地理指向功能和地理标志保护的可行性。要解决这一问题，只存在一种假设的可能性，即湖北省或鄂州市在全国范围禁止武昌鱼养殖，将武昌鱼养殖范围限定在鄂州市境内。但就武昌鱼在全国广大的养殖范围而言，这样做的可行性显然仅存在于理论上。武昌鱼的事例说明，保护优秀的地方品种和珍贵的动植物资源十分必要，地理标志保护制度可以作为一种有效的保护手段及时加以利用。地方品种一旦大范围推广，试图挽回的成本将十分高昂，甚至无法挽回。

二是处理好品种选育与品种改良之间的关系。就初级产品，尤其是植物类初级产品而言，随着市场变化和技术进步，植物新

---

❶ 王清印. 海水生态养殖理论与技术 [M]. 北京：海洋出版社，2005：7.

品种往往具有后发优势，可以不断改善产品的总体质量。如樱桃产品，国内本土品种近年来已逐步让位给外来品种，苹果早已被红富士（Malus Pumila Mill）等品种所取代。如果栽培品种变了，原有的地理标志是否就不存在了？对这个问题的理解要区分具体情况。由于产地自然条件相对稳定，适生产品种类有限，有些品种调整未必改变地理标志产品的本质属性，可以被视为技术创新的一部分；而另一些品种改变则可能影响到原有地理标志产品的本质特征，不可盲目推行。另外，时间的把控也很重要，"朝令夕改"不可取，品种的调整应是经过时间和实践检验后作出的选择。

品种调整涉及的是如何处理特色产品的"变与不变"的关系问题。毋庸置疑，地理标志保护的一个主要特点是传承历史文化积淀和当地生产传统。已经确认的地理标志产地范围、生产工艺和包括动植物品种在内的质量技术要求应保持相对稳定，没有特殊理由不得随意改变。这方面国内外在管理上均有要求，如，欧盟对于已注册的地理标志修改变更质量技术要求的规定是：有关修改不得涉及产品主要特性；不得改变产品名称；不得影响划定的产地范围；不得改变主要生产工艺等。

然而，凡事又不都是一成不变的。地理标志保护制度旨在维护产品的特色质量，并非一味因循守旧。随着时间的推移，动植物新品种不断涌现，根据市场需要，在农业生产实践中研究、实验、选取新的适生品种是完全可能的。另外，即使不改变品种选择，一个植物品种经过数年的生长周期，可能出现混杂退化现象，需要进行提纯复壮。只要实验证明新品种适合在该地域范围内生长，且质量特色得以呈现甚至更加突出，就应该允许品种优化和调整。这也是地理标志产业可持续发展的客观要求。例如，杨梅、水蜜桃等生鲜水果因不耐储运，长期以来仅限于本地及周边市场销售。一些水果，如香蕉、芒果等，若想销往外地市场，须在果实成熟前采摘，在运输过程中熟化。近年来，经过科研人员实验研究，优化改良了一些水果品种，使其较耐储存，有利于实现水果外销，部分解决了储运难的问题。当然，品种选育和改良是长期任务，需在实践中不断改进完善。提前采摘或通过技术改良品种可能影响到果实的品质和风味。北京市农林科学院研究员姜全（2020）认为，在品种选育和改良方面，有时只注重丰产、耐储运等特点，把果实特质"改丢了"。❶ 提醒科研人员，任何品种改良都不应破坏原有的品质和风味，不可顾此失彼。

另外，对于一些动植物产品，地理标志保护审核过程中所认定的，往往是当地通过长期选育确定下来的地方品种，其适生性经过当地地理环境长期实践证明，如泰和乌鸡、南阳牛、莱芜猪等。在现有条件下，变更品种意味着改变产品的主要品质特征，直接影响消费者对产品的市场认知，所以往往行不通。王清印等（2005）认为："引种有助于改善养殖品种结构，提供育种素材，但也会导致外来种与土著种的遗传混杂。"❷ 引种和品种改良在任何时候都须谨慎从事。以塞尔维亚的 Futog Cabbage（Futog 卷心菜）地理标志为例，这是当地一个卷心菜品种，品质特色是叶片轻薄、口感清甜，生产范围和规模较小。地理标志保护的主要目的就是保护该地方品种的质量特色和原产地环境，因此其质量

---

❶ 于文静. 买家说桃子越来越不好吃了？啥原因？：来自水蜜桃产业的调查［EB/OL］.（2020-09-02）［2020-09-06］. https：//baijiahao.baidu.com/s？id=1676711377245137204&wfr=spider&for=pc.

❷ 王清印. 海水生态养殖理论与技术［M］. 北京：海洋出版社，2005：7.

技术要求中明确了品种要求，不得随意改变。❶

2. 特殊配方和工艺保证特色质量

无论是农产品种养殖，还是食品、工艺品生产加工，地理标志产品的生产或使用特定品种和配方，或使用特殊工艺和生产方法。特殊的生产方式是成就地理标志产品的重要因素，但也不宜过分强调地理标志产品生产的特殊性。总体而言，地理标志的生产首先应遵守农产品和食品加工标准化生产的基本要求，而不是另起炉灶，执行完全独立的一套管理体系。在此前提下，也要承认地理标志产品生产的特殊性，主要体现在种养殖类产品的独特管理技术，以及食品加工的特殊工艺要求。这些特殊要求有机地存在于生产过程中，使产品生产既满足有关标准或管理体系的强制性要求，也满足产品特色质量对工艺的特殊要求。

例如，水果生产的通用标准和生产技术规程已基本覆盖所有果树类产品。只要严格按照相关标准和技术规程进行生产，果品质量就可以得到保证。而水果类地理标志生产的特殊性主要体现在：一是品种选育，限定在某一个或几个品种范围内；二是种植密度和树形，严格规定行间距和株间距的上限，明确树形修剪要求，保证果实质量；三是肥水管理，施用有机肥，禁用某些化肥农药；四是果实采摘，限定采摘时间、成果单果重或直径，并以此分级销售，通常仅保留二级以上成果作为地理标志保护产品。以上简单说明了水果类地理标志产品生产的一般性指标，根据当

---

❶ VANDECANDELAERE E, TEYSSIER C, BARJOLLE D, et al. Strengthening sustainable food systems through geographical indications: evidence from 9 worldwide case studies [J/OL]. Journal of sustainable research, 2020, 2 (4): 27 [2020-11-18]. https://doi.org/10.20900/jsr20200031.

地环境条件，还有其他一些特殊指标，在此不一一列举。

3. 传统工艺维护特色产品的质量特征

生产工艺在很大程度上决定着产品质量和食品安全。地理标志保护致力于合理利用土地资源，倾向于保留传统生产技术，不使用或少使用农药、化肥和食品防腐剂。这些都对生产出健康、优质的产品发挥了积极作用。上文谈及合理利用资源等问题，这里再着重讨论一下传统工艺。

所谓传统，"是从历史沿传下来的思想、文化、道德、风俗、艺术、制度以及行为方式等。……是历史发展继承性的表现。"❶ 从生产技艺的角度讲，传统是历经长年积累传承下来的经验总结。传统生产工艺往往意味着纯手工或较少使用现代机器、工具，工序较为繁复，劳动强度较大，生产成本较高。传统工艺往往与特色产品的特殊质量要求密切相关。王笑冰（2019）认为："尽管传统生产方式成本较高，但地理标志产品支配溢价的能力使这种生产方式获得了存续的经济基础。"❷ 关于如何把握地理标志与传统工艺之间的关系，重点要以能够体现和保持产品的质量特色为目的。只要被证明能够完整呈现出产品的质量特色，在地理标志生产过程中并不排斥使用现代设备和工具，否则应谨慎使用。在涉及时间、效率等问题上，不可随意改变传统工艺所要求的时长、工序等条件，不刻意追求所谓的改良工艺。无论是农产品还是加工食品，都是水土、气候与人类智慧相结合的产物，其生产过程都应尊重历史传承，强调延续传统工艺，不随意改变或摒弃。改良工艺的目的大多是提高生产效

---

❶ 夏征农，陈至立. 辞海 [M]. 6 版. 上海：上海辞书出版社，2009：321.
❷ 王笑冰. 经济发展方式转变视角下的地理标志保护 [M]. 北京：中国社会科学出版社，2019：49.

率，缩短生产时间。但经验告诉我们，农产品和食品最讲究时令和季节。以损害产品质量特色为代价，盲目提高生产效率是地理标志保护的大忌。

例如，山西老陈醋是享誉全国的地理标志产品。仅从名称上看，一个"老"字就体现着酿造时间上的要求。而通过实验分析，由于采用精选高粱、麸皮为主料，稻壳、谷壳为辅料，以大麦、豌豆为原料制作的大曲作为糖化发酵剂，经酒精发酵后采用固态醋酸发酵，再经熏醅、陈酿等工艺酿制而成，山西老陈醋与其他醋相比，含有丰富的愈创木酚类物质、四甲基吡嗪、5-甲基糠醛及苯甲醛，其可视为山西老陈醋的特色指标。❶ 根据《地理标志产品　山西老陈醋》国家标准（GB/T 19777-2013），所有标明"山西老陈醋"的商品都必须经过一系列严格的质量管控，其中之一是要经过"捞冰、伏晒"等不少于 12 个月的陈酿期。只有这样生产出的产品方可被称为"山西老陈醋"。而现实中，一些厂家为降低成本，并未完全满足这一生产要求，转而采用所谓的改良工艺，因而不符合地理标志保护要求，不能冠以"山西老陈醋"名称。这也才有了市场上名目繁多的山西"××陈醋""××老醋""××醋"等招牌。而只有"山西老陈醋"这五个字名下所收纳的才是名副其实的山西老陈醋，才是完全满足消费者对传统工艺和健康理念要求的地理标志保护产品。

酒类产品（葡萄酒、烈酒、啤酒、白酒、黄酒等）是地理标志产品的重要组成部分。虽然世界各地的酒类产品从原料选取到生产工艺存在明显差异，但由于酿酒过程与当地的自然和人文因素大都有着较为密切的联系，因此酒类产品在国际地理标志中

---

❶ 参见：深圳市计量质量检测研究院在 2010 中国地理标志保护论坛上分享材料。

占有较大份额。就我国而言,白酒酿造工艺历史悠久,地域特征显著。而民间流传的"好水出好酒"从一个侧面反映了产地水质对于白酒质量的重要影响。事实上,我国的几大名酒之所以誉满中华,与当地特殊的自然条件,尤其是水质和气候有着密不可分的关系。再加上不同白酒酿造工艺的独特性,才使优质白酒的特色质量得以长期保持,闻名遐迩。蜿蜒于贵州、四川两省的赤水河被形象地称为"美酒河",原因就在于这条河流沿岸是茅台、郎酒、习酒等多个中国久负盛名的白酒产地。

中国优质白酒的生产普遍沿用传统的蒸馏酒固态法工艺,即以高粱等粮谷为原料,采用固态(或半固态)糖化、发酵、蒸馏,经陈酿、勾兑而制成,未添加食用酒精及非白酒发酵产生的呈香呈味物质,形成具有本品固有风格特征的白酒。❶

除了对水质、原料的特殊要求外,白酒生产技术的关键流程还包括制曲、发酵和贮藏等。所谓制曲,是糖化、发酵剂在制造过程中依靠自然界带入的各种菌类或单一菌种,在不同原料中进行富集、扩大培养,再经过风干或烘干、贮藏而得到的固态物质。赖登燡等(2021)认为,大曲在酿酒中具有四大作用,即提供菌源、糖化发酵、投粮作用、生香作用。由于微生物与其存在的自然环境有一定联系,地理环境对酿酒具有重要意义。地理标志产品就是地理环境对白酒生产重要性的一个体现。❷ 不同的温度、湿度以及产地所在的"小环境"(风向、地势、植被等)都对酒曲质量产生一定影响。

---

❶ 赖登燡,王久明,余乾伟,等. 白酒生产实用技术[M]. 2版. 北京:化学工业出版社,2021:9.

❷ 赖登燡,王久明,余乾伟,等. 白酒生产实用技术[M]. 2版. 北京:化学工业出版社,2021:27,31.

再以浓香型白酒为例,其生产的一个重要特点是窖池和窖泥技术。窖池是将泥窖作为发酵容器,窖泥是白酒产生香味成分的微生物培养基,是浓香型白酒生产最关键的物质基础。离开了优质窖泥就不可能生产出优质浓香型白酒。而黄泥的自然老熟需要很长时间。通过大量研究实验,现在可以模拟自然老窖成熟的条件,用人工方式缩短窖泥成熟周期。窖泥培养的实质是通过培养有益菌群,并使其成为窖泥中的优势菌群,从而产生合理的香味成分,并能使这些菌类保持长期、合理、有效的生长。❶

值得一提的是,中国优质白酒的生产过程是自然因素与人文因素的有机结合,具有典型的地理标志产品特征。其中蕴含的是对自然环境的敬畏和尊重,也是历史文化和传统技艺的延续和传承。一个有趣的现象是,不少名酒产地都拥有较为丰富的旅游资源,在保障食品安全的同时,实现了真正意义上的"好山好水出好酒"。

4. 规范行业管理,完善保护机制

地理标志保护是一个系统工程,其中包括对产业上下游的规范管理,是政府监管、行业监督和企业自律的综合管理。

南溪豆腐干是四川一特色小吃,2008年9月获批为地理标志保护产品,并在随后的实践中形成了地理标志保护阶段的工作模式。具体的做法是:

(1) 健全保护机构。建立了政府负责、协会指导、同行监督、企业自律的保护工作机构。政府负责宏观层面的保护和南溪

---

❶ 赖登燡. 王久明,余乾伟,等. 白酒生产实用技术 [M]. 2版. 北京:化学工业出版社,2021:59-64.

豆腐干整体品牌的宣传、提升和产业发展等工作，成立了"南溪豆腐干地理标志产品保护委员会"，制定并发布了《南溪豆腐干地理标志产品保护管理办法（试行）》和《地理标志产品南溪豆腐干专用标志考核细则》，以规范性文件的形式建立健全了地理标志产品保护工作制度。南溪县食品工业协会是南溪豆腐干地理标志产品保护的参与部门，其作用包括加强地理标志产品的同行监督和行业自律，协助管理地理标志产品的市场准入、标准体系建设、信息收集、会议联系等，协会以企业为主体，加强自身建设，做到"自主、自立、自强、自养"。

（2）加强标准体系建设。南溪豆腐干除按照《南溪豆腐干质量技术要求》制定了《地理标志产品 南溪豆腐干》地方标准外，还制定了《地理标志产品 南溪豆腐干生产工艺技术要求》地方标准。各专用标志申请企业在递交申请后，必须经地理标志产品保护办公室按照《地理标志产品 南溪豆腐干》《地理标志产品 南溪豆腐干生产工艺技术要求》，结合 QS 市场准入和食品安全的相关要求进行现场核查合格后才向四川省质量技术监督局推荐，从源头确保了地理标志产品的质量特色及其公信力。

（3）提高检测和研发技术水平。建设了"四川省（南溪）豆类制品质量检测检验中心"和"四川南溪食品研发中心"，推进农业科技成果的转换，提高对豆腐干食品安全的监控能力。依托骨干企业，开展豆腐干自动化生产的自主创新，并鼓励企业与高等院校、科研院所开展产学研合作，形成集政府、主管部门、企业、科研机构为一体的地理标志产品技术创新体系，一方面确

保了食品安全，另一方面也构建了一个很好的发展服务平台。❶

再以汉源花椒为例，据汉源县人民政府提供的信息，自汉源花椒 2005 年获得地理标志保护后，汉源县在规范汉源花椒行业管理、完善保护机制上采取了以下措施：

（1）成立了汉源花椒协会，主要从事汉源花椒优良品种引试、提供花椒种植技术和品牌推广等工作。

（2）成立了花椒产业推进领导小组、花椒产业发展局、花椒产业发展中心，设立花椒产业发展基金，把花椒产业作为加快全县中高山区农村经济发展的战略重点和突破口，推进花椒产业发展。

（3）探索出了"政府扶持、龙头企业带动、椒农广泛参与、社会化服务"的产业化发展模式。

（4）形成了"培训为先、示范带动、平台建设、科技支撑、补贴跟进、校企合作"的多元化推动格局，在加快新农村建设中发挥重要作用，成为中高山区群众致富、地方财政增收的有效途径。

上述两个地理标志产地的案例具有一定代表性，其运行管理机制具有借鉴参考价值。实践中，不少地理标志产地通过借鉴先进经验，摸索出适合当地特色产业发展的途径。地理标志保护机制的建立和完善有效保证了地理标志产品的质量安全，提高了产品声誉和消费者信心。

---

❶ 参见：四川省宜宾市南溪质量技术监督局在 2010 中国地理标志保护论坛上分享材料。

第二节　地理标志保护促进健康事业发展

目标3：良好健康和福祉

联合国官方统计显示，2019年，"（世界各国）改善了数百万人口的健康状况，在提高人口预期寿命、减少产妇和儿童死亡率、抗击传染性疾病等领域取得了很大进展。但在消除某些病患，如痢疾和肺结核方面出现停滞不前的状况。全世界仍有一半以上人口享受不到基本医疗服务，其中很多人因负担不起医药费而可能陷入极端贫困。需要各国齐心协力实现基本医疗全覆盖，并提供可持续经费保障，解决日益增加的包括精神健康问题在内的非传染性疾病负担，应对抗生素类抗药性，以及空气污染和饮用水卫生问题。"[1]

健康生活是人类社会的永恒追求和共同目标。人类健康离不开卫生、清洁的饮用水、食物和健全的医疗保障。作为地理标志的主要产品类别，农食产品为消费者提供绿色、环保、优质的商品。毫不夸张地说，由于普遍采用优化、特殊的生产方法，世界各地的地理标志产品比其他同类产品更加符合健康生活理念，可以更好地满足消费者需求。同时，虽然地理标志保护不属于医疗卫生范畴，但提供道地药材等制药原料、促进各年龄段人口的卫生健康，是地理标志保护的目的和重要内涵之一。

---

[1] Knowledge Platform［EB/OL］.［2020-07-24］. https：//sustainabledevelopment. un. org.

草本药材在中国和其他一些国家有着悠久的栽培种植历史,在世界范围拥有广大的市场需求,也是地理标志产品类别之一。鉴于中医药在我国医药市场上的重要地位,药材种植在我国一直是一个大产业,影响面广,涉及人口多,并且与实现脱贫增收目标关系密切。

由于不同地方生产出的药材存在质量差异,因此不同产地的药材可呈现出药效差异,进而影响治疗效果。中医建议尽可能使用"道地药材",也就是在特定产地栽培种植的优质药材。道地药材的概念与地理标志如出一辙。中国在发展地理标志保护的进程中,已将许多道地药材纳入保护范围,既划定了产地范围,防止遭受侵权假冒,也保证了道地药材的质量特色,确保了药材药效。前文介绍了礼县大黄的事例,其他如岷县当归(岷归)、蕲艾、霍山石斛、西峡山茱萸、封丘金银花等一大批道地药材获得地理标志保护,使众多患者吃上了"放心药",促进了中医药事业的健康发展。

草本药材在世界范围均有种植栽培。以西红花(saffron)(别名番红花、藏红花)为例,这种原产于西亚的草本药材,具有活血化瘀、凉血解毒、解郁安神的功效。古代或由西域经青藏高原传入中原地区,因此在我国被广泛称为藏红花。现今的西红花产地主要分布在伊朗、希腊、印度、摩洛哥、阿富汗、尼泊尔、中国等国家,是当地百姓的重要收入来源。在我国,真正原产于西藏的藏红花数量较少。随着市场需求的不断增长和科技进步,其种植范围近年来已延伸至上海、浙江等地,使得市场上销售的"藏红花"相当一部分产自西藏以外。西藏政府部门和行业组织近年来开始加大投入,扩大生产,恢复藏红花的市场地位。2017年,西藏藏红花获得地理标志产品保护。

西红花在国外的发展也与地理标志保护密切相关。Krokos Kozanis 西红花是希腊著名地理标志保护产品（PDO）。在西非国家摩洛哥，西红花 2008 年年产量约为 3 吨，位居世界前列，其中 1.8 吨产自一个省的 560 公顷产区。地理标志的发展促进了可持续生产体系建设，对经济、文化、生物多样性以及与西红花相关的农业旅游产生了积极影响。❶ Taliouine 西红花是摩洛哥的地理标志产品，产地生产者达 2300 人。实施地理标志保护的目的是促进当地经济发展，阻止落后地区农村人口外流。地方公共政策大力支持个体农户组织化建设，产地成立了 35 个合作组织。2000~2014 年，通过合作组织销售的西红花收购价格翻了 5 倍，而同期未加入合作组织的收购价格仅增长 40%。与此相对应，2000~2014 年，非合作组织销量下降 26%，合作组织销量增加 10.75 倍，合作组织数量由 2000 年的 5 个增加到 2014 年的 35 个，并且成立了一个覆盖全体西红花生产者的行业协会。❷

Rooibos 是南非一种具有芳香味道的健康茶饮，在许多国家受到欢迎。这种茶叶仅在南非出产，并且是南非所有茶叶品种里唯一具有保健功能的茶饮。20 世纪六七十年代，科学家发现，它富含抗氧化成分，不含咖啡因，具有保健作用，可用于缓解婴幼儿食物过敏、皮肤干燥、失眠、多动症等症状，也可用于美容和护肤。经过长达 8 年的研究和倡议，2014 年 Rooibos 终于成为

---

❶ 联合国粮农组织. 可持续食品体系的自愿性标准：机遇与挑战 [M]. 王永春，等，译. 北京：中国农业出版社，2019：89.

❷ VANDECANDELAERE E, TEYSSIER C, BARJOLLE D, et al. Strengthening sustainable food systems through geographical indications: evidence from 9 worldwide case studies [J/OL]. Journal of sustainable research, 2020, 2 (4): 8, 16, 30, 33 [2020-11-18]. https://doi.org/10.20900/jsr20200031.

南非的地理标志保护产品。❶

　　天然矿泉水是我国地理标志保护对象之一。健康、清洁、富含有益矿物质的天然矿泉水水源地分布较广，尤其是人迹罕至的高原和山区，是天然矿泉水的重要产地。西藏作为地球第三极，素有"亚洲水塔"之称，冰川资源较多，河流、湖泊密布，天然矿泉水水源丰富。曲玛弄矿泉水（5100）水源地位于西藏当雄县公塘乡，念青唐古拉山脉南麓当雄断陷盆地北侧地带，海拔5100米。该矿泉水富含偏硅酸、锂、锶，这三项矿物质均达到国家标准，年产量约20万吨。偏硅酸、锂、锶具有与钙、镁相似的生物学作用，有利于骨骼钙化，有一定保健作用。曲玛弄矿泉水于2009年11月获得地理标志保护，在其质量技术要求中明确规定，水源地7个泉眼海拔为5000米以上，日开采量不超过3000立方米，并规定了严格的水源地保护措施。❷ 曲玛弄矿泉水是我国天然饮用水地理标志保护的一个代表。地理标志保护有助于实现在保护水资源环境的同时，让更多消费者喝上优质健康的放心水。

---

❶ WIPO. Disputing a name, developing a geographical indication [EB/OL]. [2022-01-08]. https：//www.wipo.int/ipadvantage/en/details.jsp?id=2691.

❷ 关于曲玛弄矿泉水地理标志产品保护公告，参见：《国家质量监督检验检疫总局公告》（2009年第104号）。

CHAPTER 04 >> 第四章
地理标志制度促进经济增长和社会公平

第一节 地理标志保护促进实现性别平等

目标 5：性别平等

男女平等是社会文明进步的标志。当今社会性别不平等现象依然存在，在有的国家和地区甚至非常严重。世界银行《2019年性别数据手册》(*the Little Data Book on Gender 2019*) 指出：虽然性别平等取得了一定进步，尤其在教育和健康卫生方面。然而，发展并不平衡，低收入国家，主要是非洲撒哈拉以南地区，男女不平等现象尤为严重。

实现可持续发展目标离不开广大妇女的积极参与。而现实中，性别歧视现象依然很多，其表现形式之一便是对妇女工作权利的歧视和剥夺。在一些国家和地区，妇女往往只能从事家务和简单农业劳动，缺乏经济自立的能力。改变性别不平等现象需要全社会的共同努力。可行的途径包括扩大妇女就业范围，增加就业岗位，通过技能培训，提高妇女劳动技能，满足社会生产需要。

在许多国家，手工艺品是地理标志的重要组成部分。资料显示，印度约 60% 的地理标志为纺织品和工艺品。[1] 在我国，刺绣、手编、陶瓷等特色工艺品皆可受到地理标志保护。而无论是过去还是现在，相当一部分手工艺品的劳动者主体是妇女。这一现象客观反映了手工艺品发展的历史沿革，以及妇女心灵手巧的天资特性。妇女的直接参与推动了地理标志产品的传承与发展，对于实现男女平等具有特殊意义，发挥了积极作用。

具体来讲，地理标志在促进男女平等方面具有以下作用。

1. 促进女性参与就业，提高妇女经济自立水平

地理标志产品以农产品、食品和手工艺品为主，农产品中又以经济类作物、果蔬、林下产品居多。这些产品的生产或对体能、力量的要求不高，适合女性的生理特点，女性参与生产劳动基本不存在障碍。另外，不管是农田管理还是食品生产加工，生产过程中都需要细心和耐力，而这也正是女性的长处所在。现实中，手工艺品制作、食品加工领域以及农产品播种、采收、分级等工种的女性占比较高。可以说，地理标志产业发展创造更多就

---

[1] BAGADE S B, METHA D B. Geographical indications in india: hitherto and challenges [J]. Research journal of pharmaceutical, biological and chemical sciences, 2014, 5 (2): 1235-1236.

业岗位，直接影响妇女参与就业，可以带动更多劳动妇女加入生产经营过程中去，使地理标志保护产生的经济回报惠及产地广大妇女。

2. 促进发展职业教育，提高女性职业技能

地理标志保护带来的影响不仅包括产品的生产经营，而且可促进与之相关的包装、物流、旅游等产业协同发展。这势必给产地及其周边地区带来连锁反应。地理标志生产绝不仅仅是简单体力劳动。从落实质量技术要求到科学管理田间地头，从创新营销手段到发展特色文化产业，所有这些都需要参与者经过业务培训和技能教育，否则难以有效实施地理标志保护的各项要求，实现地理标志产业链协同发展。女性劳动者可在此过程中学习、实践新知识，掌握新的劳动技能。这对于女性自身和整个家庭来说都是好事，对于改善产地经济社会面貌，实现男女平等都产生积极作用。

3. 摆脱家务局限，实现本地就业

近年来，我国越来越多的农民工选择返乡就业，原因之一是子女教育和老人赡养等问题。妇女普遍担负着生儿育女、赡养老人等家庭重任。家务在客观上限制了女性走出家门，到远离家乡的地方打工就业，实现经济上的自立。地理标志生产对于解决这一困局有着十分现实的价值和意义。地理标志产地妇女可在家门口实现就业，在不影响照顾家庭的前提下，从事力所能及的工作。

从地理标志产品的性质来看，无论是农业生产还是食品加工，其生产大都具有季节性。而刺绣、编织等一些工艺品的制作生产对场地并无特殊要求，可居家完成。这从另一方面给女性就业带来了便利，即可以利用上述生产的季节性或适宜于居家从业

的特点,从自身家庭条件出发,自主选择就业时机,灵活参与地理标志生产经营。正如黎锦(海南)生产者所说:"带着娃,绣着花,挣着钱,养着家。"❶

镇湖是江苏无锡市太湖东岸的一个小镇。镇上有个传统手工代代相传,这就是镇湖刺绣。镇湖刺绣是闻名遐迩的苏绣的一个地方分支。镇湖古时湖岸绵长,河道纵横。特殊的地理位置使之成为沟通苏州古城、联络太湖沿岸城市的水路要道,贸易十分发达,催生了刺绣行业的形成和发展。又因镇湖位于苏州市西部伸入太湖中的一个半岛,地形狭长,南、北、西三面环水,使得镇湖自古以来以刺绣为农家主要副业的传统得以完好保留。太湖水乡的滋润,养育了宛如流水一般柔美的镇湖绣娘。镇湖绣娘世代以刺绣为生,为保护祖辈传下来的技艺,镇湖地方政府还创造性地将刺绣技艺列入小学课程。❷ 当地政府为保护和传承这一文化瑰宝,申请地理标志保护。镇湖刺绣具有厚重的历史文化积淀和广泛的社会参与度,尤其是以"八万绣娘"为代表的劳动妇女,为镇湖刺绣产业的发展奠定了牢固的基础,也为扩大妇女就业树立了榜样。

"庆阳香包"是甘肃庆阳市的地方传统手工艺品,庆阳香包生产技艺已被列入第一批国家级非物质遗产名录,2014 年 4 月庆阳香包获得地理标志产品保护。香包,古名香囊,又叫荷包。庆阳香包制作的历史渊源与农耕文化里男耕女织这一特点关系紧密。庆阳民间一直沿袭着妇女制作香包比手工,和端午节赠送、佩戴香包祛邪纳福的传统习惯。当地妇女通过细心观察,把身边

---

❶ 参见:2020 年 7 月 18 日 CCTV-4 的《中国新闻》。
❷ 何斌,吴森明.对加强传统手工艺品地理标志保护的建议[J].中国检验检疫,2010(11):19-20.

看到的素材画出来，然后再绣出来。香包制作按照剪纸图样，在丝绸布料上用彩色纱线绣出各种图案，然后缝制成不同造型，内芯填充上丝绵和草药香料，成为小巧玲珑的刺绣品。草药被称为"香草"，而药袋变为"香包"，寄托了劳动人民驱邪、避灾、祈福的美好愿望，是庆阳妇女世世代代对原始、传统手工技能的传承，也是个人技能和智慧的再现。庆阳香包的发展历程充分体现了中国劳动妇女的勤劳智慧和创作才能。如今，庆阳香包已发展为覆盖庆阳市 5 个区县近 80 个乡镇，拥有 200 多家生产企业的地方产业，从业人员近 4 万人。2008 年，庆阳香包民俗文化产业群被文化部命名为"国家文化产业示范基地"。❶

事实上，除手工艺品外，我国在采茶、传统医药、食品加工等涉及地理标志生产的领域都吸引了大量妇女就业。妇女的广泛参与促进了地方特色产业的协调发展。

第二节 地理标志保护促进区域经济发展

目标 8：体面工作和经济增长

伴随着经济增长和工业化进程，外出务工，到经济发达的地方去，早已是欠发达地区普遍存在的社会现象。以我国为例，据国家统计局统计，2019 年全国共有 2.9 亿农民工，其中，1.7 亿

---

❶ 陈亮洲. 蓬勃发展的庆阳香包民俗文化产业 [EB/OL]. (2018-03-19) [2022-01-03]. http://wtgdly.zgqingyang.gov.cn/xwzx/hyxx/content_70981.

农民工选择了外出就业,剩下的约1.2亿则选择留在当地劳动力市场,留下的农民工占比约为41%。❶ 据《经济观察报》记者分析,平均每名外出农民工每月可以获得4427元的收入,本地农民工则为3500元。在过去的10年时间中,选择留下的比例在不断增加。国家统计局统计显示,2011~2018年,在本地就业的农民工数量占农民工总数的比例从37.25%不断上升至40.12%,每年本地农民工数量的增速也均大于外出农民工数量的增速。

《经济观察报》记者引用中国社会科学院农村发展研究所研究员李国祥的观点,认为尽管受到新冠肺炎疫情影响,选择回流的人数在增多,但长期来看,外出务工依然会是大部分农民的选择。李国祥提示,到2019年已经出现了本地农民工数量增速小于外出农民工数量增速的情况。农民工选择外出就业主要因为三点,即本地就业机会不多、当地工资水平低,以及在城镇化推进过程中国家大力发展区域经济,如发展长三角、粤港澳大湾区等造就的吸引力。而未来不同区域经济发展的潜力将决定农民工未来的流动趋势。因此,农民工外出就业机会更多的长期趋势未必会改变。❷

农民工是改革开放以来促进经济快速增长的一支重要力量,发挥了突出作用。但也应该看到,青壮年人口长期外出务工造成家乡劳动力大量外流,使得农村"空心化",出现"空

---

❶ 国家统计局. 中华人民共和国2019年国民经济和社会发展统计公报[EB/OL]. (2020-02-28)[2020-04-30]. http://www.stats.gov.cn/tjsj/zxfb/202002/t20200228_1728913.html.
❷ 田进. 2.9亿农民工的艰难选择:本地就业,还是外出打工?[N]. 经济观察报, 2020-06-12.

巢村",留守老人、留守妇女和儿童现象日益突出。外出务工在改善家庭经济条件的同时也带来新的社会问题。研究和探索如何实现就地致富,返乡创业、返乡就业已成为社会关注的话题。58同城、安居客发布的《2019—2020年返乡置业调查报告》显示,有68.6%倾向于选择回乡置业,想在工作城市(非家乡城市及家乡省会城市)的人群占比为29.8%。子女教育、房价、工作机会、照顾家人等因素是人们决定是否返乡的主要因素。孔祥智等(2019)引用人力资源和社会保障部监测统计数据,显示在2017年第四季度返乡农民工中,有10.9%的农民工选择了创业。截至2018年1月,返乡创业的农民工已经超过了700万人。❶

  国家近年来对于返乡创业出台了涉及税费减免、贴息贷款、创业补贴等一系列鼓励和优惠政策。而不管是自主创业,还是返乡就业,都离不开发展当地产业作支撑。这其中尤以挖掘自然资源优势、发展特色产业为优先考虑之一。孔祥智等(2019)指出了农民工返乡创业的四种典型形式,即家庭农场、农村电商、休闲农业和农产品加工业。❷ 这四种形式都以当地特色资源为主要依托。因地制宜发展特色产业为欠发达地区脱贫致富找到了一条出路,也在一定程度上解决了本地就业的问题。

  黄冈是湖北传统农业大市,地理环境独特,农产品资源丰富,但长期以来,黄冈的特色产品"大名气"与特色产业"小块头"形成强烈反差,影响了农民收入,阻碍了经济发展。全市11个县、市、区,有5个被定为国家级贫困县,1个被定为省级

---

❶ 孔祥智,等.农业经济学[M].2版.北京:中国人民大学出版社,2019:78
❷ 孔祥智,等.农业经济学[M].2版.北京:中国人民大学出版社,2019:78-79.

贫困县。当地党委、省政府审时度势，把实施特色农产品地理标志保护战略作为促进老区跨越式发展的着力点，全面推进质量建设，助推农业农村经济跨越发展。

一是把实施地理标志产品保护与提高农业产业化水平相结合。坚持用工业化的理念谋划农业，将分散的农户以地理标志为纽带、以龙头企业为通道连接到市场，积极推广"地理标志+龙头企业+农户"的新型农业产业化模式，促进了农村经济结构优化升级和山区农民脱贫致富。在罗田板栗获得地理标志保护后，当地先后引进加工企业3家。罗田全县板栗栽培总面积发展到7万公顷，板栗年产量达到3万吨，居全国各县之首，板栗系列总产值7亿元，占农业总产值40%；全县人均板栗收入1000多元，板栗产业成为该县经济最具活力的增长点。

二是把实施地理标志产品保护战略与品牌农业、创汇农业、休闲农业建设相结合。英山茶借地理标志这张名片，开发建设乌云山茶叶公园，已成为大别山区重点生态旅游线路，促进了该县旅游经济发展。

三是坚持实施地理标志产品保护与促进农业增效、农民增收相结合。以加快优势特色地理标志产品保护、使用为手段，以提高产品质量和市场竞争力为目标，用现代工业的思维和方法把地理标志保护产品纳入工业企业的生产体系，初步实现了"借助一件地理标志，带动一个产业，富裕一方百姓"的目标。黄州萝卜借助地理标志走向市场，从过去论"堆"卖到现在的论"个"卖，按品质差别，一个萝卜一般要卖到2~3元钱，成为农民致

富的新门路。❶

四川是我国农民工输出大省，每年有数百万人外出务工，在为家庭带来可观经济收益的同时也改善了家乡面貌，但多数农民工终会面临回乡发展的问题。作为解决这一问题的手段之一，四川实施的地理标志产品保护战略，在促进农民本地就业增收上发挥了积极作用。四川农业人口占比较高，2019年达3870.1万人。❷ 农村人口就业问题突出。四川政府部门认识到地理标志保护对于乡村振兴和农业发展的重要意义，大力宣传推广地理标志保护制度，使四川地理标志产品数量领跑全国，为解决农村人口在当地就业开辟了一条新路。以蒲江雀舌为例，在2008年获得地理标志保护后，规范了茶叶种植生产，提高了产品附加值和品牌知名度，同时还带动了乡村旅游和包装、物流等产业发展，年接待游客超过100万人次。越来越多的农户在当地就业，围绕茶叶、茶场做文章，人均收入显著提高，安逸地在家门口工作不再是奢望。

汉源花椒在2005年获得地理标志保护后，当地按照"因地制宜，应种尽种"的原则，制定花椒产业发展规划，对汉源全县花椒产业进行统一布局，对海拔1200米至2500米的适生区进行重点发展，以63个贫困村为中心，辐射全县中高山所有区域。2012年以来，累计发展花椒种植面积10.39万亩。据汉源县人民政府提供的数据，初步统计，2021年花椒种植基地县内种植面积20.4万亩，全县鲜花椒产量2500万千克（折合干花椒产量500万千克），综合产值26亿元。每年7~9月，甘

---

❶ 参见：2009年10月27日，湖北省黄冈市人民政府代表应红在地理标志产品保护实施十周年纪念会议上的发言。
❷ 参见：《四川省2019年国民经济和社会发展统计公报》。

孜州、凉山州以及云南、贵州部分县区大量花椒采摘工人来到汉源县花椒基地采摘花椒，提供就业岗位3万余个，采摘工经济收入合计超2亿元。

地理标志保护对就业的促进作用主要体现在以下几个方面。

（1）劳动密集型特点创造更多就业岗位

地理标志产品是高附加值产品的代表，地理标志产品的影响力波及供应链各环节的企业和个人。地理标志产品多为农产品和食品的特点又决定了该产业用工量较大，劳动密集程度较高。食品加工是典型的劳动密集型行业。即便是农产品，个体农户在自己的土地上从事农业生产虽不额外增加用工岗位，但产品的收获、筛选、包装等环节或仍需使用较多人力。王笑冰（2019）认为："地理标志特有的支配溢价能力不仅能提高农业劳动收入，而且其劳动密集型特点吸纳了更多的农业劳动力。"❶ 这方面的案例很多，都江堰猕猴桃地理标志保护带动就业3.2万人，人均年收入7000多元。在郫县豆瓣获得地理标志保护后，当地产业吸纳、聚集近100家行业龙头企业共同发展，辐射带动上游、下游、平行产业的若干生产性服务业繁荣发展，形成了强大的规模经营优势和品牌集群效应。❷

（2）地理标志相关产业吸引更多非农就业

2020年6月习近平总书记在宁夏视察时指出，乡亲们在家门口就业，虽然收入不比进城务工高，但省去了住宿、伙食、交

---

❶ 王笑冰.经济发展方式转变视角下的地理标志保护［M］.北京：中国社会科学出版社，2019：37.

❷ 刘忠俊.成都推动地理标志发展促进民众就业增收［EB/OL］.（2014-04-23）［2021-12-04］.http://www.chinanews.com.cn/df/2014/04-22/6091613.shtml.

通等费用，还能照顾家庭，一举多得。❶ 而地理标志对产地带来的积极影响并不局限于产品的生产和经营。地理标志的地域特色是典型的文化旅游资源。产地赋予地理标志的历史文化底蕴、环境友好贡献和人文技艺展示可催生乡村旅游和多种文化体验，带动产地居民参与餐饮、民宿、交通、导游、娱乐等就业活动，实现在家门口挣钱养家、增收致富的目的。

福建是中国茶文化发达的省份，是安溪铁观音、武夷岩茶、正山小种等享誉世界的名茶产地。地理标志保护促进当地发挥资源优势，在种好茶、做好茶的基础上，顺应市场需求，延伸茶经济产业链，提高茶产品的加工深度，从第一产业（茶叶生产）向第二产业（茶饮料、茶叶深加工）及第三产业（茶文化、茶艺、茶馆、茶旅游）延伸扩展，形成了一条茶生产、茶加工、茶机械制造的传统核心茶产业链，还外延出一条旅游、会展、博览、公路服务等相关联产业链。❷

（3）地理标志就业较少受性别和年龄限制

地理标志农产品、食品生产往往对从业者文化程度和职业技能要求不高，即使是工艺品等传统手工技能（如刺绣、织毯），经过培训也可逐渐上手。与此同时，农业生产基本不受性别和年龄限制，手工艺制作或更适合女性参与。这就意味着，地理标志产地可因地制宜，充分吸纳当地人口参与到生产过程中，从事相应的工作。这方面的事例很多，如富平柿饼地理标志产地在陕西省富平县，柿饼生产传统上在一家一户的庭院晾晒完成，其中一

---

❶ "让人民群众奔着更好的日子去"——习近平总书记考察四川纪实［EB/OL］.（2020-06-11）［2021-12-04］. http：//www.sohu.com/a/556167970_121400326.

❷ 参见：福建南平顺昌县质量技术监督局地理标志产品保护交流材料。

些工艺要求，如"揉捏整形"等，主要由妇女和老人完成，许多老人参与到富平柿饼的生产中来，传授制作技艺，指导年轻人操作，甚至加入产品的网络直播中，形成独具特色的富平柿饼产业现象。

第三节　地理标志保护促进减少不平等

目标 10：减少不平等

可持续发展第 10 项目标旨在减少国内省份之间，以及国与国、地区与地区之间存在的发展不平等现象。发展不平等是世界各国，尤其是发展中国家普遍存在的问题。联合国报告指出，新冠肺炎疫情所造成的失业和无收入来源使得全球的不平等程度正在加剧，导致严重的社会经济危机。❶ 随着新冠肺炎疫情在全球蔓延，失业或半失业人口激增，多个行业遭受重创，考验各国的应对能力和恢复经济能力。新冠肺炎疫情对于最不发达国家和其他发展中国家的冲击后果尤为严重，给原本就脆弱的经济造成巨大破坏，削弱各国减贫脱贫的努力。

党的十九大报告指出："中国特色社会主义进入新时代，我国社会主要矛盾已经转化为人民日益增长的美好生活需要和不平衡不充分的发展之间的矛盾"。习近平总书记 2020 年 8 月 24 日在经济社会领域专家座谈会上进一步指出："我国发展不平衡不

---

❶ Knowledge Platform ［EB/OL］.［2020－07－24］. https：//sustainabledevelopment. un. org.

充分问题依然突出,创新能力不适应高质量发展要求,农业基础还不稳固,城乡区域发展和收入分配差距较大,生态环保任重道远,民生保障存在短板,社会治理还有弱项。"❶

关于发展不平衡问题,张占斌(2017)认为:"不平衡问题,主要包括经济不平衡、社会不平衡、制度不平衡等重要领域。其中经济不平衡主要包括产业不平衡、区域不平衡和动力不平衡等。"❷ 从区域发展的角度分析,我国东、中、西部经济社会发展长期处于不平衡状态,且在某些领域呈现差距逐步拉大趋势。从发展的质量和效益角度分析,不少地区仍普遍存在产业结构不平衡、一些产业占据过多资源、质量效益不高的问题。从城乡发展和收入分配角度分析,存在城乡居民收入不平衡、消费不充分的问题等。

区域发展不平衡有多方面原因。如前文所述,落后地区往往地处偏远,交通不便,缺少产业支撑和人才资源。为发展产业,吸引人才,很多地方政府下大力气开展招商引资,制定优惠政策引进人才。偏远落后地区吸引投资主要凭借资源优势、较低人力成本,以及涉及土地、税收等方面的优惠政策。而随着近年来国家在环境保护上的要求日趋严格,对矿产开发、煤化工等项目限制越来越多,一味攫取落后地区自然资源的做法已难以为继。落后地区发展的出路指向合理利用当地自然资源,生产经营与当地物产密切相关的优质特色产品,并发挥历史文化传承优势,充分利用当地资源发展文化、旅游产业。综合分析,地理标志保护在解决地区发展不平衡问题上具有以下作用。

---

❶ 参见:习近平总书记于2020年8月24日在经济社会领域专家座谈会上的讲话。
❷ 张占斌. 正确认识中国新时代的社会主要矛盾 [J]. 人民论坛,2017 (31):2.

1. 促进产业结构调整，提升特色产业规模和质量效益

促进特色产业发展是地理标志保护的主要目的和优势所在。地理标志保护制度从发现优质特色产品入手，通过挖掘质量特色、规范生产管理、优化资源配置、提高质量效益、打造区域品牌等措施，提升特色产品的产业规模和质量效益，促进解决一些地区部分产业过多占据资源、破坏生态环境等问题。改善产业结构，使之朝着可持续的方向调整和发展。

辽宁抚顺市是国务院2009年公布的第二批32个资源枯竭型城市之一，经济曾长期依赖煤炭等矿产资源开发，第一产业基础薄弱，第二产业比重偏大。为实现经济转型，促进资源型城市可持续发展，抚顺市人民政府着手调整和优化产业结构，发挥当地森林覆盖率较高、林下资源丰富的优势，巩固农业的基础地位。抚顺市先后有10个产品获得地理标志保护，在给当地带来经济效益的同时，坚持保护生态、绿色发展的理念，科学合理利用森林资源，发展林业及林下经济产业，大力推动以林下种植、林下养殖、林下产品采集加工、森林景观利用等为主的林下经济规模化、标准化、产业化发展，推动生态优势转化为发展优势。❶

云南石屏县地处偏远，交通不便，但石屏豆腐却在云南省远近闻名。得益于当地特有的地下水质，以当地地下酸水作为凝固剂点制豆腐是石屏豆腐生产的一大特色，生产历史长达400多年。2012年12月，石屏豆腐获得地理标志保护❷。到2018年，全县共生产石屏豆腐产品20万吨，实现产值23.6亿元，带动全

---

❶ 参见：抚顺市农业农村局的官方介绍，http://www.fushun.gov.cn/.
❷ 参见：《国家质量监督检验检疫总局公告》（2012年第218号）。

县从业人员9000余人。按照"一园三区"的布局，石屏县先后实施了松村豆制品加工区、石屏豆腐文化产业园、石屏豆腐创意园建设工作，石屏豆腐产业实现了从分散式生产向园区集中发展的转变，产业集聚度得到了极大提高，产业布局不断优化。通过技术创新，石屏豆腐产业从传统的初级加工逐步向精深加工方向发展，产业链不断延伸，产品附加值不断提高。❶ 如今的石屏豆腐产品行销全国，各大商超都能见到它的身影。石屏县利用当地特有资源发展出的特色产业具有较强的生命力。因为具有鲜明特色，所以受到市场追捧，又由于质量特色与产地历史人文的密切关联，豆腐产业在当地"开花结果"。特色产业的健康发展较好地解决了地区发展不平衡的问题，为偏远落后地区经济社会发展提供了借鉴。

2. 促进农村经济发展，拓宽农民增收渠道

地理标志产品的地域性特征决定了地理标志保护制度主要面向广大农村地区。党的十九大报告指出，农业、农村、农民问题是关系国计民生的根本性问题，必须始终把解决好"三农"问题作为全党工作的重中之重，实施乡村振兴战略。2018年9月，中共中央、国务院印发了《乡村振兴战略规划（2018—2022年）》，2018年9月21日，中共中央政治局就实施乡村振兴战略进行第八次集体学习。习近平总书记在主持学习时强调，乡村振兴战略是党的十九大提出的一项重大战略，是关系全面建设社会主义现代化国家的全局性、历史性任务，是新时代"三农"工作总抓手。《乡村振兴战略规划（2018—2022年）》第六章

---

❶ 云南石屏大力发展豆腐产业［EB/OL］.（2019-10-09）［2020-04-23］. http：//www.shipingdoufu.com/nd.jsp?id=32#_np=2_789.

远景谋划中提出,到 2035 年,乡村振兴取得决定性进展,农业农村现代化基本实现。农业结构得到根本性改善,农民就业质量显著提高,相对贫困进一步缓解,共同富裕迈出坚实步伐;城乡基本公共服务均等化基本实现,城乡融合发展体制机制更加完善;乡风文明达到新高度,乡村治理体系更加完善;农村生态环境根本好转,生态宜居的美丽乡村基本实现。实施地理标志保护能够在落实《乡村振兴战略规划(2018—2022 年)》中发挥重要作用,尤其体现在质量兴农、绿色发展、乡村文化和减贫脱贫等方面。

土地是农民收入的主要来源。影响农民收入增长的因素很多,其中之一是农业劳动生产率偏低,规模小,成本高。以我国为例,家庭联产承包责任制在全国农村已实施 40 多年,对于调动广大农民的生产积极性、实现脱贫增收发挥了重要作用。与此同时,随着经济社会发展,家庭联产承包制单元分散、耕地不匀、规模小、效率低、不适合现代化农机设备、集约性差的缺点逐渐显露出来。江珊珊等(2011)认为"农民从农业耕作中所获得的收益仍然远低于外出打工所获得的报酬。"解决这一问题的关键,是要"引导农民走合作化道路,通过农村互助组织,逐渐地实现规模化生产,并且自发地与市场接轨。"❶ 要实现规模化、集约化生产,克服一家一户生产造成的劳动生产力低下、效率偏低的问题。

《中华人民共和国农民专业合作社法》2007 年 7 月开始实施。农民专业合作社是在农村家庭承包经营的基础上,同类农产

---

❶ 江珊珊,黄雅虹,高定慰,等. 农民收入问题调查报告[EB/OL]. (2011-07-28)[2020-11-11]. https://wenku.baidu.com/view/87c0f9c10522192e453610661ed9ad51f11d54ec.html.

品的生产经营者或者同类农业生产经营服务的提供者、利用者自愿联合和民主管理的互助性经济组织。农民专业合作社以其成员为主要服务对象，提供农业生产资料的购买，农产品销售、加工、运输、贮藏以及与农业生产经营有关的技术、信息等服务。据统计，截至2017年，全国已有农民专业合作社193.3万家，涉及超过1亿个农户。❶

地理标志保护制度倡导建立地理标志产品农民专业合作社等合作组织，实施统一农资、统一品种、统一播种、统一收获、统一标识、统一销售等多项统一生产制度，保护和提高农产品质量特色，提升农产品市场附加值和竞争力。如前文所述，地理标志具有集体属性，只有调动起广大农户，使之与产地其他企业或个人形成集体意识，发挥集体作用，捍卫集体权利，才能真正实现地理标志保护的目的。而一旦落实地理标志保护的各项措施，地理标志产品既有的特色质量优势可有效提高产品附加值，以高出同类产品的价格回报产地生产和经营者。这已被世界各国的地理标志保护实践反复证明。

林芝市位于西藏东南部，平均海拔3000米，是西藏平均海拔最低的地级市。境内河流密布，雪山冰川众多，自然环境优美，森林资源丰富，素有"西藏的江南"的美誉。但在过去，林芝虽然享有西藏境内海拔相对较低、林下资源丰富等有利条件，却未能转化为百姓增收致富的现实生产力。近年来，林芝市提出质量强市战略，大力发展林下特色产业，开展地理标志产品保护，塑造林芝区域品牌形象。迄今已有林芝松茸、林芝天麻、林芝灵芝等10个特色产品获得地理标志保护。地理标志保护极

---

❶ 孔祥智，等. 农业经济学［M］. 2版. 北京：中国人民大学出版社，2019：180.

大地释放了当地百姓参与特色产业发展的积极性，缓解了当地农村人口就业问题，为农民增收致富创造了条件，也为地方经济社会可持续发展作出了贡献。

以林芝松茸为例，松茸被誉为"菌种之王"，林芝市工布江达县拥有独特的气候条件和丰富的森林资源，松茸产量较高，但当地松茸市场长期处于群众自发采集、出售的状态，没有形成产业化发展。近年来，伴随着林芝松茸获得地理标志保护，工布江达县成立了松茸采集加工农民专业合作社，建立加工基地，购置冻干、冷储、物流设备，开展松茸收购、加工、包装和统一销售。合作社已由最初 5 户股东发展到现在 167 名会员，固定资产达 4360 万元，年产值 1100 万元，年经营利润 163 万元。年均吸纳农牧民就业 300 余人，人均年增收 3.7 万元。同时，合作社辐射带动全县 1600 户 4600 名农牧民，人均增收 2800 元。❶

3. 促进消费升级，缓解消费不充分问题

经济发展不平衡还体现在消费不平衡不充分这一问题上。广大消费者日益增长的生活需要呼唤市场不断提高供给水平，持续提高产品质量，实现消费升级，满足不同层次消费者的市场需求。地理标志产品作为优质特色产品和拥有较高附加值的生活消费品，目标市场为中高收入者以及追求高质量生活的群体，它满足了市场细分和差异化需求。

关于营销管理，扎卡伊（2012）认为，营销管理就是要识

---

❶ 王淑，贾华加．西藏工布江达：深山走出"致富菇"［EB/OL］．（2020-07-17）［2020-07-23］．http://www.tibet.cn/cn/news/yc/202007/t20200717_6820561.html．

别细分市场和目标市场。❶ 艾米丽·凡德肯德莱尔等（2020）认为："消费者可通过地理标志（专用标志）识别出某种独特品质，继而提高支付购买的意愿。"❷ 调查显示，欧洲消费者普遍愿意以高出同类产品 15%~30% 的价格购买地理标志保护产品。我国的情况与之相仿，地理标志产品价格普遍高于同类产品。地理标志产品所形成的市场溢价可从品牌影响力的角度解释说明。俞吉兴（1996）认为，品牌更像是一种声望。❸ 卫军英、任中峰（2013）认为，品牌作为一种概括，其本身就具有质量和信誉的暗示。品牌对消费者来说是一种保证和信赖，对于企业来说则是一种责任，而这种暗示的强度也决定了品牌影响和品牌竞争的力度。❹ 地理标志保护产品所代表的是一个地方的优质物产和特色质量。它向消费者传递的信息非常明确，是对产品质量信誉的保证，可促使消费者产生更多信赖。中高端消费者通过购买地理标志保护产品，在提升生活品质的同时，更好地满足了对绿色、健康生活的追求。这在一定程度上有助于缓解消费不充分的问题。

---

❶ 扎卡伊. 可持续消费、生态与公平贸易 [M]. 鞠美庭，展刘洋，薛菲，等，译. 北京：化学工业出版社，2012：6.

❷ VANDECANDELAERE E, TEYSSIER C, BARJOLLE D, et al. Strengthening sustainable food systems through geographical indications: evidence from 9 worldwide case studies [J/OL]. Journal of sustainable research, 2020, 2 (4): 19 [2020-11-18]. https: //doi. org/10. 20900/jsr20200031.

❸ 俞吉兴. 市场价格 [M]. 北京：中国商业出版社，1996.

❹ 卫军英，任中峰. 品牌营销 [M]. 北京：首都经济贸易大学出版社，2013：21.

第四节　地理标志保护促进可持续生产和消费

目标12：负责任的消费和生产

联合国在回顾目标 12 的执行情况时指出，世界范围的物质消费规模正迅速扩大，严重威胁着联合国可持续发展目标的实现。需要采取行动，确保当今的物质需求不会导致资源过度开采，环境遭受破坏。这其中应包括改善资源利用率和减少浪费的政策，并应覆盖各经济领域。可持续消费和生产旨在"降耗、增量、提质"，即在提高生活质量的同时，通过减少整个生命周期的资源消耗、环境退化和污染，来增加经济活动的净福利收益。可持续消费和生产也要求从生产到最终消费这个供应链中各行为体的系统参与和合作，包括通过教育让消费者接受可持续的消费和生活方式，通过标准和标签为消费者提供充分的信息。[1]

这又是一个涉及优化资源利用效率的目标。与目标 1、目标 2 相比较，目标 12 提出的"降耗、增量、提质"和实现可持续的生产和消费，既针对发达国家，也针对发展中国家和最不发达国家，重点是发达国家。1992 年里约热内卢联合国环境与发展大会通过的《21 世纪议程》讨论了影响全球可持续发展的两个主要因素，即发展中国家人口增长过快和发达国家的过度消费和浪费。《21 世纪议程》第 4 章的标题为"改变消费形态"，聚焦

---

[1] Knowledge Platform［EB/OL］.［2020-07-24］. https：//sustainabledevelopment. un. org.

不可持续的生产和消费方式，研究制定转变不可持续消费形态的国家政策和战略。第4章第4.3条指出：贫困与环境恶化密切相关，全球环境恶化的主因是各国不可持续的消费和生产方式，尤其是工业化国家。第4.5条指出，改变消费形态需要多方面战略，聚焦需求，满足穷人的基本需要，在生产过程中减少废弃物和资源利用。第4.8条进一步指出，所有国家都应推广可持续消费方式，发达国家应率先实现可持续消费方式。第4.15条要求重新定位现有工业化社会已产生并在世界其他地区被照搬的生产和消费模式。改变消费形态涉及社会各方面，包括行业、政府、家庭和个人。关于减少浪费，第4.19条要求政府、行业、家庭以及社会公众共同减少浪费和废弃物品。第4.24条要求制定价格激励机制，向生产者和消费者发出明确的市场信号，指出能源消费的环境成本、物质和自然资源成本，以及所产生的浪费，只有这样才能转变现有的消费和生产形态。此外，第4.27条还特别强调了女性和家庭作为购买力较强的消费群体所发挥的潜在影响力。❶

关于地理标志在合理利用资源方面发挥的作用，本书前文已作探讨，这里重点讨论一下地理标志与推进绿色发展、实现可持续消费和生产之间的关系。

党的十九大报告提出，要推进绿色发展。加快建立绿色生产和消费的法律制度和政策导向，建立健全绿色低碳循环发展的经济体系。倡导简约适度、绿色低碳的生活方式，反对奢侈浪费和不合理消费。习近平总书记2020年8月作出重要批示，要求厉行节约、反对浪费。他指出，餐饮浪费现象触目惊心、令人痛

---

❶ 参见：https://sustainabledevelopment.un.org/milestones/unced/agenda21.

心！要进一步加强宣传教育，切实培养节约习惯，在全社会营造浪费可耻、节约为荣的氛围。❶

扎卡伊（2012）认为，全球消费量剧增对生态的影响是可持续发展概念产生的重要历史根源。负责任的消费者承担的是一个采取具体行动的问题，需要通过日常行为来完成，强调个人的执行能力。❷ 推进绿色发展，实现负责任、可持续的消费意味着要尽可能减少对自然资源的索取，减少人类消费活动对环境造成的负面影响，以最少的资源消耗满足人们的日常生活需要。要厉行节约、反对浪费，建设资源节约型社会。邢秀凤（2013）论述了资源节约型社会的特点，认为"所谓资源节约型社会，是指社会经济发展要建立在节约资源和能源的基础上，在社会生产和社会生活的每一个领域，都应该采取一种综合性的措施，力求以最小的资源能源消耗获取最大的经济社会效益，以实现经济和社会的可持续发展。"❸ 她认为，可以从企业、区域和社会三个层次来理解。其中，社会层次的资源节约型社会是节约社会的最高层次。从社会角度来看，要求摒弃奢侈消费和浪费问题，倡导一种科学、合理、适度、文明的消费风尚，形成健康的消费模式。要做到这一点，首先必须不断改进生产方式，提高生产效率，转变消费理念，追求绿色健康的生活方式。其次，要理性看待生活中的物质需求，减少浪费现象，减少不可再生能源的消耗和碳排放，培养负责任、可持续的消费理念。

---

❶ 习近平作出重要指示强调：坚决制止餐饮浪费行为切实培养节约习惯 在全社会营造浪费可耻节约为荣的氛围［N］.人民日报，2020-08-20（1）.
❷ 扎卡伊.可持续消费、生态与公平贸易［M］.鞠美庭，展刘洋，薛菲，等，译.北京：化学工业出版社，2012：3，130.
❸ 刘爱军.生态文明研究［M］.济南：山东人民出版社，2013：151-152.

杨家栋、秦兴方（2000）把可持续消费定义为："既符合代际公正，又符合代内公正原则，能保证人类物质和精神生活不断由低层次向高层次演进的，能促进可持续发展战略实现的消费。"❶ 他们将可持续消费分为物质、精神和生态消费三种形态。根据内容，把可持续消费分为广义和狭义两类。广义的可持续消费包括可持续的资源消费、生产资料消费、商品消费和劳务消费（旅游、文化、服务性消费）四个方面。狭义的可持续消费主要指可持续的商品消费和劳务消费，并在一定范围内涉及自然资源消费。孙启宏、王金南（2001）认为："可持续消费是指家庭、公司和公共部门购买产品和服务用于满足其对食物、住房、交通、休闲和通讯的基本需求的同时，要最大限度地降低所购买产品和服务的生命周期全过程的环境损害。"❷ 他们认为，与可持续生产相比，可持续消费强调经济活动中需求的一面。

与可持续、负责任消费概念密切相关的还有"绿色消费主义"和分享型经济（共享经济）。绿色消费主义要求消费者不购买那些在生产过程或使用过程中造成污染和破坏生态的产品。孙启宏、王金南（2001）引用英国约翰·艾尔金盾（John Elkington）和尤利娅·海尔斯（Julia Hailes）于 1988 年出版的《绿色消费者指南》中的观点，提醒消费者如何用自己的购买行为鼓励生产经营者付出环保努力。❸ 除此之外，近年来兴起的共享经济已渗透到日常生活的方方面面，除了城市常见的共享单车、共享汽车、共享充电宝等载体以外，已深入商品交换使用、住房分享、家庭餐食分享等广泛领域。

---

❶ 杨家栋，秦兴方. 可持续消费引论［M］. 北京：中国经济出版社，2000：172.
❷ 孙启宏，王金南. 可持续消费［M］. 贵阳：贵州科技出版社，2001：9-10.
❸ 孙启宏，王金南. 可持续消费［M］. 贵阳：贵州科技出版社，2001：3.

根据《剑桥英语词典》给出的定义，共享经济（sharing economy），或分享型经济，是基于人们分享个人财产并提供服务的经济体系，它或收费或免费，通常经由互联网组织上述活动。我国是共享经济最为发达的国家。据报道，共享经济在中国国内生产总值中的占比已达到 10%，比其他任何国家都要高。2020年共享经济用户达 8.3 亿人，市场交易额约 4706 亿欧元。❶

现实中，一些共享活动并不完全等同于商品租赁。例如，在德国，双方可在网上商定某一物品（如书籍、充气钻等）的使用和交接时间，使用者无须付费。再以房屋分享为例，依业主意愿，房客有时无须支付任何费用。也就是说，共享行为或不以营利为目的，而主要为提高闲置资源的使用率，减少资源浪费和任何被认为是不必要的消费。德国可持续发展与生产合作组织发起人指出，共享经济由组织方提供互联网平台，参与者提供个人信息、兴趣爱好和拟交换分享的内容，既可以是普通商品交换，如书籍或工具，也可以是服装，还可以是房主分享的住房，甚至是家庭主妇主动向外人提供的拿手菜。可以说，共享经济体现了可持续消费的理念，追求的是商品使用价值的最大化。鉴于它与本书主题关联性不强，不再赘述。

可持续消费的理念正逐步走进日常生活，其中所涉及的商品可能与地理标志密切相关。《联合国气候变化框架公约》第二十六次缔约方大会（COP26）于 2021 年 11 月在英国格拉斯哥召开。会议期间有一个细节值得关注，即，COP26 的餐饮供应商在菜单上标明每份餐食的碳足迹数字。食品供应商与有关公司合作，由其计算某种食物对气候产生的影响。计算须考虑

---

❶ 德朗格拉德. 中国，共享经济王国 [N]. 参考消息，2021-12-16 (15).

食品生产过程中每个阶段——从栽培耕作到加工运输——的温室气体排放量，将国家和当地市场数据考虑在内，然后得出最终的排放量。结果显示，低碳足迹食品（以植物为基础）每千克排放 0.1~0.5 千克二氧化碳当量。高碳足迹食品每千克排放量超过 1.6 千克二氧化碳当量。低碳足迹食品使用当季食材，且大多是本地产品或仅经过短途运输的产品。❶ 而本地生产、就地消费正是许多地理标志产品的重要特点之一，与低碳的理念不谋而合。

客观分析，低碳、环保等可持续消费理念的形成和培养与经济社会总体发展水平密切相关。《参考消息》援引《华盛顿邮报》的报道指出，2019 年，约 80% 美国人认为人类活动正在加剧气候变化，但与此同时，只有不到一半的受访者认为应对气候变化需要他们作出"重大牺牲"。皮尤研究中心近日公布的一项大规模调查显示，最发达经济体中有近 3/4 的居民担心，气候变化有朝一日会给他们的生活带来灾难。然而，只有 55% 的日本人愿意改变生活方式以应对气候变化，为受调查国家中最低。在瑞典，这一数字为 85%。报道还指出，总体而言，关于气候变化对个人的影响，年轻人比老年人表现得更为担忧，女性大多比男子更担忧。❷ 这一结果与杨家栋、秦兴方（2000）的研究观点基本吻合，他们认为："处于不同发展水平的国家对环境的态度是不一样的，越是富裕国家越重视环境保护。"❸

---

❶ 亚当，韦斯特福尔. COP26 菜单将碳足迹计算在内 [N]. 参考消息，2021-11-08（11）.
❷ 丹尼斯，泰勒. 皮尤民调发现，全球民众越来越把气候变化视为对个人的威胁 [N]. 参考消息，2021-11-05（7）.
❸ 杨家栋，秦兴方. 可持续消费引论 [M]. 北京：中国经济出版社，2000：172.

中国作为世界上最大的发展中国家,可持续消费大众化虽已起步,但相当一部分人口群体正处于消费上升阶段。这在一定程度上表现为物质追求持续升高、消费规模不断扩大。与此相伴的负面问题则是一些浪费现象屡禁不止,大众消费中的环保、低碳意识仍显不足,可谓有悖于可持续、负责任消费的理念。同时,必须承认,这是发展过程中产生的问题,需要在发展中逐步加以解决。

扎卡伊(2012)引述大量欧洲研究成果来说明负责任的消费与人口群体之间的关系[1],本书归纳为以下几点:

(1) 人口因素并未成为识别负责任消费者的重要标志;
(2) 负责任的购买行为不受性别影响;
(3) 受过高等教育似乎与更多负责任的消费行为相关;
(4) 收入水平是最重要的影响因素,较高收入者比低收入群体更关注环境友好。

以上研究成果反映了欧洲发达国家负责任消费的一般状况。可见,即使在发达国家,在负责任消费方面,也尚未形成全社会普遍关注并采取一致行动的消费行为。

转变人们的消费理念和生活方式绝非易事,需要全社会的共同努力和宣传引导,以加深人们对可持续消费的认识和理解,进而形成消费者自觉行为的动力。地理标志保护作为一个与这一努力高度契合的制度设计,在运行中体现着负责任和可持续生产、消费的理念。

首先,地理标志保护有助于解决生产和消费信息不对称的问

---

[1] 扎卡伊. 可持续消费、生态与公平贸易 [M]. 鞠美庭,展刘洋,薛菲,等,译. 北京:化学工业出版社,2012:92.

题。实施地理标志保护制度的目标之一是持续完善产品的质量保证体系，其中包括建立地理标志保护产品的溯源体系，加强产品标识管理，提高产品信息公开透明程度。扎卡伊（2012）列举了与可持续消费相关的10对矛盾，其中之一是"消费者缺乏判断哪些产品更符合可持续消费需求的分析方法"。他认为，单纯告知消费者改变消费习惯（并影响市场）并不十分有效。而公共政策导向和信息沟通却能持续发挥作用。他在谈及欧盟生态产品标签的作用时认为，（相对于能源标识）生态标签的市场表现一般，但有助于减少信息成本，即减少消费者找到一个符合生态环境标准产品所需要的时间。❶ 艾米丽·凡德肯德莱尔等（2020）认为，消费者在购买时无法评价商品质量，经销商可能隐瞒商品缺陷，影响市场作用的正常发挥。同时指出，标准化、监控和标识可平衡这一市场失灵现象，而地理标志可使消费者解决在售货地点难以通过感官评价了解产品"质量"信息的问题。❷

丰富地理标志保护标签标识信息属于公共政策的具体措施，这些措施旨在更好地保护消费者权益，提高商品和地理标志保护制度的可信度，维护地理标志产品的市场信誉，"降低消费者的信息成本和选择成本"。❸ 产品信息公开透明有助于消费者在作出消费决定前，充分了解产品产地、环境、声誉、原料成分、传

---

❶ 扎卡伊. 可持续消费、生态与公平贸易［M］. 鞠美庭，展刘洋，薛菲，等，译. 北京：化学工业出版社，2012：2，6，92.

❷ VANDECANDELAERE E, TEYSSIER C, BARJOLLE D, et al. Strengthening sustainable food systems through geographical indications: evidence from 9 worldwide case studies [J/OL]. Journal of sustainable research, 2020, 2 (4): 4 [2020-11-18]. https://doi.org/10.20900/jsr20200031.

❸ 王笑冰. 经济发展方式转变视角下的地理标志保护［M］. 北京：中国社会科学出版社，2019：27.

统工艺等真实信息，促使关心生态环境保护和产品质量安全的消费者选择购买地理标志保护产品，以自身消费体验来体现可持续消费理念。虽然世界各个国家和地区在地理标志保护管理水平上存在差异，但越来越多的国家和地区要求地理标志保护产品施加专用标志，有的还对地理标志的产品标签内容作出具体规定，生产者须提供关于产品原料来源、地理方位图示等附加信息。❶

其次，地理标志保护或有助于实现公平消费。所谓公平消费，是从消费中人与人之间关系的角度出发，即当代人与后代人都有平等追求生活质量的权利。任何人都不应由于自身的消费而危及他人的生存和消费（代内公平），当代人也不应由于自身消费而危及后代人的生存与消费（代际公平）。客观来讲，公平消费的理念要求消费者具有较高的思想认识水平和公德意识。从平衡消费总量、抑制过度消费的角度分析，地理标志保护可间接影响人们的消费习惯，促进公平消费目标的实现。

孙启宏、王金南（2001）认为，价格是引导消费以及消费者和生产者行为的有利因素。价格偏低，会造成自然资源过度开发和不可持续消费，但价格过高又可能引起自然资源交易量下降，给严重依赖资源出口的发展中国家带来难题。❷ 俞吉兴（1996）认为，市场环境下，"合理的价格一般是既能正确反映商品价值，又能正确反映市场供求变化状态的价格。"❸ 他归纳了农产品的生产成本，包括物质费用和人工费用。物质费用包括：生产资料费用（种籽、肥料、饲料、燃料、固定资产折旧等）；人工费用（人员劳动报酬、管理费用、保险、贷款利息

---

❶ 参见：欧盟 1151/2012 号条例第 12 条。
❷ 孙启宏，王金南. 可持续消费［M］. 贵阳：贵州科技出版社，2001：18.
❸ 俞吉兴. 市场价格［M］. 北京：中国商业出版社，1996：3，66.

等）。进一步细化，人工成本又可细分为直接成本和间接成本。以种植业为例，直接人工成本包括平整土地、播种、田间管理、收获用工等；间接人工成本包括积肥用工、初期生产用工、经营管理用工、销售用工等。

如前文所述，地理标志农产品在诸如种籽选育、肥料或饲料标准、田间管理、收获、分级、择优销售等环节都有严格要求，势必造成生产成本提高，继而推高产品售价。因此，与同类产品相比，地理标志农产品通常以高于同类产品的市场价格销售。食品和工艺品生产虽与农业生产性质不同，但工艺上以手工为主，同样推高生产成本。地理标志产品较高的市场定位意味着它的消费主体为中高收入群体，而非大众消费者。购买、消费地理标志产品的行为是以较高的付出获得更加优质的服务，也就是优质优价的概念。与此同时，这种服务在提供过程中更好地体现了节能、减排、降耗和绿色且有机的发展理念。

赖德胜（2001）把浪费分为配置性浪费、生产性浪费和消费性浪费三个层次。[1] 他认为，社会关注的通常是消费性浪费，而配置性浪费和生产性浪费往往不被重视。本书前文探讨了地理标志保护对于资源配置和集约生产方面的积极贡献。关于消费性浪费，意大利"零浪费运动"发起人认为，相较于食物在生产和流通环节的损失，消费端的浪费情况最为严重。[2] Hannah Ritchie 援引 Joseph Poore 和 Thomas Nemecek（2018）发表在《自然》杂志的一份研究报告，认为全球食品供应链上产生的损失和消费者

---

[1] 赖德胜. 关注浪费 [M]. 北京：中国财政经济出版社，2001：1.
[2] 意大利"零浪费运动"发起人塞格雷：中国反对浪费食物的行动具有积极意义 [EB/OL]. (2020-08-16) [2020-12-20]. https://baijiahao.baidu.com/s?id=1675168501352290153&wfr=spider&for=pc.

食物浪费贡献了世界上6%的温室气体排放量。❶

  虽然尚无证据表明地理标志产品能够有效抑制浪费现象,但从消费心理和消费行为的角度分析,优质优价的商品更有可能促使消费者在购买时谨慎选择,在使用时减少废弃,从而在某种程度上抑制消费中存在的浪费现象。

---

❶ RITCHIE H. Food waste is responsible for 6% of global greenhouse gas emissions [EB/OL]. (2020-03-08) [2021-11-17]. https://ourworldindata.org/food-waste-emissions.

第五章 地理标志制度助力保护地球生态环境

第一节 地理标志保护促进应对全球气候变化

目标 13：气候行动

联合国报告指出："温室气体排放持续升高，气候变化的速度超出预期，其后果正在世界各地显现。尽管在气候金融融资上，国家层面决定的捐资取得了积极进展，但仍需更大规模的计划，并加快减缓和应对的行动速度。金融以及加强能力建设，尤其对于最不发达国家和发展中的岛屿国家来说应更快提高。"❶

---

❶ Knowledge Platform [EB/OL]. [2020-07-24]. https://sustainabledevelopment.un.org.

目标 13 呼吁世界各国立即采取行动，应对气候变化及其影响。对气候产生影响的人为因素很多，除了工业化和人类活动产生的温室气体排放持续走高以外，人口增长、城市化进程、乱砍滥伐、粗放式的农业生产、对海洋和水体的污染等都可对环境和气候造成不利影响。"气候变化"已不再仅仅是专家议论的话题，越来越多的人正切身感受到气候变化所带来的影响。越来越多的消费者开始关注所购买产品与环境相关的问题。

联合国环境规划署（UNEP）2020 年 9 月 1 日引用一份联合研究报告的观点，认为在应对气候变化方面，如采取措施转变各国食品消费体系，或可为 2050 年全球减排目标贡献 20%。该报告认为，各国现有涉及食品领域减排的工作重心放在了农业上（如畜牧养殖业），而食品损耗和浪费对气候所造成的影响普遍被忽视。实际上，食品体系（包括食品生产、加工、运输、仓储、消费等）占所有温室气体排放总量的 37%。减少食物损耗和浪费，或转向更为可持续的食谱（以植物类食物为主，减少肉食）的作用普遍被忽视。❶

前文提到地理标志保护在优化资源配置、改进生产方式、提高有限资源的收益率方面的特点和优势。下面再以实际事例进一步说明地理标志对于应对气候变化所发挥的积极作用。

Madd（Saba senegalensis）是一种黄色野生水果（果实形状类似于山竹），生长在西非布基纳法索、塞内加尔、几内亚、马里等国家的林地或草原上，果实所在的枝条呈藤缠树的形态。其

---

❶ WWF, UNEP, Climate Focus, et al. Improved climate action on food systems can deliver 20 percent of global emissions reductions needed by 2050 [EB/OL]. (2020-09-01) [2020-10-21]. https://www.unep.org/news-and-stories/press-release/improved-climate-action-food-systems-can-deliver-20-percent-global.

中生长在塞内加尔南部 Casamance 一带的叫作 Madd de Casamance。该产地针对该产品，于 2017 年启动了地理标志注册申请，其有望成为西非首个野生水果地理标志保护产品。由于 Madd de Casamance 是野生水果，当地百姓对其生长环境格外注意保护，因为这关系到个人和家庭的生计。据统计，自从当地开始将 Madd de Casamance 作为商品采摘销售以来，未发生任何一起森林火灾，这也是 2019 年塞内加尔全国唯一未发生森林火灾的区域。可以说，保护当地生产环境已在老百姓中形成广泛共识，因为这样做"不仅仅是对环境的道德义务，（更重要的是）这关系到切身经济利益"。申请地理标志保护的过程协调统一了当地百姓以及各利益相关方的立场，使其更加珍惜这一自然禀赋，并由此对保护环境产生积极作用。❶

蒲江雀舌产自四川，是四川茗茶。蒲江县境内森林覆盖率达 48.31%，土壤、气候都适宜茶树生长。当地种茶历史悠久，起源于唐，距今已有一千多年，具有厚重的人文底蕴。蒲江县还是国家级生态建设示范区，是马尾松林的原产地。地理标志保护促进了蒲江雀舌产地集约化发展。

一是在全国率先进行茶林混植试点。蒲江雀舌茶树的生长环境非常特别，茶树或栽植在马尾松树林中，或簇拥在松树下，呈不规则的混合栽植状态。当地人认为，因茶树喜阴怕晒，这种混栽模式有利于茶树更好地汲取养分，获得适当的光照。采取茶林混植模式，优化了茶树生长环境，促进茶树健康生长，提升茶叶品质，增加茶叶产量，并提高了单位土地面积经济效益和林木覆

---

❶ WIPO. Supporting environmental sustainability with GIs: the case of Madd de Casamance［EB/OL］.［2021-11-20］. https：//www.wipo.int/ipadvantage/en/details.jsp?id=11582.

盖率，实现了产业发展和环境保护双赢。

二是在全国首创了茶园托管经营、统防统治管理模式。按照"公司+合作社+基地"的发展模式，与茶农建立合作双赢的利益联结机制，激励茶农将自己的茶园交由托管公司管理，统一施肥，统一病虫害防治技术，保证了茶叶企业拥有稳定、可控的原料基地，解决了投入品管理和技术规范问题，实现茶叶质量安全可溯源。❶

归纳起来，地理标志保护对于应对全球气候变化可以发挥以下作用。

1. 传统生产方式有助于减少温室气体排放

如前文所述，地理标志多采用传统工艺和生产方法，较少使用现代化机器设备，这在客观上减少了能源消耗和温室气体排放。传统工艺通常指纯手工或使用传统加工器具。这些加工器具在使用过程中往往主要依靠人力，对体力要求较高，且工艺较为繁复，生产效率相对偏低。国内这方面比较有代表性的包括宣纸的制作，锦、绣织物生产，白酒制曲、窖藏、蒸馏，黄酒和食醋酿造，以及植物油榨取等传统生产工艺。以宣纸为例，宣纸地理标志保护质量技术要求规定的工艺要求为：

选料：

青檀皮料加工程序

伐条、蒸煮、浸泡、剥皮、日光晒干、皮坯

燎草加工程序

选草、切草、捣草（破节）、埋浸、洗涤、渍灰、堆积、洗涤、日光晒干、草坯

---

❶ 参见：成都市质量技术监督局在 2010 年中国地理标志保护与发展论坛经验交流材料。

蒸煮、涤、日光摊晒、蒸煮、洗涤、日光摊晒、燎草

制浆：

青植皮料

皮坯—浸泡—蒸煮—洗涤—压榨—选检—漂白—洗涤—压榨—选检—打料—洗涤—漂白檀皮纤维料

草料

燎草—鞭草—打料—洗涤漂白—漂白草纤维料

配料：

草料粉碎—配合筛选—打匀洗涤全料

青檀皮料

制纸：

全料配水—配胶—捞纸—压榨焙纸—选纸—剪纸—成品[1]

  上述工艺流程基本依靠纯手工完成。之所以仍采用人工而非现代化设备，主要在于手工对质量特色所产生的影响无法被机器所取代。这种"逆潮流"而动、固守传统的生产方式虽然生产效率偏低，但由于保留了产品的品质特色，使之历经时间考验不发生改变，因此受到市场欢迎和消费者信赖。当然，地理标志并非一味固守传统，不采用新技术和创新科技成果。对于农业生产而言，现代农业技术已经彻底改变了落后的生产方式，极大地提高了农业综合效率和农产品质量。地理标志农产品生产并没有固守传统，而是走在了新技术应用的前面，是创新技术的重要实践基地。但在农作物病虫害防控等处理上则十分慎重，不用或少用农药、化肥，不片面追求提高产量，减少对土壤和环境的损害。

---

[1] 关于宣纸原产地域产品保护公告，参见：《国家质量监督检验检疫总局公告》（2002年第75号）。

总体而言，在全球气候变化加剧的形势下，发展地理标志产业，继承传统工艺，弘扬传统文化，有助于节能减排降耗，有利于减少人类活动对地球环境造成的不利影响。

"哈里斯花呢（Harris Tweed）是世界上唯一受特定法律保护（指1993年颁布的哈里斯花呢保护法案）的一种布料。正宗的哈里斯花呢加盖哈里斯花呢主管部门批准使用的证明商标。它保证花呢布料使用100%羊毛生产，并且在苏格兰外赫布里底岛纺织工家里手工染色、纺织。布料的最后清洗和整理也在位于该岛上的工厂完成。只有符合上述条件的布料方可由哈里斯花呢主管机构检验并准予（在布料上）施加印章。"❶ 哈里斯花呢依照特定的法律保护其正宗真品。这是国外对一些传统手工产品的保护形式之一，涉及的其他产品还有 Bordado da Madeira 陶瓷（葡萄牙）、Solingen 刀具（德国）等。❷ 王醉山（2016）认为，一个多世纪以来，哈里斯花呢的手工捻纱、染色、纺织技术从未发生改变。哈里斯花呢采用纯手工制作，使用人力驱动的踏板纺织机，不借助自动化或电力设备。又由于原料和燃料均取自自然、可生物降解、可吸收挥发性有机物，无致敏性，生产过程十分节能，因此对生态的影响较低。❸

2. 采用当地原料有利于减排降耗

这里指的是加工食品或手工艺品生产。我们知道，地理标志产品加工大体分为两类：一类是全部采用当地出产的原料，并且

---

❶ 参见：https：//www.harristweedboutique.com。
❷ 欧盟关于非农产品地理标志保护的研究报告认为，对这三种产品的保护不属于专门法保护，只是规定了质量技术要求。Study on geographical indications protection for non-agricultural products in the internal market Final report［EB/OL］. (2013-02-18)［2021-12-12］. https：//ec.europa.eu/docsroom/documents/14897。
❸ 参见：http：//www.360doc.com/content/16/0403/08/30237147_54749146.shtml。

在原料产地完成生产加工全流程，如葡萄酒、干酪等。另一类是既采用当地原料，也采用外地原辅料生产，如白酒、黄酒、食醋等。前者的生产完全在原料产地完成，其间基本不需要物流运输，且倾向于采用传统手工操作，因而排放和能耗极其有限。后者虽部分采用了外地原料，但本土成分仍占较大比重，且同样采用传统工艺。进一步分析可知，地理标志产品或多或少存在市场销售"本地化"现象。许多产品，尤其是生鲜类地理标志，优先满足的是本地或邻近地区的消费市场。例如，石屏豆腐的销售范围主要是石屏县和周边县市，过去最远也只是销往昆明市场。再比如，岗巴羊地理标志虽然市场需求很大，但由于养殖范围和产量受限，始终难以满足西藏以外的市场需求，甚至在西藏本地市场上也不多见。

　　上述两个例子说明，一方面某些生鲜类地理标志产品不耐储存，贮藏技术有待提高，市场辐射范围有待扩大；另一方面也与一些地理标志产品产量、规模严格受控有关。当然，除此之外，也有市场宣传推广方面的问题。这些特点对于地理标志产品市场营销而言或许是个问题，但产品稀缺和销售范围较小在客观上有助于减少温室气体排放，对环境和气候产生了正面影响。

　　La Ruche Qui dit Oui（蜂巢）❶ 是法国一个专供本地食品和农产品交易的网络平台，可谓"本地化"网络营销的典型代表。该平台使广大农户和厂商实现在网上与消费者直接交易，按每笔交易额的 20% 收取费用，用于纳税和平台运行维护，其余 80%全部归生产者所有。由本地的"蜂巢"设立的线下店铺负责收集农户的产品，消费者在网上下单，在约定时间内前往线下店铺取货。为宣传和保护本地特产，保证产品的生鲜品质，该平台仅

---

❶ 参见：https://laruchequiditoui.fr/fr/p/provide.

供销售本地生产的食品和农产品,产地和网点的平均距离为43千米。蜂巢的主要特色是服务当地农户和消费者。所有产品均产自当地,产品的消费者也在当地。这也就意味着,蜂巢在法国全境布局设立的线下网点所经营的产品各不相同,且都只销售当地出产的农副产品。因此,消费者大都对产品质量特色十分了解。农户或厂商按订单备货,交由蜂巢线下店铺,消费者前往就近的线下网点取货。该销售模式类似于国内的网上直销,不同点在于其产品来源和销售对象都集中于原产地,这对于当地小微企业经营、解决广大农户销售难的问题具有一定积极意义。当然,由于本地市场容量较小,因此这种销售模式显然并不适用于大宗农产品和食品销售。大宗商品须在更大的范围去开发外部市场。

3. 生态农业缓解气候变化影响

发展可持续农业是实现可持续发展目标的重要内容。欧盟共同农业政策(CAP)指出,良好的环境条件是农业活动可持续的基础,使农民可以开垦自然资源,生产出产品维持生计。反过来,农业生产带来的收入支撑起农民家庭和农村社会,而依靠农业生产出的食物支撑着整个社会。❶ 环境条件影响农业可持续发展。工业化造成的环境污染对农业生产影响巨大。

张天佐(2018)引用原农业部对湖南、湖北、江西、四川4省88个区(县)的水稻产地污染区进行的专题调查,结果显示土壤污染超标面积较大,重点污染区超标率高达68%。他还引用原环境保护部和原国土资源部2014年公布的全国首次土壤污染状况调查公报,显示全国重金属污染土壤占总面积16.1%,

---

❶ European Commission Sustainable Agriculture in the CAP [EB/OL]. [2021-01-29]. https://ec.europa.eu/info/food-farming-fisheries/sustainability/sustainable-cap_en.

耕地土壤污染点位超标率高达 19.4%，其中中度污染为 1.8%，重度污染为 1.1%。综合多部门调查结果，当前我国耕地重金属污染比例为 10%~15%，以镉污染最为普遍。污染区域主要为工矿企业周边农区、污水灌区、大中城市郊区。"由此可见，我国耕地重金属污染不容乐观，形势严峻。耕地污染量大面广，隐蔽性强，治理难度大，事关农产品产地环境安全和人民群众健康安全，已成为最突出的农业环境污染问题之一。"❶

治理农业环境污染，大力发展绿色农业、生态农业是农业可持续发展的必由之路。但绿色农业、生态农业普遍存在投入高、见效慢、不易被农民接受等问题。张天佐（2018）列举了农民不愿参与绿色生产的几个主要原因，包括：

（1）农民认为自身素质或技能无法达到绿色生产的技术要求，实际操作中存在困难；

（2）技术投入成本增加，如果缺乏外部激励和经济补偿，农民不愿主动采纳绿色生产方式；

（3）不清楚绿色生产是什么，不感兴趣。❷

这说明，开展绿色生产需要地方政府和行业组织持续加大宣传教育和推广力度，同时应辅之以一定的激励机制。

农产品是世界各国地理标志保护的主要产品类别，其中又可分为种植类和养殖类产品。鉴于地理标志对于生产环境和工艺的严苛要求，相当一部分种植类地理标志产品产地通过了有机认证，采用的是有机农业的生产方式。使用有机肥或有机饲料，基本不

---

❶ 张天佐. 转变农业发展方式与农业绿色发展 [M]. 北京：中国农业出版社，2018：66.
❷ 张天佐. 转变农业发展方式与农业绿色发展 [M]. 北京：中国农业出版社，2018：32-33.

使用人工合成肥料、农药或饲料添加剂，避免使用农药、化肥对环境造成的污染和能源消耗。地理标志产品在制定质量技术要求时对生产方式都有明确规定，产地专业合作社和行业协会负责督促落实，地理标志管理部门开展符合性监督检查，督促各项要求落到实处，使地理标志的品质特色得到保障，总体质量保持稳定。有机生态农业可有效减轻污染，有利于保护环境，恢复生态平衡。

与生态种植业严格管控化肥、农药使用，保护土壤和环境相一致，养殖类地理标志产品多采用散养或半散养辅以补饲的方式，有助于减少大规模集中饲养所产生的甲烷等温室气体。同时，遵守严格的管理措施，规定养殖密度上限和养殖环境条件，限定饲料内容物和喂养（补饲）方式，保证产品质量。

以当雄牦牛为例，其地理标志保护质量技术要求包括：

一、品种

西藏高山牦牛

二、养殖环境要求

海拔 4200 米以上，高山草甸放牧草地充裕，以桑曲河、拉曲河、布曲河、秀古河和高山融雪为水源。

三、饲养管理

（一）饲养方式：天然草地放牧饲养。

（二）饲料条件：放牧饲养以天然草地饲草为主，归牧后补饲本地产精粗饲料。

（三）饲养管理要点：

犊牛断奶管理：犊牛 6~7 月龄断奶，断奶犊牛与母牛群分群饲养，犊牛群补饲当地产青干草、青贮料和精饲料。

暖季育肥：在牧草生长季节，以天然草地放牧方式育肥，其间仅补饲矿物质饲料。

（四）出栏要求：

出栏年龄5~7岁，出栏活体重母牛180~200千克，公牛250~300千克。

四、环境、安全要求

饲养环境、疫情疫病的防治与控制必须执行国家相关规定，不得污染环境。

五、屠宰加工及贮运

（一）牛源标准：产自保护范围内符合前述第一至第四条规定要求的健康牦牛。

（二）屠宰加工工艺要点：

1. 静养待屠：停食静养24小时，宰前3小时停止饮水。

2. 屠宰方式：按当地传统方式屠宰。

3. 排酸：胴体在0至5℃，相对湿度85%~90%的环境下排酸48小时。❶

由此可见，当雄牦牛地理标志质量技术要求不仅规定了养殖环境和饲养管理要求，甚至对屠宰方式等都作出了明确规定，体现了保护养殖地自然环境、尊重少数民族风俗习惯等人道主义精神，是养殖类地理标志产品生产的范例之一。

4. 优质地理标志产品生产和消费有助于实现可持续发展目标

食品消费与地域、种族、饮食习惯有着密切联系。前文引述联合国环境规划署研究报告的观点，认为转变饮食习惯，增加植物类食物消费占比有助于减少全球温室气体排放，实现可持续发展目标。联合国粮农组织2021年11月发布的《2021统计年鉴》

---

❶ 当雄牦牛质量技术要求摘选，参见：《国家质量监督检验检疫总局公告》（2016年第128号）。

指出，2000~2019年，全世界农业用地温室气体排放量下降了2%，但农产品生产温室气体排放量实际上升了11%，其中约55%来自畜牧业。❶

我们知道，地理标志产品中包括大量动植物产品，进一步研究分析可知在畜禽产品中，大多为地方土生品种，生产规模普遍较小，且以散养、半散养牛、羊、猪以及家禽为主。大宗圈养和舍饲类产品，如普通生猪、肉鸡等均不具备地理标志保护条件。这意味着对温室气体排放产生较大影响的畜牧养殖业，尤其是大型舍饲类畜禽养殖基本未涉及地理标志产品。当然，这并不等于说发展地理标志养殖业可以不考虑对环境气候的影响。不能排除个别养殖类地理标志产品不严格执行地理标志保护质量技术要求、未将养殖数量控制在合理区间内的可能性，因此，必须持续改进养殖技术，严格管控负面影响。

与畜禽产品相比，种植类地理标志产品占比更高，包括了粮食、油料作物及其产品，以及蔬菜、水果等多种植物类生鲜和加工食品。地理标志产品的生产管理和溯源体系的建立和完善，在有效减少农业生产对土壤、水源、环境的影响下，保证了食品安全和消费者健康。

以富平柿饼为例，其质量技术要求包括：

（一）原料品种

富平尖柿。

（二）立地条件

土壤类型为灌淤土、洪淤土、黄绵土、褐土、垆土，有机

---

❶ FAO. World food and agriculture: Statistical Yearbook 2021 [M/OL]. Rome: FAO, 2021 [2021-12-20]. https://www.fao.org/3/cb4477en/online/cb4477en.html.

质≥0.8%，pH 7.0~8.0，海拔高度400~1000米。

（三）种苗繁育

以君迁子为砧木，从无检疫性病虫害的富平尖柿母株上采接穗进行嫁接繁殖。

（四）栽培管理

1. 栽植密度：根据不同树形、地形，合理密植，每公顷栽植株数≤840株。

2. 整形修剪：冬、夏修剪结合，树形结构合理，保证树冠通风透光。

3. 施肥：每年每公顷施用腐熟的有机肥不少于20吨。

4. 环境、安全要求：农药、化肥等的使用必须符合国家的相关规定。

（五）采收

果面呈橙红色，果实充分成熟，10月中下旬手工采摘。

（六）加工

工艺流程：选果→洗果去皮→自然晾晒→揉捏整形→剪柄下架→无霜饼（吊饼）→回软潮霜→霜饼→吊饼→捏饼→合儿饼

1. 选果：选择成熟充分、质地尚未软化、形状整齐、无病虫害、无碰伤的果实。

2. 洗果去皮：去皮时要求柿蒂周围果皮残留不超过1厘米。

3. 自然晾晒：晾晒时最低离地高度不小于50厘米，露天自然曝晒2~3天，然后用篷布覆盖遮阳，自然风干。

4. 揉捏整形：在晾晒一周左右，果面发白，果肉微软时，用手轻轻揉捏，挤压果肉，促进软化。

5. 剪柄下架：果肉完全软化、无硬芯，含水量≤35%，剪除果柄，下架收果，产品即"无霜饼"。

6. 回软潮霜：将晒好的无霜饼装入干净容器中苫盖，置于阴凉的室内，经 4~5 天，柿饼回软后放置在通风阴凉处摊晾进行潮霜，产品即"霜饼"。

7. 贮存：常温或冷藏条件下贮存，库房应清洁干净，干燥通风，不得与有毒、有害、有异味的商品混存，贮存温度应小于 10℃。❶

不断提高全社会环境保护的意识，适度增加地理标志产品消费，鼓励消费者优先选购地理标志保护产品，在一定程度上有利于减少温室气体排放，实现可持续发展目标。

第二节 地理标志保护促进保护海洋渔业资源

目标 14：水下生物

该目标旨在保护并可持续地利用海洋、海水和海洋生物。联合国报告指出，虽然海洋生物多样性保护区正在扩大，但现有的政策和国际条约在鼓励合理利用海洋资源方面仍显不足，无法应对过度捕捞和气候变化造成的海洋酸化，以及海岸的富营养化。鉴于数千万人口依靠海洋谋生并获取食物，又鉴于海洋之间融为一体的性质，各个层面都需以更大的努力和干预来保护海洋资源的可持续利用。❷

---

❶ 参见：《国家质量监督检验检疫总局公告》（2008 年第 92 号）。
❷ Knowledge Platform ［EB/OL］.［2020-07-24］. https：//sustainabledevelopment. un. org.

影响可持续利用海洋资源的人类活动主要是海洋捕捞和海水养殖。海洋占地表总面积70%以上，可持续利用海洋资源是可持续发展的重要组成部分。海洋渔业与人类生活密切相关，人类社会发展到今天，海洋捕捞、海水养殖和水产加工仍然是沿海国家和地区的重要经济领域，从业人口多，涉及范围广。陈作志（2008）指出："海洋渔业是人类的重要产业，渔业直接为2亿人提供就业岗位，并提供人类消费的动物性蛋白质总量的19%。"❶ 与之相适应，海洋渔业规模持续扩大，产量不断增加，给全球生态环境带来不可忽视的负面影响。人类对于海洋资源的攫取量成倍扩大，严重威胁海洋资源生存。过度捕捞破坏海洋的生物多样性，海水养殖泛滥加剧海水污染进程。有人甚至认为，海水养殖的副作用大于其实际贡献。❷ 约翰·克拉克（2000）认为："海水养殖既是污染的原告，也是清洁环境的被告。一方面，海水养殖获得成功，需要周围环境的清洁水供应；另一方面，海水养殖强化了本身对沿海水域造成的污染，使生物多样性减少。"他同时指出："世界范围的渔获量在下降，如果缺乏有效的环境管理，海洋食物的产量很难保持目前水平。"❸

世界上的海水养殖系统，大多已进入半集约化或集约化养殖，饵料的投入和残饵的生成是促成养殖自身污染的一个重要因素。鱼类除了残饵以外，还包括鱼类的粪便及其排泄物。总体来

---

❶ 陈作志. 捕捞对北部湾海洋生态系统结构与功能的影响［D］. 上海：上海海洋大学，2008：1-2.

❷ MERCOLA J. Farmed salmon=most toxic food in the world［EB/OL］.（2018-07-25）[2021-07-03]. https：//www. organicconsumers. org/news/farmed-salmon-toxic-flame-retardant.

❸ 克拉克. 海岸带管理手册［M］. 吴克勤，杨德全，盖明举，译. 北京：海洋出版社，2000：4-8.

说，养殖自身污染属于有机污染，其主要形式是增加了氮、磷的环境负荷量。

我国是世界上水产养殖发达的国家，养殖面积和总产量均居世界首位。联合国粮农组织的统计资料显示，2019 年我国水产养殖总产量为 4824.6 万吨。❶ 我国的海水养殖业是一个以贝藻养殖为主的行业，在品种上还有很大的发展空间。我国的水产养殖业经历了从污染到治理再到持续改善的过程。吴军等（2013）认为，虽然我国海洋环境污染的治理近年来取得了一定成绩，但是我国近岸海域污染总体形势依然严峻。❷ 但随着我国大力实施环境保护战略，我国近海及海岸污染问题正逐步得到改善。《2017 年中国海洋生态环境状况公报》显示，2013~2017 年，我国海水增养殖区环境综合质量等级为"优良"和"较好"的比例分别为 91% 和 96%，呈增加趋势。2017 年我国管辖海域劣于第四类水质的总海域面积为：夏季 33720 平方公里，秋季 47310 平方公里，呈逐年下降趋势。❸

海水养殖产品是地理标志保护的重要类别之一，品种繁多，涉及范围很广。以我国为例，已获得地理标志保护的海水养殖产品包括鱼、虾、贝类等多种类别，如程村蚝、台山鳗鱼、烟台海参、三门青蟹等。这些地理标志产品的养殖生产大都遵循严格的管理措施和质量控制标准，把对生态环境的影响降到最低。正如前文所述，地理标志保护促进可持续利用自然资源，其中包括对海洋资源的可持续利用。本书认为，地理标志保护对可持续利用

---

❶ 参见：https://www.fao.org/fishery/en/countrysector/cn/en.
❷ 吴军，陈克亮，汪宝英，等. 海岸带环境污染控制实践技术 [M]. 北京：科学出版社，2013：4.
❸ 参见：自然资源部官网，http://gc.mnr.gov.cn.

海洋资源的作用体现在以下几个方面。

1. 严格控制养殖密度和养殖规模，最大限度降低对海水的污染

这里涉及海洋环境容量的概念。吴军等（2013）认为，所谓海洋环境容量，是在充分利用海洋的自净能力和不造成污染损害的前提下，某一特定海域所能容纳污染物质的最大负荷率。人类对海洋的开发必须控制在海域环境容量范围内，它是海洋可持续发展重要的判断依据。[1] 因此，海水养殖业需要解决的问题，是把养殖规模控制在海洋环境容量以内，使其不对可持续利用海洋资源造成不良影响。

根据《2017中国海洋生态环境状况公报》，我国海域的主要污染物为无机氮、活性磷酸盐和石油类污染物。影响海水质量状况的主要原因是水体呈富营养化状态以及沉积物中粪大肠杆菌群等超标。造成污染的原因与海水养殖不无关系。"有的养殖场放苗过密，造成环境恶化。水域环境质量差，控制、保持健康环境的能力不足。一些地方对资源管理和近海环境的改良重视和支持不够。"[2] 在水产养殖、水产品加工以及销售等许多方面，存在滥用药物、过量用药和滥用添加剂的问题。[3]

地理标志保护十分关注养殖密度和养殖规模，对饲养环境有明确要求。这也是质量技术要求中必须限定的内容。限定养殖密度和规模的目的，一是保证在有限的水体内养殖产品获得充足的营养；二是确保水体水质保持在正常水平；三是将排泄物对水体

---

[1] 吴军，陈克亮，汪宝英，等. 海岸带环境污染控制实践技术 [M]. 北京：科学出版社，2013：9-11.
[2] 浙江省海洋与渔业局. 海水养殖 [M]. 杭州：浙江科学技术出版社，2006：4-5.
[3] 王清印. 海水生态养殖理论与技术 [M]. 北京：海洋出版社，2005：2.

的污染控制在合理范围内。例如，烟台海参海底增养殖工艺要求选择风浪小，水质清澈，潮流畅通，流速缓慢，海底有岩礁、砾石、硬沙且海藻丛生的泥沙底质的海区，放苗密度：2~4头/平方米。底播增殖区严禁拖网渔船作业。❶ 台山鳗鱼质量技术要求规定："养殖地周边生态环境良好，养殖用水符合国家渔业水质标准的规定；……放养密度为2000至3000尾/亩；饲料投喂鳗鱼的专用配合饲料；饲养环境、疫情疫病的防治与控制，必须执行国家相关的规定，不得污染环境。"❷

2. 注重标准化生产，完善海水养殖标准体系建设

完善标准体系建设，组织开展标准化生产是我国实施地理标志保护的基本要求。世界上其他国家和地区在管理上虽然各具特色，但标准化理念和管理措施是地理标志保护的惯常做法。标准化生产对于海水养殖业来说尤为重要。海水养殖业曾长期存在管理粗放的问题。张岩等（2005）认为："很多管理还以养殖者的经验积累为主，没有科学统一的操作技术规范。"❸ 赵法箴（2005）认为：存在"盲目追求产量，随意发展养殖面积，养殖布局和养殖密度不合理，饵料质量差，养殖管理水平低等问题。""配合饲料质量不稳定，饲料系数偏高，残饵及粪便的代谢终产物易于造成污染，导致病害的发生。"除此之外，"不重视养殖废水的处理，导致近海水域环境的破坏，并致养殖生态系统失衡。"❹

通过实施地理标志保护，开展海水养殖标准化生产，对于减少养殖污染、保护海洋生物多样性具有重要意义。海水养殖标准

---

❶ 参见：《国家质量监督检验检疫总局公告》（2009年第32号）。
❷ 参见：《国家质量监督检验检疫总局公告》（2011年第175号）。
❸ 王清印. 海水生态养殖理论与技术 [M]. 北京：海洋出版社，2005：13.
❹ 王清印. 海水养殖研究新进展 [M]. 北京：海洋出版社，2008：4-5.

体系建设涉及养殖方法、水环境调控、饵料研发生产等多个方面的技术研究和标准制定。赵法箴认为，要完善养殖保障体系，包括环境保障体系、病害控制体系、种苗保障体系和产品保障体系。要大力发展健康养殖，须做好包括养殖设施、苗种培育、放养密度、水质处理、饵料质量、药物使用、养殖管理等在内的诸方面。"要研制开发优质配合饵料，大力开发和研制质量高，稳定性、诱食性和吸收性好，并有助于提高免疫功能和抗逆能力，饵料系数低的环保型饵料。"❶ 张岩等认为："饵料的质量不但决定了饵料的转化效率，而且对水环境起着决定性影响。"❷ 由此可见，解决海水养殖对于生态环境影响问题的关键在于发展健康养殖，完善养殖保障体系建设。这与地理标志保护的要求和目的不谋而合。海水养殖类地理标志保护产地已采取措施，落实生态健康养殖理念。

3. 促进可持续海洋捕捞，维护海洋生态多样性

联合国粮农组织报告指出，非法捕捞，不报告或任意捕捞构成对可持续捕捞的最大威胁。❸ 陈作志（2008）认为："海洋捕捞通过直接或间接作用改变或恶化了海洋生态系统，特别是捕捞活动及其他人类活动最为集中的海域，捕捞直接影响了海洋生物多样性，并通过副渔获、栖息地恶化以及生物学关系等间接影响生态系统，造成了世界范围海洋食物网的简化和渔获物营养级的降低。"❹ 海洋捕捞的负面影响显而易见，但问题的解决涉及面

---

❶ 王清印. 海水养殖研究新进展［M］. 北京：海洋出版社，2008：6-7.
❷ 王清印. 海水生态养殖理论与技术［M］. 北京：海洋出版社，2005：16.
❸ 参见：https://www.fao.org/fisheries.
❹ 陈作志. 捕捞对北部湾海洋生态系统结构与功能的影响［D］. 上海：上海海洋大学，2008：2.

广,是人类共同面临的挑战。科学规划,适度捕捞,最大限度地维护海洋生态多样性是每个海洋渔业国家的责任和义务。

海洋管理委员会(Marine Stewardship Council,MSC)❶ 把可持续海洋捕捞定义为:"使海洋拥有充足的鱼类,尊重鱼类栖息环境,同时保证以海洋捕捞为生的人们可维持生计。"❷ 这其中包含三方面内容:一是保证鱼类种群数量。捕捞应控制在一定范畴,既保证捕捞可持续,也保证鱼群可继续繁殖和健康生长。二是最大限度降低对海洋生态的影响。捕捞活动须谨慎开展,以确保生态系统中其他种群和栖息地维持健康发展。三是实施有效管理。按照有关法律法规进行管理,并根据环境变化适时调整管理规范。

地理标志保护对于海洋捕捞可持续发展的促进作用充分体现了上述发展理念,具体表现在:一是合理规划捕捞区域;二是严格控制捕捞数量;三是合理安排捕捞时间。

总的来看,相对于海水养殖,通过海洋捕捞获取的野生地理标志产品种类和数量较少(我国仅有舟山带鱼注册地理标志证明商标),地理标志保护的成功案例有限,但仍不失为维护海洋生态多样性的有效方法。以 Bulot de la Baie de Granville(格朗威尔海湾螺贝)为例,这是一种野生螺贝,2019 年 2 月注册欧盟地理标志保护(PGI,Official Journal L35,07,02,2019)。其捕获地位于法国 Cotentin 半岛西侧划定的区域范围内,距离卸货海岸陆地(共规定 44 个登陆卸货地点)不超过 30 海里。该野生螺贝地理标志规格为 47~70 毫米,但捕获时约有 8% 小于 47 毫米,15% 大于 70 毫米。在品质特色上,该螺贝具有碘、海水和海藻

---

❶ 这是一个独立的非营利组织,总部位于英国。
❷ 参见:https://www.msc.org。

的气味。经烹制入口后，肉质细嫩，富含水分和碘化物，具有海洋和坚果的味道。Bulot de la Baie de Granville 地理标志产品的捕捞活动充分考虑了环保因素，要求所有捕捞船只长度小于 12 米，以便作业后可拖至陆地放置，还规定了捕捞工具（特制的瓶、罐）和具体时间季节。由于当地盛行西风，因此规定捕捞船只全部沿陆地一侧（偏东方向）排开，这也是确定众多陆地卸货地点的原因。除此之外，还规定了渔民分拣、清理等活动的场所地点，以保护当地环境。相对较小的捕捞海域保证了将捕获数量稳定控制在较小范围。[1]

这个案例对于海洋野生地理标志产品保护具有一定示范意义，值得从业者和相关管理部门学习借鉴。

第三节　地理标志保护促进保护陆地资源环境

目标 15：陆地生物

正如联合国报告指出的，这里指的是保护、恢复和促进陆地生态系统的可持续利用，可持续管理森林，对抗沙漠化，阻止、扭转土地退化，阻止生物多样性遗失。

联合国《2020 年可持续发展目标报告》指出："保护陆地生态系统和生物多样性正在全球取得积极进展。森林砍伐速度放缓，更多的生物多样性关键区域得到保护。然而，联合国为

---

[1] 参见：SINGLE DOCUMENT 'BULOT DE LA BAIE DE GRANVILLE' EU No：PGI-FR-02319 — 4.8.2017, Official Journal of the European Union 29.8.2018.

2020年设定的可持续发展目标仍难以完成，土地退化在继续，生物多样性正以惊人速度遗失，外来物种和非法盗猎继续抵消保护和恢复生态和物种系统的努力。"❶ 经济合作与发展组织（OECD）告诫"七国集团"（G7）首脑，称许多生态系统正朝着不可逆方向发展，以至于恢复代价过高，已无可能。2019年生物多样性和生态系统服务政府间科学政策平台（The Intergovernmental Science-Policy Platform on Biodiversity and Ecosystem Services，IPBES）报告指出，在全球范围，人类栖息地变化（尤其是原有自然区域被农业大量占用）、气候变化、外来生物入侵、过度消耗以及污染是最主要原因。❷

地球是人类的共同家园。目标15所提出的要求既涉及环境保护，也包括自然资源的可持续利用。要实现这一目标，重点之一是要转变经济发展方式，改变大众消费习惯。转变经济发展方式涉及方方面面，其中包括合理利用土地资源，实现农业可持续发展。关于合理利用土地资源，本书此前已有讨论。这里重点探讨地理标志保护对于保护环境和生物多样性、实现农业可持续发展所起到的作用。

首先，地理标志促进保护森林资源。柯水发、李红勋等（2019）指出，全球有16亿人依赖森林所提供的产品和服务为生。他们认为，林业在应对气候变化、保护生物多样性和保持水土等方面发挥了重要的生态和社会效益。"林业是绿色经济发展

---

❶ 参见：https://www.un.org.
❷ SETTELE J, DÍAZ S, NGO H T. Global assessment report on biodiversity and ecosystem services of the Intergovernmental Science-Policy Platform on Biodiversity and Ecosystem Services [EB/OL]. (2019-05-04) [2022-03-24]. https://doi.org/10.5281/zenodo.3831673.

的循环经济体。林业产品的可再生、可回收、可降解的特点，使其成为一个最大的自然循环经济体。林业生产过程实现了'资源—产品—再生资源'，达到了低消耗、高利用、低排放的物质和能量循环利用，对生态和环境的影响小，为人类提供了绿色经济发展必须的生物质材料和能源。"❶

林下产品是林下经济产业的组成部分。顾晓君等（2008）从农业经营的角度将林下经济定义为"是借助林地的生态环境，利用林地资源，在林冠下开展林、农等多种项目的复合经营。"❷柯水发、李红勋等（2019）认为："发展林下经济、森林旅游等绿色产业，可以给农户带来多元化的收入和就业，有效地帮助他们抵御市场风险。"❸

依靠森林所提供的水分涵养、光照条件和优质土壤腐殖质，优质食用菌、坚果、草本药材、蜂产品等林下产品十分丰富，是我国地理标志保护的重要产品类别之一。林下产品的生长很大程度上依赖于自然环境，生产过程中的人为干预较少。有些林下产品，如松茸、松露、野山参等，呈完全野生状态，尚无法人工繁育。这些产品因资源稀少，附加值较高，市场行情长期看好。

柯水发、李红勋等（2019）总结了福建发展林下经济的成功经验和林下经济模式，主要有：林药模式、林菌模式、林游模式、林蜂模式和林禽模式。以林菌模式和林禽模式为例，林菌模式就是"利用森林环境，在郁闭的林下种植香菇、木耳等食用

---

❶ 柯水发，李红勋，等．林业绿色经济理论与实践［M］．北京：人民日报出版社，2019：17-20.

❷ 柯水发，李红勋，等．林业绿色经济理论与实践［M］．北京：人民日报出版社，2019：169.

❸ 柯水发，李红勋，等．林业绿色经济理论与实践［M］．北京：人民日报出版社，2019：22-34.

菌。或者利用林下原有的菌群，做好菌群基地管护工作，适时采摘收获。林禽模式是在林下透光性、空气流通性好的环境条件下，充分利用林下空间及林下丰富的昆虫、杂草等资源，放养或圈养鸡、鸭、鹅等禽类。"而林禽模式养殖产生的粪便和林菌模式产生的培养基废料也可作为林地肥料使用，促进林木生长，还可作为水产的饲料来源。顾晓君（2008）认为，广西浦北县坚持以林为主、保护生态、突出特色的原则，因地制宜发展林下经济。推动林下经济园区化、基地化发展，建成了七大产业基地。形成特色明显、辐射力强、多业发展的良好态势，促进了农民增收，产生较好的效益。❶ 这其中就包括了15万亩地理标志保护产品浦北红椎菌产业基地。浦北县有20多万亩连片原始红椎次生林。红椎菌，又名红蘑菇，是在漫长的岁月里形成的红椎林土壤腐殖层于高温高湿的特定气候条件下，自然生长的纯天然食用菌，目前仍无法进行人工栽培。2013年12月，浦北红椎菌获得地理标志产品保护，成为地理标志保护促进森林资源保护的范例之一。

国外通过地理标志保护森林资源同样不乏范例。前文提到的塞内加尔Madd de Casamance产地生产者以申请地理标志保护为契机，使当地百姓认识到，只有保护好宝贵的森林资源，才能保证Madd de Casamance这一野生水果的特色质量不受影响。保护森林资源与生产优质产品、增加个人收入形成互惠共生的关系，促使当地百姓自觉加入保护森林资源的行动中。值得关注的是，该产地所在区域的森林成为2019年塞内加尔全国唯一未遭受火

---

❶ 柯水发，李红勋，等. 林业绿色经济理论与实践［M］. 北京：人民日报出版社，2019：124-129，170.

灾的省区。❶

上述所有林下经济模式赖以生存的基础都是森林所提供的优质环境条件。因此,林下产品的地理标志保护更侧重于对自然环境的维护,保证其原有生长条件不被破坏。在相关地理标志产品质量技术要求中,明确保护生长环境的内容。因为只有保护好产品的生长环境,才能够可持续利用地理标志资源。事实上,地理标志产地的百姓也已意识到保护环境对于增收致富的重要性,十分注重保护产地环境。例如,林芝松茸产地的百姓在采挖后会自觉将表面土层复原,据说只有这样,来年才会在相同的地方长出松茸。那曲冬虫夏草的采挖方法也十分相似。当地百姓在生产实践中深切认识到,只有尊重自然,才能收获大地回馈的财富。地理标志保护的过程,就是保护森林资源的过程,二者相得益彰。

其次,地理标志保护促进防治土地退化。随着中国城市化和工业化发展,土地退化问题日益严重,保持现有农业产出能力面临威胁。人类过度利用土地资源是土地退化的重要原因。虽然干旱、洪水、大风等自然影响可导致土地质量下降,但人类的过度开垦、农药化肥使用不当等因素同样会造成土地沙化、土壤肥力下降、盐碱化等。土地退化的后果包括产能下降、粮食安全受到威胁、生态系统遭到破坏、生物多样性遗失等。解决土地退化问题需要多措并举,其中之一是解决农牧业过度利用土地的问题。

土地的生产能力并非取之不尽、用之不竭的。正常情况下,一块土地的生产能力,取决于种植、栽培的作物品种和数量,以

---

❶ WIPO. Supporting environmental sustainability with GIs: the case of Madd de Casamance [EB/OL]. [2021-12-05]. https://www.wipo.int/ipadvantage/en/details.jsp?id=11582.

及常年利用的时长。大家知道，农业生产离不开轮作。轮作的目的是以地养地，实现均衡利用土壤养分，防治病虫害，改善土壤理化性状，调节土壤肥力，实现丰产增收。由于不同植物对土壤养分的需求存在差异，某些植物（比如人参、山药）对地力的需求较高，收获之后往往需要土地"休养"数年方可再次耕种，否则将直接导致产量和质量下降，严重影响产地经济收益。

与之相仿，过度放牧同样可造成草场退化，形成荒漠草原，无法继续开展牧业生产。过度放牧的事例很多，其中一些与饲养的品种有关，比如，山羊因喜食草根，对草场的破坏力大于绵羊。还有一些与放养密度有关，单位面积放养数量过多，导致牛羊营养不良，品质下降。张天佐（2018）认为："草原作为畜牧业的基础，对于草地资源的放牧利用一定要控制在其承载范围之内。引进适合舍饲、半舍饲，经济效益较高的肉用或乳用品种，大力发展羔羊养殖，改部分放养为养奶牛，实现农牧结合饲料多元化，放牧与舍饲结合科学化，通过季节性轮牧建立节约型畜牧业，保护草原生态系统。这样既保障了草原生态系统的平衡，又可不降低牧民收入。"❶

为保护草原生态，实现畜牧业可持续发展目标，从 2011 年起，国家在河北、山西、内蒙古、辽宁、吉林、黑龙江、四川、云南、西藏、甘肃、青海、宁夏、新疆等 13 个主要草原牧区省（区）和新疆生产建设兵团、黑龙江农垦总局，全面建立草原生态保护补助奖励机制。根据草场面积核定放养数量，杜绝过度放牧，保护天然草场；鼓励牧民科学放牧，可持续利用天然草场资

---

❶ 张天佐. 转变农业发展方式与农业绿色发展 [M]. 北京：中国农业出版社，2018：113.

源。这一机制对于保护草原生态发挥了重要作用。"尤其是项目区草原生态状况呈现区域性好转，草地产草量和载畜能力在近几年均有所提高。"2018 年，国家继续在上述省（区）、兵团、农垦总局实施农牧民补助奖励政策。中央财政年度补助资金 155.6 亿元，落实禁牧补助 90.5 亿元，草原平衡奖励 65.1 亿元。通过落实补奖政策，牧区农牧民户均增加政策性收入近 1500 元，补助资金已成为农牧民增收的重要补充。❶

畜禽类产品属于地理标志保护对象之一。饲养在世界各地的牛羊以及其他畜禽产品品种繁多，各具特色。有观点认为，畜禽类产品的差异主要取决于品种，与产地环境关联度小。也有人认为，这其中既有品种带来的固有差异，也与地理环境和气候存在一定的关联度，即，同样的品种在不同的地理条件下可呈现出品种以外的质量差异。例如，市场上普遍认为，盐碱地上放牧的羊群，肉质更加鲜美，且无膻味。这正是宁夏"盐池滩羊"地理标志产品的质量特色之一。产自西藏的"岗巴羊"也存在类似情况。这从一个侧面说明了畜禽产品地理标志保护的可行性。

前文提到，开展畜禽产品地理标志保护的目的之一是保护优良品种的种质资源，将其保留在原产地适生环境下，不盲目对外引种和推广。目的之二是合理规划饲养规模，优化饲养方法，保持产品的特色质量，持续提高市场溢价能力。这其中就包括要杜绝过度放牧，保护原产地草场环境不被破坏，防止土地退化，促进特色畜牧业可持续发展。为此，针对每一个畜禽产品在制定地理标志保护质量技术要求时，都需要规定养殖密度上限，保证将

---

❶ 中国优质农产品开发服务协会. 中国品牌农业年鉴 2018 [M]. 北京：中国农业出版社，2019：73，99.

种群数量控制在合理范围内。此外，还要规定不同季节、不同育龄的饲养要求，明确放牧、补饲、育肥和出栏条件。有了上述保障，畜禽类地理标志才得以健康发展，达到以质量换效益的目的。我国畜产品地理标志已发展成为相关农牧区百姓脱贫致富的拳头产品，在保护环境的同时，产生了可观的经济社会效益。

最后，地理标志制度促进保护生物多样性。关于生物多样性，克里斯蒂昂·莱韦克（2005）认为，生物多样性由基因（遗传）多样性、物种多样性和生态系统多样性共同组成。他引用联合国《生物多样性公约》给出的定义："来自地球生态系统、海洋和其他水生生态系统，以及由它们形成的生态复杂系统的所有活性组织的多变性，这包括物种内部和物种之间的多样性，以及生态系统之间的多样性。"❶ 安妮·马克苏拉克（2011）认为："生物多样性指的是在地球上或者在某特定地区内生存的所有物种。如果在一个区域内有着丰富的物种和繁荣的种群，那么我们就说该地区具有生物多样性。"❷

地理标志保护有助于维护遗传基因和生态系统多样性。王笑冰（2019）认为，"地理标志体系有助于保持生物多样性，尤其是基因资源的多样性"。❸ 如前文所述，地理标志保护十分关注动植物品种的选育和培养，这有利于保护遗传基因的多样性，对于维护畜禽种群的遗传基因多样性尤其重要。充分研究分析产地环

---

❶ 莱韦克. 生物多样性［M］. 邱举良，译. 北京：科学出版社，2005：2-4.
❷ 马克苏拉克. 生物多样性：保护濒危物种［M］. 李岳，田琳，等，译. 北京：科学出版社，2011：1.
❸ 王笑冰. 经济发展方式转变视角下的地理标志保护［M］. 北京：中国社会科学出版社，2019：49.

境特点与土生品种之间的关联，限定产地范围，保持本土品种的质量特色，避免不必要的引种推广是地理标志保护的基本原则。

地理标志对于保护生态系统的多样性同样发挥着积极作用。地理标志生产有赖于产地独特、完整的生态系统。以白酒生产为例，固态发酵工艺下生产的白酒对产地环境的要求十分苛刻，其中一些工艺依靠特定温湿度条件下所产生的微生物种群间的相互作用，是产地独特的自然环境和气候条件造就了中国优质白酒的特色质量。一旦产地生态系统发生改变，优质白酒的品质必然遭受重大影响，这一点已为名酒生产企业所公认。张嘉涛、崔春玲、童忠东等（2014）认为："茅台镇酿酒环境的微生态与其他酿酒微生态的明显差异，主要体现在极端的嗜热菌和嗜酸菌方面。茅台长期的高温生态环境、高温制曲和高温堆积发酵环境，驯服了一些极端的微生物，不但增加了微生物的热稳定性，而且加快了微生物的代谢率。"[1] 因此，保护生态系统就是保护地理标志的现在和将来。

---

[1] 张嘉涛，崔春玲，童忠东，等．白酒生产工艺与技术［M］．北京：化学工业出版社，2014：45．

第六章
建立伙伴关系，促进地理标志保护国际合作

目标 17：促进目标实现的伙伴关系

联合国《2020年可持续发展目标报告》指出："强化实施手段和方法，巩固全球为实现可持续发展而建立起的伙伴关系。当前，实施层面进展迅速，其中个人捐资达到历年新高，上网人口比例逐年增加，同时还设立了最不发达国家技术银行。但仍面临许多挑战：政府开发援助有所减少，个人投资与可持续发展结合程度不高，网络建设分化严重，贸易争端日趋激烈。因此，需大力加强国际合作，确保将有效的实施方法提供给相关国家，以实现可持续发展目标。"[1]

联合国可持续发展目标是人类社会的共同奋斗目标，与世界各国息息相关，没有任何国家可置身度外。应广泛深入地开展国际合作，交流实

---

[1] 参见：https://www.un.org.

施方法，相互学习借鉴。尤其要帮助最不发达国家，结合可持续发展目标，完善发展规划，提高实施能力。17项可持续发展目标涵盖了经济、社会各主要领域。可以预见的是，实施中会出现很多问题，各国协调难度很大。作为与可持续发展总目标相关联的发展目标之一，协调世界各国共同推进地理标志保护国际合作，在当今国际环境下仍面临诸多困难。

中国改革开放40多年的历程告诉我们，发展是解决一切问题的关键。要实现可持续发展目标，必须紧扣"发展"这一主题，使发达国家和发展中国家在不同背景下实现共同发展目标。各国自然条件和政治、经济、历史、文化宗教等因素差异很大，没有普遍适用的简单方法，但广泛开展国际合作无疑是实现发展目标的必要举措。地理标志属知识产权范畴，是与贸易有关的知识产权。因此，地理标志保护国际合作首先涉及国与国之间的贸易往来，以及由此产生的保护地理标志知识产权的必要性。正是基于上述原因，中国与欧盟、美国、日本等国家或经济体深入开展了地理标志保护交流，2019年底完成了中欧地理标志协定谈判，深化了中欧战略合作机制，标志着中欧知识产权保护合作进入了新阶段。可以预见，我国将不断深化地理标志保护合作，与世界上关注地理标志保护、重视地理标志产业发展的国家或经济体广泛开展对话交流，促进双多边贸易往来，维护国际经济贸易秩序。

鉴于地理标志在国际上的发展历史较短，引起广泛关注仅仅持续20年左右时间，笔者认为，开展地理标志保护合作可关注以下几个方面的问题。

一是可将重心放在深入开展多双边交流和经验分享上。在地理标志保护制度上，各国或地区做法不一，笼统归纳也有3~4

种法律体系：既有专门法律制度，如欧盟、瑞士、日本、印度；也有商标法保护，如美国、加拿大等移民国家；还有使用反不正当竞争法或消费者权益保护法的国家。即便在同一类法律体系下，关于地理标志保护的规定也不尽相同。例如，瑞士在《贸易标记法案》（*Trade Mark Act*）中规定，货物及服务类来源标记（indication of source）无须申请即可获得保护，但同时也可申请注册为"地理标记"（Geographical Mark），农食类产品还可申请注册地理标志（Geographical Indication）。[1] 而我国存在《商标法》和属于专门保护体系的部门规章并行的双重保护形式。WTO 尊重各成员现有的法律制度，并未要求或鼓励采用任何一种统一的保护形式。因此，开展地理标志保护交流合作的重心并非法律制度本身，而在于交流经验、分享成果、共同促进、协调发展。各国或地区历史文化背景不同，自然禀赋存在较大差异，但发展区域特色产业，扩大地理标志市场占有率则是世界各国的共同愿望。分享发展经验，深化交流内涵，对世界各国，尤其是发展中国家和最不发达国家来说，具有很强的借鉴意义。交流合作形式多样，如人员互访、短期培训、项目合作等。通过交流合作，地理标志保护相对滞后的国家学习掌握地理标志保护制度和管理、经营理念，在合作伙伴的协助下，开展地理标志保护实践活动。这方面联合国粮农组织等国际组织以及欧盟投入较大，已在东南亚、中亚、非洲等国以项目援助的方式组织地理标志培训，协助开展地理标志申报，与当地主管部门建立合作机制。

---

[1] 参见：https://www.ige.ch/en/protecting-your-ip/indications-of-source/protecting-geographical-indications/protection-in-switzerland.

二是可深化合作内涵，促进有关国家完善地理标志保护制度，开展地理标志保护实践。地理标志保护的最终目的是实现经济社会可持续发展，为使更多人口摆脱贫困作出贡献，并在此过程中履行知识产权保护义务。WTO成员积极开展多边交流，及时通报地理标志保护动态，有利于各成员因地制宜，发展、完善各自的地理标志保护制度，加强对国际贸易伙伴的知识产权保护。

亚洲国家间广泛开展地理标志保护交流与合作具有特殊意义。由于历史、语言、文化等因素影响，在地理标志保护领域，亚洲国家普遍与WTO成员围绕地理标志的矛盾和纷争少有关联。虽然地理标志是知识产权的重要组成部分，但亚洲国家当前面临的首要任务是如何更好地运用地理标志制度，挖掘本国地理标志资源，提高产品质量效益和管理水平，提升区域品牌价值，促进区域经济持续健康发展。近年来，一些国家已经逐渐认识到地理标志保护对于自身发展的重要性，积极完善本国法律体系，出台地理标志保护法律法规，注册保护本国地理标志产品。从目前情况来看，越来越多的亚洲国家倾向于采取制定专门法或条例保护地理标志。例如，日本于2015年颁布了地理标志保护法，印度早在1999年即发布了地理标志条例。东盟国家中的泰国、印度尼西亚（以下简称"印尼"）、马来西亚、老挝、柬埔寨、新加坡、越南也陆续制定了地理标志专门保护法律法规。❶ 上述东南亚国家的地理标志法律体系建设受欧盟影响较大，得到了联合国粮农组织和欧盟的项目支持。法律制度虽然是地理标志国际交流

---

❶ MALIK M. Updates on the Geographical Indications in the ASEAN Region [EB/OL]. (2019-07-02) [2021-04-25]. https：//www.wipo.int/edocs/mdocs/sct/en/wipo_geo_lis_19/wipo_geo_lis_19_6.pdf.

合作的重要内容，但大可不必将精力过多地投入在研究各国法律体系的异同上，而应更加注重开展实践交流，探讨项目合作的可行性，在实践交流中增进彼此了解，深化互利合作。

"南南合作是国与国之间开展合作，实现各国经济发展和全球发展目标的榜样。通过南南合作展示的国际间团结协作也是有效应对全球新冠肺炎危机的关键。"❶ 受发展水平所限，许多发展中国家，尤其是最不发达国家，在能力建设上普遍与发达国家存在差距和困难，很难凭借自身力量有效发展地理标志产业。这方面可以借鉴联合国粮农组织和欧盟的做法，在积极吸引民间和社会力量参与的同时，更好地发挥政府和行业作用，建立专家咨询机构，主动参与发展中国家，尤其是最不发达国家的地理标志保护项目建设，从项目提出到实地考察、产品梳理、产地划定、规范制定、实施支持等各环节给予帮助，配合打造属于当地的特色产品和产业。

三是可深化与发展中国家之间的地理标志合作。地理标志保护对于任何一个发展中国家都具有重要意义和发展潜力。发展中大国，如"金砖五国"（中国、印度、俄罗斯、巴西、南非），和印尼、越南、埃及、肯尼亚、秘鲁、墨西哥等具有一定代表性的国家，所处的地理环境和发展水平各异，但都拥有丰富的自然资源，具备地理标志产业发展潜力。以印尼为例，印尼是东南亚最大的发展中国家，岛屿众多，人口密集，热带物产丰

---

❶ 参见：https://www.un.org.

富。印尼于2016年颁布了商标与地理标志法❶，2019年发布了有关实施条例❷。印尼迄今已对66个本国地理标志、8个国外地理标志实施了保护。咖啡、胡椒等印尼地理标志在国际市场上崭露头角。据东盟统计，截至2019年1月，东盟国家已有346个地理标志获得注册保护，其中包括37个东盟以外国家的地理标志。❸ 再比如墨西哥地理标志虽然数量不多，但拥有"龙舌兰酒"（Tequila）这一享誉世界的品牌优势，在烈酒地理标志保护方面具有成熟的发展经验。交流实施经验，学习方法手段，可以有效加快本国地理标志发展速度，少走弯路。

四是可强化中日韩关于地理标志保护的合作。地理标志保护与历史文化关系密切。欧美之间围绕地理标志的争论，反映出移民国家与传统欧洲国家由于语言文化相似而产生出的关于地名和产品名称的争议。一方面，中日韩三国文化相近，虽然存在地名重名现象，但三国间在贸易往来中关于产品名称方面的争议并不多见。另一方面，相较于东西方饮食文化差异，中日韩三国居民的饮食习惯相近，其中一个国家的特色产品很可能在另一国家同样受到欢迎，如黄酒、大米、泡菜等。与此同时，中日韩三国同属贸易强国，三国间贸易额巨大，人员往来频繁，并且都是近年来才开展地理标志保护的国家，正处于积累经验和完善制度阶

---

❶ MIRANDAH D, DEVINA R P. Indonesia：Implementing regulations for geographical indications [EB/OL]. (2020-04-13) [2021-09-24]. https：//www.mirandah.com/pressroom/item/indonesia-implementing-regulations-for-geographical-indications/.

❷ 参见：Ministry Regulation No. 12 of 2019 implementing the specific provisions regarding geographical indications.

❸ MALIK M. Updates on the Geographical Indications in the ASEAN Region [EB/OL]. (2019-07-02) [2021-04-25]. https：//www.wipo.int/edocs/mdocs/sct/en/wipo_geo_lis_19/wipo_geo_lis_19_6.pdf.

段。开展三国间的地理标志保护合作具有十分有利的基础条件和特殊意义。地理标志保护交流合作既可有效保护有关产品的知识产权，又可促进相关地理标志产品扩大外销渠道，满足邻国市场对地理标志产品的需求。

五是继续开展多双边交流，适时建立合作机制。在多边领域，WTO 知识产权理事会围绕地理标志议题展开的谈判已持续多年，但收效甚微。谈判争论的焦点有两个：一是是否建立具有法律约束力的地理标志多边注册登记制度，二是是否将对葡萄酒、烈酒的高水平保护扩展到其他产品范围。之所以谈判无果，主要在于欧美国家，即欧洲所谓"旧世界"国家与美洲、大洋洲等所谓的"新世界"国家在地理标志名称上的固有矛盾难以调和。而与众多亚非国家和地区的经济利益并无太大关联，既不影响亚非国家间开展地理标志双边合作，也不影响这些国家与欧美国家开展交流与合作。

事实上，伴随着国际多边谈判陷入僵局，越来越多的国家和经济体转而投向地理标志双边合作。这当中最值得关注的是欧盟与多国签署的地理标志合作协议。据不完全统计，欧盟已完成与中国、越南、新加坡、日本、韩国等国的地理标志双边谈判，签署了合作协议。可以预见的是，更多国家可能加入这一行列中来。

中欧地理标志交流合作始于 20 世纪 90 年代，原国家技术监督局颁布的《原产地域产品保护规定》正是在借鉴法国原产地监控命名制度的基础上起草发布的。原国家质检总局 2001 年组建成立后，与欧洲委员会贸易总司、农业总司等部门广泛开展了地理标志保护交流，举办了一系列中欧地理标志保护合作论坛、研讨会，开展了人员互访和技术磋商。2005 年，原国家质检总局与欧洲委员会贸易总司签订了《中华人民共和国国家质量监督检验检疫总局与欧洲委员会贸易总司关于地理标志的谅解备忘录》，并从2006年起开展了中欧10+10地理标志保护产品互认互保试点项目（EU-China 10+10 Pilot Project），双方各有10个地理标志产品在对方获得注册保护。这次合作是双方在技术层面的全面交流，中欧针对对方提交的10个产品，完全按照各自当时法律法规规定的审核程序进行了书面审查，欧方还与中方10个产品的产地代表进行了面对面交流，并实地考察了地理标志产地。欧方对中方地理标志产品保护的做法和成绩给予了充分认可，中方也从中了解到欧方地理标志保护的具体做法和成熟经验。可以说，双方这次合作交流非常成功，为日后深化中欧地理标志保护合作、签订双边协定奠定了基础。❶ 2011年，中欧在更高层面启动了地理标志协定谈判。双方经过8年时间多轮磋商，于2019年底宣布结束谈判，并在2020年9月14日中欧领导人峰会上正式签署《中华人民共和国政府与欧洲联盟地理标志保护与合作协定》（以下简称为《中欧地理标志协定》），双方各有100个地理标志产品将在对方境内获得保护。该协定生效4年后，中欧将各自再增加175个地理标志产品，纳入在对方境内保护范畴。

《中欧地理标志协定》在知识产权保护水平上相当于WTO/TRIPS第23条所规定的对葡萄酒和烈酒的高水平保护，高于第22条所规定的对地理标志的一般性保护，也是双方首次在国家

---

❶ EU and China sign landmark agreement protecting Geographical Indications [EB/OL]. (2020-09-14) [2020-09-01]. https://ec.europa.eu/commission/presscorner/detail/en/ip_20_1602.

层面签署地理标志合作协议，具有里程碑式意义。❶ "这是中国对外商签的第一个全面、高水平的地理标志双边协定，也是近年来中欧之间首个重大贸易协定，对深化中欧经贸合作具有里程碑式的意义。该协定包括十四条和七个附录，主要规定了地理标志保护规则和地理标志互认清单等内容，具有保护数量多、保护丰富、保护待遇高等亮点。"中国国际问题研究院欧洲研究所所长崔洪建分析认为，《中欧地理标志协定》有助于满足中欧双方对高品质产品的需求，为双方民众带来实实在在的福祉。从更深层次看，《中欧地理标志协定》的签署向世界释放出三重信号。一是推动中欧经贸关系高质量发展。二是表明中欧在知识产权方面取得了积极进展。三是将推动整个世界范围内对地理标志的认可和重视。❷ 从技术层面分析，中欧签署地理标志协定还将对国际地理标志保护格局产生影响，或有利于地理标志专门保护体系在更多的国家和地区生根发芽。

前文提到，WTO 成员在地理标志保护议题上存在较大分歧，欧洲国家与美国、澳大利亚、新西兰、智利、阿根廷等所谓的"新世界"国家存在矛盾。争论的焦点是地理标志保护的法律约束力，以及是否将 TRIPS 第 23 条规定的对葡萄酒和烈酒的高水平保护扩展到其他产品。换言之，欧洲国家希望强化对地理标志名称的法律保护，以保护其内部相关产业，不断增强其国际市场竞争力。而"新世界"国家由于受移民文化影响，生产了一些

---

❶ EU and China sign landmark agreement protecting Geographical Indications ［EB/OL］. (2020-09-14)［2021-02-22］. https：//ec. europa. eu/commission/presscorner/detail/en/ip_20_1602.

❷ 栾雨石，牛宁. 海外网评：中欧地理标志协定正式签署释放三重信号［EB/OL］. (2020 - 09 - 15)［2021 - 02 - 22］. http：//opinion. haiwainet. cn/n/2020/0915/c353596-31876382. html.

与欧洲国家地理标志同名或名称近似的食品和农产品，因此强烈要求弱化保护举措，认为相关产品属于通用名称，地理标志保护阻碍其产业发展和国际贸易。地理标志保护反映在法律层面是采用什么样的法律体系。欧盟采用的专门法律体系是严格保护地理标志的主要范例，欧盟官方也在不遗余力地宣传推广其地理标志保护手段，并在世界范围取得了一定成效。中欧签署地理标志协定或将影响其他国家，尤其是发展中国家地理标志保护制度和国际立场，促使有关国家更加关注地理标志的作用和影响，完善本国地理标志保护法律体系。

中国根据自身国情开展地理标志保护。经过20多年的探索、尝试和发展，社会各界逐渐形成共识，认识到加强地理标志保护对于减贫脱贫、促进特色产业发展所发挥的积极作用，以及对于知识产权保护、国际贸易扩大的重要意义。与欧盟签署地理标志协定有利于进一步完善国内地理标志法律体系，适时制定地理标志保护法。至于该协定对于国际贸易的具体影响程度，需要持续关注和研究评估。可以预见的是，与列入《中欧地理标志协定》保护清单的产品名称相同，或标注有同名产品"类""型"等近似名称的产品将难以再进入中欧市场。

双边合作强调的是互利互惠。开展地理标志双边合作既有利于相互保护对方重要地理标志产业的经济利益和知识产权，也有助于开展经验交流，相互学习，共同发展。在地理标志保护过程中探索与可持续发展目标相结合，交流借鉴可持续发展经验，使地理标志成为可持续发展具体实践的重要载体。

结　语

　　笔者通过对地理标志相关概念、保护制度内涵以及相关问题的讨论，试图客观分析地理标志保护制度的独特价值及其对于实现可持续发展目标的正向意义。鉴于本书主题是地理标志与实现可持续发展目标之间的关系，笔者省略了有关地理标志法律制度和知识产权保护案例的介绍，旨在强化读者对于地理标志制度促进经济社会可持续发展的理解和认识，并对致力于地理标志保护实践的读者提供借鉴和参考。

　　地理标志制度的初衷，一方面是保护优质特色产品的知识产权；另一方面是维护原有生产条件和生产方法不因时间的推移而被改变，从而使产品的特色质量得以保持和传承。经过一个多世纪的发展，尤其在WTO成立后的20多年时间里，地理标志保护逐渐引起世界范围的广泛关注。越来越多的国家和地区将其与区域经济增长和国际市场竞争力联系起来，延伸、强化了地理标志保护的意义。从世界范围来看，欧洲国家，尤其是法国、意大利、希腊、西班牙等国家，以及发展到后来的欧盟各成员国，既是地理标志保护制度的发源地和最先实践的地方，也是迄今为止收效最为显著的国家和经济体。地理标志作为欧盟共同农业政策（CAP）的组成部分，与传统特色保证（TSG）、有机产品等质量保证机制一道，成为提升食品和农产品声誉、保护特色产品质量和知识产权、扩大国际市场份额的有效工具。我国作为后来者，在过去20多年的探索发展中，学习借鉴了国外的有益做法，从无到有建立并逐步完善国内的地理标志保护制度，在全国范围付诸实践，积累了丰富经验。但与欧盟相比，还存在一定差距。一方面，我国现有的地理标志专门保护法律层级偏低，一定程度上影响知识产权保护效力。另一方面，各地对于地理标志保护制度的认识不一，政策支持不平衡，尚未形成统一、清晰、明确、可持续的地理标志发展战略，不利于区域经济高质量发展进程。

　　关于地理标志保护制度在我国的实施效果，实事求是地讲，各地情况参差不齐。本书选取了一些好的范例，但现实中也有不成功的案例。不成功的原因无外乎产地管理部门后续跟进不够、生产者参与程度低、制度宣传推广不到位，或者产品本身底蕴不足，难以为继。事实上，即使在欧盟国家，地理标志保护制度的实施也并非无懈可击，其影响力和实际成效在成员国之间存在差距。

　　总之，地理标志保护制度的有效性取决于产地实施水平，取决于各利益相关方是否能够形成共识，共同发力，认真落实制度安排所涉及的各环节要求。由于体制上的差异，国外地理标志保护的做法往往是自下而上，由产地组织发起，通过宣讲、辅导、研讨等方式吸引利益相关方广泛参与申请注册过程。这种方式相当于把地理标志保护措施的"宣贯"前移。其优点是覆盖面较广、基础工作比较扎实。缺点是过程可能较长、效率偏低。我国的做法有所不同,虽然也是自下而上,由地方政府或行业组织启动申报工作,但申报过程中主要依靠当地专家和技术人员编写申报材料,申报成功后再组织开展实施宣传、培训和技术辅导。这一方式的申报效率较高,但缺点也很明显,即,前期基础较弱,群众参与度不高,后续实施宣传、培训、监督等任务繁重。地理标志保护成功与否很大程度上有赖于地方政府发挥引领作用,持续给予人力、财力和政策支持。

总体来看,我国在开展地理标志保护上仍具有一定制度优势。地理标志这一概念从不为人知到引起广泛关注仅用了十几年时间。在不到20年时间里,全国共批准、注册了数千件地理标志(含地理标志保护产品、地理标志集体/证明商标、农产品地理标志登记),成绩斐然。主管部门、地方政府和行业组织开展了行之有效的地理标志保护宣传推广工作,地理标志产品遍地开花,实现了全国31个省、自治区、直辖市(不含港澳台)全覆盖。笔者认为,接下来有待进一步完善的工作:一是提高地理标志保护法律层级和保护效力;二是加强地理标志品牌建设,更好地将其作为区域品牌建设的重要抓手;三是优化市场环境,提升消费者信心,使更多消费者乐于购买国内外优秀地理标志保护产品,让地理标志这一传承历史文化记忆的区域品牌成为实现可持续发展目标的有生力量。

Introduction

The protection system for geographical indication (hereinafter referred to as the GI system) was originated in the 19th century from l'Appellation d'origine Contrôlée (AOC) practiced in France for the protection of wines and cheeses whose characteristics were linked to the geographical conditions of the producing areas.The basic mindset of AOC and the GI system is-by designating the geographical areas where it is produced-to set up legal means to protect a product named after its geographical location,its characteristics being closely related to the natural and human factors of its origin.Non original products of the same kinds are prohibited from using the 'registered' name, including names that look alike.The exclusive right of the original product is thereby established to prevent from any infringement and misuse.Meanwhile,by setting up specific technical regulation, namely the specification,the source of raw materials,techniques and characteristics,as well as packaging and marketing rules are all regulated and monitored to guarantee the preservation of unique characteristics of the protected product.

The basis of geographical indication and l'appellation d'origine (AO) is 'soil' or 'terroir'.Defined by l'Institut National de l'origine et de la Qualite(INAO) of France, "a terroir is a specific geographical area where production takes its originality directly from the specific nature of its production area.Terroir is based on a system of interactions between physical and biological environment,and a set of human factors within a space which a human community built during its history with a collective productive knowledge.There are elements of originality and typicality of the product."[1]

The idea of terroir has a significant impact on the *sui generis* protection system of geographical indication. It points out the intrinsic links between the soil,the environment and the quality of a product, which is helpful for our comprehension of the fundamentals and principles of the GI system.

The Uruguay Round of Multilateral Trade Negotiations was concluded in 1994.Members signed the *Final Act* at the Marrakesh Ministerial Conference in April 1994 and announced the *Marrakesh Declaration* before adopting the resolution to establish the World Trade Organization (WTO).The *Agreement of Trade-Related Aspects of Intellectual Property Rights* (TRIPS) was among the 60 documents that were compiled into Annex 1c.[2] Articles 22 to 24 of TRIPS lay down the definition of geographical indication,along with the clause on high-level protec-

---

[1] See:https://www.inao.gouv.fr/eng/official-sign-identifying-quality-and-origin/PDO-AOC.

[2] See:https://www.wto.org/english/docs_e/legal.

tion for wines and spirits,and the clause for exceptions.As is defined in Article 22,

> Geographical indications are, for the purposes of this Agreement, indications which identify a good as originating in the territory of a Member, or a region or locality in that territory, where a given quality, reputation or other characteristic of the good is essentially attributable to its geographical origin. ❶

TRIPS serves as the primary legal basis that WTO Members shall abide by when it comes to the protection of geographical indications.It also serves as the most significant international convention to date regarding the protection of intellectual property rights.

Geographical indication is place-based exclusive right.GI's quality is attributable to the unique geographical conditions - the soil,temperature, humidity, altitude, terrain, rainfall, water, forest coverage etc. - and special techniques as well as other human factors.Natural conditions cannot be replicated, so are such human factors as traditional techniques and inherited elements that are invaluable assets closely associated with history and geographical conditions.It denies the theoretical claim that the production could be replicated or transferred to other places,for the change of specific geographical conditions coupled with a lack of human inheritance may well paralyze the attempt.Therefore, GI protection emphasizes uniqueness and exclusive right.GI products make distinctions with others of the same kind, thereby accentuating their characteristics and outstanding values so that to gain higher price surplus.

GIs are now increasingly perceived as an opportunity in many other countries

---

❶ Page 10, TRIPS, the Chinese version, 23 Jan. 2017.

that have unique physical and cultural attributes that can be translated into product differentiation. ❶

Apparently, such a 'privilege' to distinguish itself from other products of the same kind is only acceptable when proper criteria and legal frameworks are put in place. They ensure effective protection as well. A geographical indication may thus evolve into a popular regional brand and a symbol of the geographical origin. It could be a driving force for local employment while, through GIs' overflow effect, fostering the coordinated growth of GI - related sectors such as packaging, logistics, tourism and environmental protection.

GIs possess many of the characteristics of an upmarket brand. They can have an impact on entire supply chains and even other products and services in a region and thereby foster business clustering and rural integration. Their differentiation from commodities can offer a valuable competitive advantage that is difficult to erode. ❷

The strong links to geographical areas imply that GIs are primarily in relation to agricultural products, foodstuffs and, some, if any, handicrafts, albeit less relevant to industrial and service products,❸ for the latter's production is barely influenced by geographical conditions or techniques of geographical nature. Agri - food GIs cover a wide range. They may roughly be divided into primary products of plant or livestock, or foods that merely undergo physical changes from their primary status (slaughter, slice, peel, cut etc.), or processed foods that have

---

❶ See: http://www. intracen. org/itc/market - info - tools/geographical - indications.
❷ See: http://www. intracen. org/itc/market - info - tools/geographical - indications.
❸ But there are exceptions. For instance, Swiss Watch is registered as GI in Switzerland. https://www. ige. ch/en/protecting - your - ip/indications - of - source/ protecting - geographical - indications/protection - in - switzerland.

adopted primary products as raw materials (cheese,wine,spirit,vinegar, etc.).Global practices split when it comes to whether to include handicrafts into the GI protection scheme.GI protection by trademark law or anti-unfair competition law normally do not discriminate against non-agricultural products.The *sui generis* regime,however,i.e.,specific law, act or regulation targeting the protection of GIs,is inconsistent in this regard.Some countries or regions,like China,India,Thailand,Vietnam, Laos,to name only a few,have included non-agricultural products in their GI schemes;others,like the European Union (EU),have rejected. (That said,14 countries within the EU have provided protections to non-agricultural GIs by trademark laws or anti-unfair competition laws.)❶

Non-agricultural products are excluded because their links to the natural conditions of the producing areas could hardly be identified. Their characteristics are usually determined by local historical and human factors,namely the historical and cultural inheritance of certain techniques.Some critics argue that historical and human factors are insufficient proof for a GI,meaning there is no way to prove any intrinsic link between the product and its producing areas,neither can it be proven that the producing areas cannot be duplicated or transferred to other locations.While those who are in favor of inclusion of non-agricultural products claim that TRIPS does not limit the scope of GIs,Article 22 states:

---

❶ European Commission. Green Paper on the protection of geographical indications for non-agricultural products-Frequently Asked Questions [EB/OL]. (2014-07-15) [2022-03-21]. https://ec. europa. eu/commission/presscorner/ detail/en/ MEMO_14_486.

Geographical indications are, for the purposes of this Agreement, indications which identify a good as originating in the territory of a Member, or a region or locality in that territory, where a given quality, reputation or other characteristic of the good is essentially attributable to its geographical origin. ❶

The definition uses 'or' to broaden the denotation of GIs. In other words, a product that points to its origin primarily due to reputation or human factors, albeit irrelevant to geographical conditions, is eligible to be accepted as a GI. Therefore, handicrafts with historical and human characteristics and market reputations could be covered by the GI system without the need to prove any causal link with the natural circumstances of the producing areas.

With rising number of countries joining the *sui generis* group in protecting GIs in recent years,❷ and that non-agricultural product being not excluded from their practices, EU has carried out studies and surveys on the possibility of extending GI protection to non-agricultural products. Moreover, in some signed bilateral trade agreements, EU has even skipped current legal provisions to include 2 non-agricultural products from Columbia and Peru as registered GIs to be protected in the EU.❸

A summary report on public consultation carried out by the EU in 2014 indicated that, among all the respondents, 57.1% were in favor of the extension of GI protection, 5% were against, the rest held no position. Most respondents inclined to weaken the requirements on local

---

❶ Page 10, TRIPS, the Chinese version, 23 Jan. 2017.
❷ According to EU statistics, there are about 80 countries.
❸ Guacamayas (Handicraft) from Colombia and Chulucanas (Potery) from Peru.

raw materials.❶ Instead,they gave more emphasis on such human factors as traditional techniques,which had often been taken as 'loose' connections by some orthodox GI critics.

Despite the controversy over the scope of GI protection,we may infer that:

(1) GIs are products with characteristics that are scarce resources.

(2) GIs possess distinctive geographical features that are worthy of protection from passing off and infringement.

(3) GIs are subject to historical and cultural influences, human factors such as traditional techniques should be inherited.

(4) GIs are closely related to natural environment.Protection of GIs goes hand in hand with the protection of natural environment.Only by doing so can we ensure the quality characteristics of GIs and safeguard their market reputations.

In view of the roughly twenty-year history of GI protection in China,it is still an immature scheme in progress.Therefore,before we probe into the relationships between the GI system and the United Nations Sustainable Development Goals (SDGs),and to help our readers better understand relevant issues,it is deemed necessary to analyze the technical contents of the GI system in relation to the SDGs. These technical contents include but not limited to,the designation of geographical areas,GI name(s),the specification,etc.Meanwhile,since this book is intended to focus on the practices of the *sui generis* regime of

---

❶ KOENIG M, et al. Summary of Results, Public Consultation on geographical indication protection for non-agricultural products in the EU[EB/OL]. (2015-01-19)[2021-09-13]. https://ec. europa. eu/growth/content/conference-geographical-indication-protection-non-agricultural-products-%E2%80%93-what-do-we-learn_en.

the GI system, GI schemes under other legal frameworks-for their distinctive approaches-will not be discussed.Moreover,as the emphasis of this book is on the intrinsic links and positive roles of GIs in achieving the SDGs, issues like GI's global progress, comparisons among different legal frameworks as well as their enforcement practices are not concerns of this book.

Chapter 1≫
Conditions and factor analysis of the GI system

GI protection starts with the finding of a product with territorial characteristics. By working through the application procedures, along with on-site examinations, documentation, market feedback reviews as well as laboratory analysis, experts and local authorities are expected to study the would-be GI and demarcate the producing areas objectively and lay down the specification in order to set the basis for GI protection.

Section 1 The demarcation of producing areas

The demarcation of producing areas is one of the preconditions for GI protection. It serves as the official confirmation of the geographical areas where a GI is produced. In China,the demarcation of producing areas is conductcd,as provided in the *Regulations on the Protection of Geographical Indication Products*, by the county-level (or a higher level) government(Article 9).

Now that the presence of characteristics is in connection with natural and human factors of the producing areas,it is necessary to clarify their size-villages,towns,counties or cities-that are involved,and parcels of land or waters that are to be encompassed.It is subject to surveys of its market reputation,production history,natural environment and overall production conditions.First-hand information could be obtained by on-site examinations,while the product name and history of production is available by consulting relevant literature,plus market feedback reviews and visits to the producing areas.The task aims at delineating the geographical areas that fit for the production,making sure that its historical and cultural traditions are properly inherited.Moreover,it is a conduct to exclude the geographical areas that have not been involved in any production activities.In general,it aims at protecting the GI's name and characteristics as well as traditional techniques.It is a task demanding objectivity and fairness.Any inclusion or exclusion of geographical areas must be justified.

Market reputation is one of the major concerns of the GI system. It is a demonstration of GI's value and consumers' responses to any product with characteristics.It is one of the core concerns of GI examinations as well.If we split GI products into multiple tiers based on their popularity and reputation,the top tier,or Tier One,consists of high-profile GIs that are of international appeals,like Champagne,Scotch Whisky,Columbia Coffee,Moutai Chiew,to name only a few,while the bottom tier,or Tier Three,refers to those that have very limited market influence and are known only around the producing areas or to adjacent towns and counties.Those between the above two groups are usually goods popular in neighboring cities or even provinces,yet unknown to the market beyond.In China,the middle tier accounts for a larger proportion than the other two groups.

In fact,very few products enjoy popularity in both domestic and overseas market. For those with low popularity and small market shares,the demarcation of producing areas might be conflict free,as the launching of GI application for protection will not spark uproars among local stakeholders.But for the high - profile ones, given their market influence,the demarcation act could be challenging,as it may have implications on producers' interests and consumer rights.It is also in relation to the sustainable development of renowned products and their market reputation.Moreover,it is relevant to the preservation of cultural and historical traditions.The question is:how to demarcate the producing areas?

Above all,facts must be respected.GI products are the yields of peculiar geographical conditions and human efforts.The demarcation of producing areas must be in consistent with the natural environment and must take the use of the GI name and production scale into account.For primary products,it is advised to consider such elements as the climate,soil (or water),terrain,landscape,altitude,forest coverage,etc. For processed products,it is advised to concern about the influence of water,climate - including microclimate caused by terrain and landscape-specific techniques and other human influences as well.Some characteristics can hardly be assessed by sensory examination.Demarcation of producing areas must therefore be accompanied by laboratory analysis.

For instance,Moutai Chiew (Kweichow Moutai Chiew) was registered as a Protected Designated Origin Product in China on 29 March 2001,by the former State Bureau of Quality and Technical Supervision (Announcement No.4 2001),which defined an area of 7.5 square kilometers under GI protection,namely,within the Town of Maotai,Renhuai City of Guizhou Province, starting from the Xiao He Hydropower Plant as the south end - which is in subjection to Maotai Town at the water outlet of Yanjin River-ending in the north at Yangliu Bay that is located by Workshop One of the Moutai Distillery,with Yangcha Street as the northern boundary.The eastern boundary is between the Maotai-Zunyi Highway and the south end of Yanjin River,while the western boundary is by the Chishui River,with a total area of 7.5 square kilometers.In the aftermath of GI registration,the Guizhou Provincial Government assembled an expert team to carry out surveys and verified the core biological conservation areas,with the 7.5km^2 designated areas being the center place.In addition,a biological conservation project was drafted that covered an area of over 4,800km^2 surrounding the Moutai Distillery.The project defined the so-called Chishui River Biological Conservation Areas that extended to as far as 100km south of and 50km north of the Maotai County,spanning 20km from east to west.It set the goal of industrial and agricultural development within the conservation areas and ensured the healthy development of Moutai

Chiew.❶

In 2012,the Guizhou Provincial Government filed an application to the former General Administration of Quality Supervision,Inspection and Quarantine(AQSIQ) for the extension of the producing areas of Moutai Chiew, extending southward from the original producing area of 7.5km^2, to a combined area of 15.03km^2, i.e., along the Chishui River valley,with the Zhidong Mountain and Peak of Mafuxi as the east end,the Chishui River as the west end,the Taiping villageas the south end against the Yantanggou boundary, and with the north end by the outlet of Yanjin River that joins the original designated areas.❷

It should be noted that,for the extension of the producing areas, Guizhou Moutai Co. Ltd. had carried out long-term study and laboratory analysis that compared the liquor produced in the extended area with that from the original area.Sufficient data were collected as evidence for the identical quality of Moutai Chiew (Kweichow Moutai) produced either in the original area or from the extension. AQSIQ eventually approved the extension request.

Secondly,respect for history is a must.Well-known GIs almost always enjoy a long history and have withstood times and market fluctuations,making it possible to find evidence by consulting relevant literature.Nevertheless,it remains an issue when it comes to the criterion that determines the so - called 'long history' or 'being traditional',for

---

❶ See: Ji Keliang, Speech on the Conference Commemorating the 10th Anniversary of GI Protection in China,27 October 2009.

❷ Announcement No. 44 of 2013 on the approval of amendment to the name and designated areas of Moutai Chiew (Kweichou Moutai Chiew) ,AQSIQ.

which there is no common standard to follow.The EU legal provisions state that 'traditional' means "proven usage on the domestic market for a period that allows transmission between generations;this period is to be at least 30 years".❶ Whilst China's *Working Procedures for the Regulation on the Protection of Geographical Indication Products* only describes it as 'relatively long producing history',which does not clarify specific length of time.(Article 19) In practice,a history of 30 years is a general benchmark that should be incorporated with reputation and scales.

Thirdly,dispute must be settled properly.The potential economic benefits from GI protection may have impact on local and neighboring regions,impelling relevant parties to make attempts to be included in the protected producing areas.Consequently, either unsolicited extension or narrowing of producing areas might exist. The causes behind are,

－the applicant intends to extend the producing areas so as to increase beneficiaries and scaling up;

－producers adjacent to the geographical origin want to be included and share the potential benefits;

－other problems resulted from disregard for facts.

Dispute over producing area is commonplace.It is usually associated with the following issues:

(1) If there is any quality difference between what is produced inside and outside the demarcated areas.

---

❶ Regulation (EU) No 1151/2012 of the Council of 21 November 2012[EB/OL].[2022-03-15]. https://eur-lex. europa. eu/legal-content/EN/TXT/? uri=CELEX.

(2) Producers beyond the demarcated areas have also adopted the same GI name,making it an established fact.

(3) Dispute over the legitimacy of the applicant.

Regardless of the causes of dispute,the burden of proof rests with the one who raises objection.Some disputes may be related to the historical origin of the product and its course of evolution,which could be complex and requires cautious handlings.Provisions on the designation of geographical areas vary from country to country and are determined both by the administration mode and institutional design of the GI system.No matter how it works,it is necessary to coordinate with stakeholders consisting of producers,operators,inter - governmental organizations,government agencies as well as consumers.In some cases,it is also necessary to coordinate with the stakeholders outside the demarcated origin.In EU Member States,the demarcation of origin is conducted by independent experts delegated by the GI authorities. For instance,in France it is done through the delegation of INAO. The experts' tasks include:

− defining objective criteria of demarcation (criteria based on natural and human factors and principal issues concerning the links with the origin),

− delimiting the geographical area.[1]

Being a member state,France follows EU's common GI scheme which divides GI into two categories,namely,Protected Geographical Indication(PGI)/l'indication géographique protégée (IGP) that does not

---

[1] INAO,Guide du demandeur d'une appellation d'origine protégée (AOP) ou d'une indication géographique protégée (IGP)[EB/OL]. [2022-03-16]. https://www. inao. gouv. fr.

require raw materials wholly produced in the locality; and Protected Designation of Origin (PDO)/l'appellation d'origine protégée (AOP), requiring all the raw materials being produced locally and all the processing including packaging and sometimes storage being entirely completed within the designated origin.In consistent with such requirements,the French authority sets different criteria in demarcating the producing areas, where the application for AOP, or PDO, faces more stringent requirements that are authorized and monitored by higher level administrative agencies.

In China,the demarcation task falls within the jurisdiction of administrative divisions of a city or county,with few exceptions spanning across the borders of administrative divisions of a city or even a province.Article 9 of the *Regulation on the Protection of Geographical Indications* provides,

> whereas the producing areas of a product are within the administrative areas of a county, the municipal government of the county is entitled to propose the designated areas; whereas the producing areas extend to other adjacent counties, it is up to the city's municipal government to make proposals on the designated areas; whereas it extends across cities, the proposal on the designation must be made by the provincial government.

Paragraph 2 of Article 10 requires that the applicant shall provide the official letter of designation of the protected areas by the county level or higher-level municipal government.The designated areas must specify the respective towns,and for aquaculture product,the water areas must be specified.When dispute arises regarding the designation of origin,Article 13 provides that,

> The coordination of objections follows the territorial principle. Objections re-

ceived during the objection period are coordinated,

— by relevant provincial quality supervision agencies delegated by AQSIQ, and report settlement of disputes in a timely manner. When necessary, at the request of the provincial quality supervision agencies, AQSIQ may consider to the experts' views and organize the coordination.

— by AQSIQ if the dispute relates to more than one province.

In line with this requirement, the general principle to settle a dispute is the coordination from the higher municipal government, i.e., if it happens between adjacent counties, it is up to the municipal government to address the issue and follow suit. Local government is encouraged to coordinate and settle the disputes, whereas the GI authorities are not directly involved. And when consensus cannot be reached by the parties concerned, the GI application will be suspended.

Given the diverse scenarios regarding the demarcation of producing areas, especially for products with historical traces, it could be complex in a country like China, for, inter alias, the administrative regions may have undergone constant changes. Such changes do complicate the demarcation task. The following two cases may help explain.

Case 1. The dispute over the origin of Dukang Liquor (Chinese Baijiu)

Dukang was purportedly the ancestor of ancient Chinese Baijiu (liquor). Literature about Dukang can be found in the *Analytical Dictionary of Characters* written in the East Han Dynasty. Emperor Cao Cao of the Wei Dynasty once claimed that Dukang was the very thing that might allay sorrow, indicating that Dukang as the name of liquor has had a long history. However, opinions vary when it comes to the true origin of Dukang Liquor. "The Kangjiawei Village in Baishui County,Shaanxi Province is said to be the birthplace of Dukang;while the Dukangfan in Ruyang County,Henan Province is said to be the place where Dukang made liquor;and the Shanghuang Fountain of the Huangdedi Village in Yichuan County,Henan Province is said to be the location where Dukang collected water to make liquor."[1] The above mentioned three places all claimed to be the origin of Dukang Liquor,resulting in many controversies.Yet the acceptable view is that it was not until the 1970's that production of Dukang Liquor was resumed in China.The distillery at Yichuan County was the pioneer in applying for the registration of trademark 'Dukang',making it the only liquor producer that owns the trademark of 'Dukang' and thereby triggered the lengthy dispute over the trademark right involving the three producing areas. In the meantime, the distillery at Ruyang County, Henan Province took the lead in applying for the Mark of Origin to the former General Administration of Quality Supervision,Inspection and Quarantine of China (AQSIQ) in 2001.Subsequently,the trademark holder‐Yichuan Dukang Distillery‐sued Ruyang Dukang Distillery over its infringement of the 'Dukang' trademark and its unwaranted act to apply for any registration of Mark of Origin,appealing for terminating its production of Ruyang Dukang Liquor.

Given the long history of Dukang Liquor and its market reputation,the dispute was handled cautiously.Document checking and consultations with the two parties revealed that the trademark 'Dukang'

---

[1] 张嘉涛,崔春玲,童忠东,等.白酒生产工艺与技术[M].北京:化学工业出版社,2014.

was registered in the early 1980's - an act prior to the release of the *Trademark Law* in China.❶ Dispute around trademark 'Dukang' was an issue left over from the past.Meanwhile 'Ruyang Dukang' was also a registered trademark for liquor product.The applicant claimed that the true origin of Dukang Liquor was in Ruyang County,where Ruyang Distillery was just built based on an old workshop with one ancient well as the proof.Further study indicated that both Dukang Village and the claimed fountain as well as current locations of the two distilleries used to be within the geographical boundary of Yiyang County (伊阳县)in ancient times.The supporting documents provided by both parties made some sense.Nevertheless,they had all exaggerated their own uniqueness.Ruyang Dukang's application for the Mark of Origin was considered valid.And since its designated producing area was within the boundary of Ruyang County,it was in conformity with the provisions of the *Regulation on the Mark of Origin*.In the meantime,the GI authority held that the registration intent was not an act of infringement against the trademark 'Dukang' ,the objection from Yichuan Dukang Distillery was thus dismissed. 'Ruyang Dukang' was subsequently approved to be registered as a Mark of Origin.

Case 2. The dispute over the origin of Dong E Ejiao (donkey‐hide gelatin)

This is another dispute over the origin of geographical indication. Like Case One,it also occurred soon after the GI system was practiced

---

❶ 《中华人民共和国商标法》1982 年 8 月 23 日第五届全国人民代表大会常务委员会第二十四次会议通过。

in China.Ejiao,or donkey-hide gelatin,is a traditional Chinese medicine,and Dong E Ejiao boasts the best of its kind.Ejiao producers have been concentrated in Shandong Province,with Shandong Dong E Ejiao Co.,Ltd being the largest one,whose Ejiao product branded with trademark 'Dong E' has the biggest market share in China.Dong E is a place name, while Shandong Dong E Ejiao Co.,Ltd is in Dong E County,Liaocheng City of Shandong Province.The dispute over Dong E Ejiao's GI protection started in 2001 when Shandong Fujiao Group, Ejiao producer in Dong E Town of Pingyin County,Jinan City in Shandong Province,filed an application to the former AQSIQ for the registration of 'Dong E Ejiao' as a Mark of Origin❶.It was extraordinary in that,while the two producers belonged to two separate cities, they were in a county and a town both named as 'Dong E'.As was expected,soon after the publication,Shandong Dong E Ejiao Co.,Ltd raised objection,accusing the other of infringing the trademark right of 'Dong E' and claiming that its application for Mark of Origin was unwarranted.

Studies revealed that Dong E Ejiao had a history of over one thousand years.However,Dong E County and Dong E Town belonged to separate administrative divisions of Jinan City and Liaocheng City. Geographically,Dong E Town was separated from Dong E County by the Yellow River.Meanwhile,both were producing areas of Ejiao.Further study indicated that the administrative divisions of Dong E had undergone changes that might have been related to the diversions of

---

❶ See:Mark of Origin is divided into two parts-the Mark of Geographical Indication and Mark of Country of Origin-by the *Regulation on the Mark of Origin*. In this case, it refers to the application for the Mark of Geographical Indication.

course of the Yellow River throughout history.It was significant in that such changes had not affected the inheritance of traditional techniques of Ejiao making, creating a scenario where the same characteristic product was made by producers from separate administrative regions. Therefore,both parties were deemed eligible for the application of Mark of Origin.The former AQSIQ then approved their registration respectively.

It is noteworthy that the above cases both occurred at the initial stage of China's accession into the WTO,when it was also the starting phase for China's GI system.The *Regulation on the Mark of Origin* was issued in March 2001 by the former State Administration of Entry-Exit Inspection and Quarantine of the People's Republic of China (SCIQ).Article 4 of this regulation provides,

A geographical indication is the geographical name of a country, region or specific place that is used to refer to a product originated from it with its quality characteristics totally or primarily attributable to the geographical environment, natural conditions and human factors.

This definition,being the first in specifying the term 'geographical indication' in any Chinese laws and regulations,has referred to Article 22 of TRIPS.Given that in-depth study of the GI system had barely kicked off,the *Regulation on the Mark of Origin* is not flawless in provisions like,for instance,the qualifications of applicant and specific requirements on the demarcation of geographical areas.Plus,the GI authority was not fully conscious of the relations between GIs and generic names containing place names.That said,the GI authority honored history and facts when it comes to the tracking of GI producing areas.And the handling of GI's relation with trademarks was in line with the principles of TRIPS.

Due to the special production pattern of some of the Chinese foodstuffs, the applicants of the above two cases were single firms, which, instead of being the common rule, were exceptions for GI application. For historical reasons, trademark right has always been the focus of disputes concerning processed foodstuffs in China. Trademark holders often attempt to monopolize the right of place names on ground of prior registration of trademarks containing geographical terms - an unfair and unwarranted act in many cases. The Regulation on the Protection of Geographical Indication Product published in 2005 made amendments to the qualifications of applicant, prioritizing the role of local government and inter-professional organization. Whereas in exceptional cases, single producer is eligible to be the applicant.❶ It is in line with international practice and the Chinese circumstances. For instance, the EU provides in its regulations on GI application from a single producer as:

> The conditions in which a single producer may qualify as an eligible applicant should be defined. Single producers should not be penalized if prevailing circumstances prevent the creation of a producer group. However, it should be clarified that the protected name may be used by other producers established in the demarcated geographical area provided the conditions laid down in the product specification are met, even where the protected name consists of or contains the name of the holding of the single applicant producer. ❷

---

❶ 《地理标志产品保护规定》第八条规定:地理标志产品保护申请,由当地县级以上人民政府指定的地理标志产品保护申请机构或人民政府认定的协会和企业(以下简称申请人)提出,并征求相关部门意见。

❷ COMMISSION DELEGATED REGULATION (EU) 2019/33[EB/OL].[2021-10-10]. https://eur-lex.europa.eu/legal-content/EN/TXT/? uri=CELEX%3A32019R0033.

The above two cases underscore the complexity of demarcation of producing areas. It is not only a recognition of production environment and techniques, but also an acknowledgement of local culture, history and geography. Consideration must be given to local cultural and historical heritages, focusing on major concerns of the GI system. It is essential to study cultural inheritance and make rational use of the natural endowment to fulfill the idea of sustainable development.

Section 2 Maintaining the market value of GI names

Geographical indication is an intellectual property right. One of the primary concerns of the GI system is the product name. No one beyond the geographical origin can use the protected GI name, which is considered a sign distinctive.[1] Consumers would associate a GI product with specific characteristics, whereby influencing their willingness to pay for it. Judged by market responses, products with high popularity are more likely to be infringed. The cases in Section One indicate that, theoretically at least and mostly for agricultural products, neighboring regions of a GI's producing areas might produce something with similar characteristics. In this case, demarcation of geo-

---

[1] 显著性标志最主要的作用在于能够传达有关产品来源和出处的各种信息,这些信息不仅易于辨认而且能帮助顾客进行重复购买,从而提供流通的效率。

graphical areas may extend across the administrative divisions. What justifies a GI is,in addition to natural conditions,the human factors as well as historical and cultural inheritance.Producers beyond the designated areas cannot use the GI name. But in case it is a popular name,people always have the intent to use it for marketing purposes. It is the established reputation of a GI that determines the convergence of name, and such convergence is not influenced by any change of administrative divisions.In other words,any act of passing off must be associated with popular brands rather than others.

Now that the popularity of a GI is established on the market,it is disseminated in a gradual manner through word-of-mouth act among producers and consumers.Consequently,the name of producing areas evolves into an iconic symbol of a particular product.Producers and operators voluntarily refer the product to its geographical origin,encouraging consumers to associate its geographical origin with characteristics,uplifting their willingness to buy. What makes a GI distinctive from other private rights such as trademark is,inter alias,that,initially, the use of a GI name is a free,voluntary act of GI stakeholders under market environment.They are not obliged to apply for registration before they can use the name as is the case for any trademark. A GI product is jointly produced by firms and individuals who comply with the common code of conduct.The product is then sold with the same name and marketing strategy-sale by individuals being also acceptable- the reputation of a GI and benefits therefrom are shared by all the stakeholders of the producing areas.

The reputation of a GI is essentially gained through long-term market performance rather than being either engineered or promoted by the producers and business operators.To some extent,GI producers merely inherit the unique techniques passed down through generations, keeping using the product name and moving forward along the route. In addition,the natural conditions of GI producing areas can neither be duplicated nor transferred.Provided there is no substantial environmental change and traditional techniques manage to preserve,a GI is bound to exist and prosper.It is the gift and endowment of nature and ancestors. Therefore,for the sake of GI production,inheritance plays a key role when compared with innovation.In fact,it remains controversial when it comes to the relations between GI production and innovation. Stephane Fournier (2016) quoted the remarks by van Caenegem (2003) as saying that (B)eing defined in a code of practices,which may give the impression every condition is given and fixed forever,GIs have been repeatedly criticized for their supposed negative impact on the adaptive capacity of production systems,for the 'significant brake on innovation' they may induce.Moreover,he has cited what Bowen & De Master (2011) called the 'museums of production' GIs may create. "However, some writers have shown that the innovation processes along the GI implementation and running may also have positive impacts (De Rosa et al.,2015;Fournier,2015;Barjolle and Paus,2007).GIs are sometimes used specifically to introduce and develop local innovations (Durand and Fournier,2015;Mancini,2013)".❶

---

❶ FOURNIER S,VANDECANDELAERE E,TEYSSIER C,et al. ,Geographical Indications: what institutional innovations for territorial construction of technical innovations? [EB/OL]. (2016-12-31) [2021-10-10]. https://www. researchgate. net/publication/334315727_Geographical_Indications_what_institutional_innovations_for_territorial_construction_of_technical_innovations.

By emphasizing the role of inheritance,we are by no means denying the role of innovation and transformation. GI productions have generally followed the course that integrates inheritance with innovations.They are carried out both by showing respect for traditions and by introducing advanced management as well as innovative measures. In agricultural sector,for instance,GI producers often apply cutting-edge technology and management system,eliminating outdated ones. Whereas for the food industry,a wide range of internationally recognized quality management systems are adopted,with technical means adjusted to ensure GI's characteristics are well preserved.In general,innovations for GI products are highlighted by setting up cooperatives that adopt common standards,and by enforcing process controls and by boosting bargaining power through improved organizational activities as well as enhanced marketing capacities. ❶

This book has so far reviewed the roles of GI name and the relations between inheritance and innovation.To further analyze the issue, we will go on with discussions about the following topics:

1. The problem of making up a name

It is a phenomenon prevalent in China.Some people argue that they must,above all,sort out a 'good' name for the product before applying for GI protection.For this reason,local government agencies and stakeholders would spare no effort to discuss the naming of a GI.Yet

---

❶ FOURNIER S, VANDECANDELAERE E, TEYSSIER C, et al. , Geographical Indications:what institutional innovations for territorial construction of technical innovations? [EB/OL]. (2016-12-31) [2021-10-10]. https://www. researchgate. net/publication/ 334315727_Geographical_Indications_what_institutional_innovations_for_territorial_construction_of_technical_innovations.

the name that has been 'studied' and 'decided' tends to be, in most cases, the name of a higher-level administrative division. It is a popular perception that this is appropriate to clarify the GI's geographical origin and to enable consumers to relate the origin with a particular quality. But as a matter of fact, it has neither respected the fact nor market rules and has distorted GI's essence. To be honest, the name of a GI is conferred to the product handed down through generations and recognized by consumers. It is neither studied nor decided by experts, officials or entrepreneurs. As far as chronology is concerned, the market reputation of a GI name is always established prior to GI registration. The order can never be reversed. Despite that many GIs are named after their counties or cities, there are considerable exceptions. In short, it is not an issue of whether it is pleasant to hear or whether it has contained the name of a province, a city or a county that has no inevitable connection with the GI's market reputation. Consumers' knowledge of GI's geographical origin stems from its market reputation and the sustained image and pleasant associations in consumers' minds. It is the power of market and genuine value of a GI brand. Any conduct that ignores market power and arbitrarily makes up a GI name is contrary to the principles and direction of GI's brand building.

2. The use of GI name and the application for approval (registration)

Some people claim that no GI name can be used until competent authority approves it. It is, however, another misconception. The name of a GI is the reputation and image accumulated through long-term market performance. The GI system serves for the protection of GI's intellectual property right-an act of legal recognition or administrative confirmation.In other words,whether producers apply for GI registration or not,the product itself is an objective existence.GI producers are free to use the GI name irrespective of any approval from the authority.In practice,one of the concerns of GI examination is the virtual use of a GI name in marketing activities.Any reluctant conduct in using the GI name implies weak popularity or a lack of brand awareness.The difference between an approved (registered) GI and an unregistered one lies in the legal protections provided to the former.Moreover,the post-approval GI producers must regulate the use of GI name and,as is the case in China,get permission from competent authority before any GI logo can be attached to the product.

3. 'Big' name or 'small' name?

Some people believe that a 'big' name is essential for a GI to acquire popularity.The product concerned is supposed to be named after either a city,or even a province or autonomous region within which the producing areas are located.They believe that a village name or name of a county is too 'small' to be accepted as a GI name.This is a false comprehension about the GI system that does not discriminate against any 'small' names.Nor is there any preference for 'big' names. GIs are distinctive from each other only by reputation and market performance.It has nothing to do with a name's 'geographical coverage', nor is there any justification for a 'good' name or a 'bad' name.

First,a 'small' name may not be weak in reputation.Longjing,for instance,is merely the name of a village,yet it has never affected the popularity of 'Longjing Tea' that not only stands for the tea produced in Longjing Village,but also that of the three designated GI producing areas of Longjing Tea.The same is true of Moutai Chiew produced in

Maotai Town,Renhuai County,Zunyi City of Guizhou Province,which has long been the top brand of Chinese Baijiu(liquor) enjoying worldwide reputation.What lies behind the name Moutai is the unique natural environment and human factors of the producing areas.The name itself retains huge intangible assets. Presumably, the name Moutai Chiew will withstand age and remain as it is.

On the other hand,a 'big' territory embodied in a GI name does not always denote geographical areas as big as the name itself implies. For example,Bordeaux does not encompass the whole Bordeaux administrative division.Instead,it refers to the designated geographical areas inside the Bordeaux administrative division.❶ And Shaanxi Apple (a GI in China) has not covered Shaanxi Province as a whole,but the high-quality producing areas located on the Loess Plateau to the north of the Wei River in Shaanxi Province.Again,the logic behind such a phenomenon owes to the market power.The evolving popularity of a GI name is idiomatic during the trading process and has been adopted through market activities.Indeed,a GI name that is 'big' enough to refer to a province or even a country may cause confusions among producers and consumers.Luochuan County,located in the designated areas of Shaanxi Apple,is one of the cores producing areas of Shaanxi Apple.❷ Given its renowned reputation,stakeholders prefer to call their apples as 'Luochuan Apple'.Similarly,the designated areas of Ningxia Gouqi (Ningxia Wolfberry) encompass the Yinchuan Plain and Wein-

---

❶ See:Announcement No. 71 of 2015 on the acceptance of the application of Bordeaux and its affiliated producing areas, AQSIQ.
❷ See:Announcement No. 91 of 2003 on the GI protection of Shaanxi Apple, AQSIQ.

ing Irrigated Areas containing Zhongning County,[1] the core producing area of Ningxia Wolfberry that accounts for a quarter of the total volume and boasts to be the best.The wolfberry sector therefore prefers to call it as Zhongning Gouqi (Zhongning Wolfberry) that enjoys greater popularity in Ningxia Province and is known to the rest of the country as well.

It bears on the relations between the whole producing areas of a GI and its core areas.Agricultural production is a function of terrain, topography and climate. When a GI encompasses large areas containing more than one city or county,the geographical conditions and microclimate may have impact on GI's characteristics.The question is, when such quality differences occur,shall we apply separately for GI protection? Again,the answer lies in GI's reputation.We must find out which name is more popular on the market,and,whether such a name is considered adequate to cover all the GI products concerned.We have discussed possible inconsistent references for some GI names in previous paragraphs,which serves as a reminder for the needs not to violate market rules by making up a name at ones' own preference.The cases of Shaanxi Apple and Ningxia Wolfberry,however,are somewhat different.Both names are already well-known in domestic market.Luochuan Apple and Zhongning Wolfberry stand for the core producing areas of Shaanxi Apple and Ningxia Wolfberry,respectively,with the best quality of its kind.Any policy change is subject to the consent of GI producers as well as regional branding strategy.Consequently,it is

---

[1] See: Announcement No. 54 of 2004 on the GI protection of Ningxia Gouqi (Chinese Wolfberry), AQSIQ.

important to coordinate their views before any action is taken to achieve mutual progress while safeguarding GIs' reputation. It is advised to formulate operational measures and overall planning that cover both the whole producing areas and the core areas. Moreover, producers from the coreareas should follow higher product standards to present superior qualities. Lastly, a coordinated marketing strategy that targets niche market must be in place.

4. GI product with more than one name

As has been discussed, it is essential to show respect for fact and history, including the respect for any aged use of GI name(s). Some GI products have adopted more than one name. Examples of such GIs include but not limited to, Moutai Chiew (茅台酒) (Kweichow Moutai Chiew) (贵州茅台酒), Dafang Dried Tofu (大方豆干) (Dafang Shredded Tofu) (大方手撕豆腐), Jiali Yak (嘉藜牦牛) (Nyangya Yak) (娘亚牦牛), Baoying Lotus Root (宝应荷藕) (Baoying Lian Ou) (宝应莲藕), Huangshan Dried Chrysanthemum (黄山贡菊) (Huizhou Dried Chrysanthemum) (徽州贡菊), Fengxian Dahongpao Prickly Ash (凤县大红袍花椒) (Feng Prickly Ash) (凤椒), to name only a few. What interprets this phenomenon is the customary naming of a renowned product among traders and producers. It may also be in relation to ethnic languages or local dialects. For instance, Jiali Yak, a PGI, also named as Nyangya Yak, is a local yak breed of Tibet Autonomous Region. 'Nyangya' is merely the transliteration of the Tibetan dialect. Both names are protected as GIs, for both have certain market influences.

5. GI names containing informal words or traditional expressions

Some products have adopted their names in informal words, regional dialects or colloquial expressions. To respect the history of a GI and its market reputation,it is generally acceptable to name a GI with such words or expressions.Yet there is no definite provision in current Chinese GI regulations.INAO of France,in Guide du Demandeur,states that regional language can be adopted as a GI name if it has been used in history.In addition,formal translation in French must accompany the dialectical expressions.❶

Some Chinese products,due to their long history and early exploration of overseas market,have adopted original translations of the era or transliterations based on local accent of the producing areas.Kweichow Moutai Chiew (Moutai Chiew) and Lapsang Souchong (正山小种) are typical examples that have withstood times in overseas market. Therefore,the translations will remain as they are to avoid misunderstanding among consumers,and to reduce operational cost of the stakeholders.

6. Generic name

Discussions about GI will not be complete without mentioning the relations between GI and generic name,for both are product names - including plant variety and animal breed - containing toponym or simply named after a place.The distinction is that the place names in generic names have lost their original function of geographical references.Instead, they have been reduced to proper nouns referring to plant varieties, animal breeds or specific techniques. The names have lost their original meanings either because they have been listed in the national directory of plant variety and animal breed,pharmacopoeia,or

---

❶ https://www. inao. gouv. fr/, Guide du demandeur d'une appellation d'origine protégée (AOP) ou d'une indication géographique protégée (IGP), Institut National de L'origine et de la Qualite(INAO, November 2017).

are widely accepted as specific techniques that have been relocated from their geographical origins,resulting in the gradual loss of any geographical meanings.Zang Hong Hua,or Tibetan saffron❶,for example, originated in West Asia.It was introduced to the interior regions of China via Qinghai-Tibet Plateau in ancient times.Although the name itself directly refers to Tibet,Zang Hong Hua has been listed in the *Pharmacopoeia* and China Approved Drug Names,CADN.Moreover,its plantation has been extended to Shanghai and Zhejiang Province, where it is also named as Zang Hong Hua,or Tibetan saffron.Unfortunately,Tibetan saffron has lost much of its function of geographical reference.Therefore,when saffron producers in Tibet filed the application for GI protection,they had to turn to 'Tibet Tibetan Saffron' to differentiate itself from Tibetan saffron,a generic name.

The debate over GIs and generic names is age-old,which is also one of the major controversies of WTO/TRIPS Council drawing global concerns.Now that it is barely relevant to the theme of this book,it will not be discussed in detail.In short,as far as GI protection is concerned,generic names cannot be protected as GIs.

7. Problems around the use of GI name

Given the good reputation of GI products,it is presumed that GI producers will voluntarily use the GI names for their products.Yet oddly enough,when you enter a supermarket in China to look for GI products,it is often embarrassing to see that the most eye-catching symbol or Chinese characters printed on the packages of some PGI's are not GI names but generic terms like 'mushroom' or 'black fungus'

---

❶ Saffron is almost always called Tibetan Saffron,or Zang Hong Hua,in China.

instead. Words containing geographic references are deliberately dismissed. As a consequence, consumers only get vague messages that do not point to any geographical location. They could hardly associate the quality with any producing area by only 'looking at' the packages, which may well affect their choice and willingness to buy. The phenomenon can be interpreted as: firstly, in the case of a less famous GI brand, the stakeholders have little knowledge about GI and do not have the conscience to use the GI name; secondly, proper management is not in place. Producers and operators have not followed instructions on the use of GI names; thirdly, they are unaware of the roles of the GI names; fourthly, production and marketing are disconnected, with the latter having no idea about the GI system and the role of GI names. All the defects could be attributed to management problems, or flaws of the GI practices, implying a denial of the registered GI that lacks popularity. GI stakeholders have much to do before they could find potential market for the product. Moreover, it raises alarm over the nominal existence of a GI that it is too weak to support the running of the GI system. It is a reminder for GI regulators to modify relevant criteria and introduce a cancellation mechanism for registered GIs.

Section 3　The specification

Products with territorial characteristics are gifts of nature. Local producers usually own some 'know-how' that stems from prolonged working experience under local conditions. Such 'know-how' based on experiences is, however, mostly individual practice lacking systematic review and generalization. People within the same village may have their own 'know-how' without any sharing act. The GI system, in this regard, may help optimize economic yields by making rational use of the natural resources and by enhancing the role of specific skills for the healthy growth of regional characteristic industry.

As discussed in previous paragraphs, the designation of geographical areas and recognition of GI name(s) are integral parts of the so-called specification-the guideline regulating the condition of production.

In China, 'quality and technical requirement' is the term adopted that corresponds to the specification, code of practice (COP) or code of conduct (CoC). Named differently, they all serve as a guideline for GI producers in carrying out production. They are a kind of generalization of specific conditions and techniques to ensure GI's characteristics. Emilie Vandecandelaer et al.(2018) argue that "(T)he specifications represent a crucial tool in ensuring a pay-back effect for farmers and producers by outlining their roles in providing the unique natural and human resources; they thus can bind the GI value chain to primary producers, who therefore have a say in negotiating price and more generally in managing the GI."[1]

Drafting of the specification is a process of observation, analysis, summary and mobilization for implementation. Observation refers to the study of natural circumstances and special skills. By finding out

---

[1] VANDECANDELAERE E, TEYSSIER C, BARJOLLE D, et al. Strengthening sustainable food systems through geographical indications. An analysis of economic impacts [M/OL]. Rome: FAO, 2018[2021-09-08]. https://www.researchgate.net/publication/334191901.

traditional techniques or specific methods, we could sum up the key factors. Analysis refers to the study of GI's characteristics through meticulous observation. It may include study of the causal links especially favorable elements in shaping the characteristics. Summary is, based on the above findings, the generalization of characteristics and traditional knowledge. By fixing the key factors, along with standardized management, the specification is considered a benchmark to be observed by every producer. Meanwhile, mobilization for implementation aims at disseminating the specification to all stakeholders to direct their operations followed by supervisions.

Such a process is typical of GI production. It is worth mentioning that, as a common practice, GI operators would prepare a 'manual' for implementation purposes. The manual, unlike a standard or technical regulation, is a concise guide that integrates the specification with relevant standard or technical requirements. It is more straightforward and is handed out to each producer. The drafting of a specification should be based on sufficient knowledge of the GI as well as the overall natural conditions of the producing area that must be preserved. "An agricultural product or foodstuff bearing such a geographical description should meet certain conditions set out in a specification, such as specific requirements aimed at protecting the natural resources or landscape of the production area or improving the welfare of farm animals."[1]

Therefore, it is somewhat different from laying down a standard or technical requirements. By sufficient knowledge, we refer to the full

---

[1] See: Regulation (EU) No 1151/2012 of the European Parliament and of the Council of 21 November 2012.

range cognition of the GI's characteristics,techniques,history,reputation and consumer feedbacks.The tasked team is supposed to grasp the key factors that determine the characteristics and analyze the essential techniques that influence the formation of characteristics.In addition,they are expected to determine what traditional techniques are to be inherited.Presumably,it is a task demanding both time and energy.

1. How to describe the characteristics of a GI product?

So,what are the characteristics of a GI product? GIs in general are consumer goods that are accessible in daily life.While their characteristics are shown in both the exterior and interior appearance,the most common approach is sensory description,i.e., depicting the GI product by judging from what is tangible-the exterior look,shape,size, color,odor,flavor,taste and texture.Indeed,the characteristic of a GI is also subject to physical and chemical analysis to obtain scientific proof.Nevertheless,GIs' reputation and market performance rely on consumers' recognition by looking at,touching and,for agri-food products,tasting,and by listening to comments from others.They are unlikely to conduct any laboratory analysis before buying anything.Instead, their willingness to pay mainly depends on purchasing experience and sensory recognition.Thus,sensory description is the predominant way in depicting a GI product.To be honest,some of the characteristics cannot be explicitly discerned even by laboratory analysis.

As far as the description of a GI is concerned,a good example is the tea.It is common knowledge that a plenty of tea products can be recognized by its appearance. Take the green tea as an example. Longjing (龙井),Xinyang Maojian (信阳毛尖),Huangshan Maofeng (黄山毛峰),Lu'an Guapian (六安瓜片),Taiping Houkui (太平猴魁),

Duyun Maojian (都匀毛尖) are some of the well-known green teas in China,which,due to their peculiar shapes and colors,can be recognized at first sight by tea lovers.Yet their real tastes and grades can only be tested by sipping and tasting.In this way,Pujiang Queshe (蒲江雀舌), meaning tongue of bird,is depicted as:

>green even tips with flap shape that is like the tongue of a bird;its aroma being fragrant and lofty,the color of tea water being bright green and light yellow,its taste rich and fresh,the tea leaves at the bottom of water are light green and even in size. ❶

Another example is Liupao Tea (六堡茶) which is described as:

>the tea leaves being tightly bounded with shining black and brown color,the tea water being in bright dark red color,its aroma pure and aged,its taste intensely pure,sweet and refreshing coupled with the flavor of betel nut. The bottom water appears reddish brown or dark brown. In general,it has the characteristics of being 'red,thick,pure and aged'. ❷

By summarizing the description of a tea,we may find out that the purchasing act has generated multiple functions of our sensory organs. It could be taken as a typical way in describing a GI product.

2. How to describe specific techniques and formula?

The causal links between a GI product and its production environment are also reflected in the techniques and production formula, which vary from one to another.Primary products have little to do with any formula,whereas the techniques are displayed in sorting seed (or breed) and technical procedures that must be followed.Meanwhile,the

---

❶ See:Announcement No. 119 of 2008 on the GI Protection of Pujiang Queshe,AQSIQ.
❷ See:Announcement No. 33 of 2011 on the GI Protection of Liupao Tea,AQSIQ.

contexts around processed products are more complex, yet the focus is usually on special requirements for ingredients, source of raw materials, types, and other elements differing from similar products. Emilie Vandecandelaer et al (2018) use the word 'defensive' and 'offensive' to divide GIs' techniques into two groups. Group One refers to those that have already acquired considerable reputations. Technique descriptions are supposed to write down precisely current production techniques, emphasizing inheritance and continuity. It aims at preventing counterfeiting and infringement. While Group Two refers to those with low fame or even without any popularity. In this case, the drafting process is regarded as a step to regulate techniques and optimize production to upgrade the quality and management.❶

3. Relations between the specification and a standard

GI protection cannot be fulfilled without specification that lies in the center place of the GI system. Apart from specification, the GI system in China requires an additional standard system to be completed by GI producers to enhance enforcement. *China's Law of Standardization* splits standards into five tiers, namely, national standard, industry standard, regional standard, group standard and corporate standard, among which standards regulating GI products are regional standards that fall within the jurisdiction of provincial administration for standardization. Compared to the GI schemes in other countries or economic communities, the requirement on regional standard is one of the distinguishing features of China's GI system. It aims to strengthen quality controls to

---

❶ VANDECANDELAERE E, TEYSSIER C, BARJOLLE D, et al. Strengthening sustainable food systems through geograhical indications. an analysis of economic impacts [M/OL]. Rome: FAO, 2018[2021-09-08]. https://www.researchgate.net/publication/334191901.

maintain GI's characteristics.Concerning practices in other countries, EU,for instance,publishes the specification of a PGI /PDO in the Official Journal,which acts as legally binding directives.

Section 4 Notable issues

So far,we have discussed issues pertaining to the specification.We will move on to some other issues with respect to GI application.

1. How to understand the history of a product?

First,we must correct a misconception.The history of a GI is not necessarily the history of its production.Instead,it is the existing time duration of a GI name.It appears somewhat confusing when we make distinction between the history of production and history of a GI name.The answer is,given the fact that every product has its producing time and location,there is no inherent connection between something produced in a place and its name.In most cases,producers are more likely to register trademarks to distinguish themselves from others,or,in the case of Agri-product,to be sold without any specific names except generic names.While the use of trademarks is accompanied by generic terms of specific category,like TCL TV,Samsung cellphone,Tsingtao Beer,so on and so forth.Meanwhile,some products with local characteristics may emerge as something distinctive from others and gradually acquire market recognition.It is by this moment that producers and traders incline to adopt the name of a producing area to meet the potential demand of consumers.This is the evolution of a GI name.

Hence, any introduction to the history of a GI product must highlight the origin of the GI name and its development, thereby demonstrating its market reputation and historical origin.

2. How to understand a product's popularity?

The same is true of the popularity of a GI product, which refers to the popularity of its name. One of the major concerns of GI protection is to prevent counterfeit products from infringing the GI names. Consumers are interested in the market performance of a GI and its formed image in their minds. Meanwhile, the popularity of a product denotes the reputation brought about by the GI name. In the case of the so-called 'three precious goods of Hainan' - Wenchang Chicken, Jiaji Duck, and Hele Crab - their popularity in Hainan Province is a commercial phenomenon prevailed over time. The unique characteristics of the three local specialties largely owe to the natural and human factors of the three regions. 'Taiping Houkui' (太平猴魁) in Chinese characters, looks irrelevant to any tea as it does not contain any character referring to a tea. Yet it is a well-known green tea name in China with a long history. It points to Taiping County of Anhui Province and the tea's core producing areas of Houkeng and Hougang as well. What's more, by using the character 'Kui', it signifies that the tea is of top quality of Jiancha (tea shoot), while Kuicheng was the name of its creator. Taiping Houkui was named during the Qing Dynasty and has prevailed to date. The name itself embodies profound traditional culture that has witnessed the tea's ups and downs. That said, when highlighting the role of a product's existing popularity, we should be conscious of the role of GI protection in promoting the popularity of a GI. Some characteristic products, their popularity being low, though, are eligible for GI protection.Emilie Vandecandelaere et al.(2018) argue that,by GI registration,products with low popularity may create it.❶ Of all the successful cases,several China's GI products,their popularity used to be confined to neighboring counties or cities prior to the application for GI protection,have dramatically raised their market popularity and gained economic rewards there afterwards.

3. How to set quality parameters?

Oddly enough,some applicants prefer,either deliberately or by accident,to set quality parameters higher than the original figures or simply adopt the 'best' figures in order to showcase the GI's outstanding quality,ignoring that once the parameters are written down in the specifications,they must be observed without exception.Regulators would monitor the GI according to,among other things,the parameters set out in the specifications.Thus,applicants are reminded not to pursue any parameter beyond their capacities.Instead,only the real characteristics are to be identified even if the figures are not perfect or the best of all. Any conduct to exaggerate the fact will undermine GI's reputation and damage consumer rights.Moreover,the applicant involved will have to file formal request to make amendment to the specification before any meaningful protection could be carried out.

The causes behind this problem are,in terms of local experts,either misapprehension of the GI system or poor knowledge of the GI product,or simply out of a confusion with any award event which al-

---

❶ VANDECANDELAERE E,TEYSSIER C,BARJOLLE D,et al. Strengthening sustainable food systems through geographical indications. An analysis of economic impacts [EB/ OL]. (2018-02-28) [2021-05-10]. https://www.researchgate.net/publication/ 334191901.

ways prefers superb parameters. Consequently, most yields of the GI product cannot satisfy the specification, making them virtually nonconforming products. It damages the GI's reputation, violating consumer rights and creating obstacles for monitoring activities.

A tough task as it is, setting the parameters requires in - depth knowledge of the characteristics. The technical staff is expected to represent the general interests of the GI producers rather than spokesman for any specific groups, for GI producing areas often involve more than one administrative division. It leaves no room for any hasty generalization of the characteristics and quality parameters, indicating that the task cannot be accomplished overnight. Instead, it is a time - consuming activity requiring thorough discussions over the testing results of the yields of the designated areas. Only those parameters that are representative and inclusive of the entire yields of the GI product are to be written in the specifications.

4. Products that are unfit to apply for GI protection

It is about the applicability of the GI system. This book so far has analyzed the popularity of a GI product with a view to emphasizing the significance of reputation. Those that are only known within a town or nearby villages are generally not advised to apply for GI protection, for the cost of promotion and overall investment that follows GI registration could be too much for the applicant even if the technical requirements are satisfied. Its popularity and market share could hardly be raised only through GI registration, nor can it attain the potential profit thereby. In addition, scale matters, too. Products confined to local households or workshops are not encouraged to apply for GI protection. It is true that the GI system may help improve quality and reputation.Nevertheless,it is a prerequisite to be equipped with some basis, such as a moderate scale and marketing strategy as well as follow-up controls.Although products lacking popularity may improve it by GI registration,as remarked by Emilie Vandecandelaer et al, "investment and financial ability is key to GI's economic development as well".[1] Small-scale products are immature,for they lack the backing of policy and finance.As a compensation,these products may be grouped as the 'potential candidates' that may apply for GI protection later.

5. The relations between geographical indication and intangible cultural heritage (ICH)

The Convention for the Safeguarding of the Intangible Cultural Heritage was adopted by the United Nations Educational,Scientific and Cultural Organization (UNESCO) in October 2003.Clause One of Article 2 provides that,

1. the 'intangible cultural heritage' means the practices, representations, expressions,knowledge,skills-as well as the instruments,objects,artefacts and cultural spaces associated therewith-that communities,groups and,in some cases,individuals recognize as part of their cultural heritage. This intangible cultural heritage, transmitted from generation to generation,is constantly recreated by communities and groups in response to their environment, their interaction with nature and their history, and provides them with a sense of identity and continuity, thus promoting respect for cultural diversity and human creativity. For the purposes of this Convention, consideration will be given solely to such intangible cultural heritage as is compatible with existing international human rights instruments, as well as with the requirements of

---

[1] VANDECANDELAERE E, TEYSSIER C, BARJOLLE D, et al. Strengthening sustainable food systems through geographical indications:an analysis of economic impacts [M/OL]. Rome:FAO,2018[2021-05-10]. https://www.researchgate.net/publication/334191901.

mutual respect among communities, groups and individuals, and of sustainable development.

2. The 'intangible cultural heritage', as defined in paragraph 1 above, is manifested inter alia in the following domains:

(a) oral traditions and expressions, including language as a vehicle of the intangible cultural heritage;

(b) performing arts;

(c) social practices, rituals and festive events;

(d) knowledge and practices concerning nature and the universe;

(e) traditional craftsmanship. ❶

The above definition does refer to instruments, objects and art facts. However, it emphasizes the association with skills. And Clause Two of Article 2 further clarifies the scope of protection that is unrelated to any concrete object. It seems that intangible cultural heritage (hereafter 'ICH') emphasizes the protection of intangible assets of traditional techniques and cultural activities which, though relevant to GI protection, differs from each other. The traditional techniques and cultural content embodied by ICH are crucial human factors for GI products that might be considered as the materialized results of ICH. The GI system targets a product, i.e., a commodity stemming from the interaction of geographical conditions, techniques, history and culture. Meanwhile, the protection of ICH focuses on the inheritance and development of traditional techniques and human activities. Presumably, ICH covers a wider scope, as traditional techniques highlighted by GI pro-

---

❶ Convention for the Safeguarding of the Intangible Cultural Heritage 2003[EB/OL]. [2021-05-10]. http://portal. unesco. org/en/ev. php - URL _ ID = 17716&URL _ DO = DO _ TOPIC&URL_SECTION=201. html.

tection are merely one of the concerns of ICH.Others include languages of ethnic groups,religions,artistic forms,to name only a few.It is therefore safe to say that GI protection and the protection of ICH are interrelated yet different from each other.Both make contributions to the inheritance and healthy development of human civilization.

As of Dec.31,2019,there are 40 Chinese elements inscribed on UNESCO's Representative List of the Intangible Cultural Heritage of Hunanity.A total of 1372 items were registered as representative elements of the National ICH List,which contain 3145 sub-items concerning 10 categories,i.e.folk literature(230),traditional music(401),traditional dance(324),traditional Chinese opera(445),Quyi(193),traditional sports,games and acrobatics(124),traditional fine arts(359),traditional medicine(137),traditional techniques(506),and folk customs(426).❶ Of all the above 10 categories,traditional techniques,traditional fine arts and traditional medicine are the only areas that are associated with GIs.In addition to traditional techniques that have been discussed about in previous paragraphs,GIs in relation with traditional fine arts are traditional handicrafts,such as paper-cut,embroidery,stone carving, wood carving, clay sculpture, bamboo weaving, Xiang Bao (incense bag),etc.While the GI-related traditional medicines mainly refer to the herbal medicinal materials.

6. Relations between GIs and local snacks or business brands containing place names

Local snacks or business brands containing place names are com-

---

❶ Intangible Heritage of China[EB/OL]. [2021-05-01] http://www.ihchina.cn,2020. 7.22.

monplace in China. The name itself normally refers to the merchants engaged in making the food from the place where it is originated. Although the food itself clearly points to a geographical location, it is a local specialty that, due to its reputation, is often made beyond its origin. Then is it eligible to be protected as a GI? The answer is negative. Despite its local characteristics and connection with a particular place, plus traditional skills passed down from masters, the food is merely an imitation of relevant skills, its characteristics being discrepant even for the same brand. On one hand it is almost impossible to replicate the original foodstuff barring the original materials, water and climate that have impacts on the characteristics. It is essentially an intangible heritage, or inheritance of techniques. On the other hand, there is hardly a consistent standard to follow even within the same industry at its origin. Or it is precisely because of the inconsistent characteristics that have created the segment market for diverse consumption demands.

Again, despite their geographical references, these products are traditional local specialties that are, as practiced in the EU for instance, regulated by Traditional Specialty Guaranteed (TSG) - a separate scheme parallel to the GI system protecting traditional techniques and ingredients without restriction on geographical areas.[1] Whereas in China, it is not regulated in the GI system. Article 3 of the *Trademark Law* defines collective trademark and certification trademark. Article 10 permits collective/certification trademark containing geographical name. While Article 4 of the *Regulation on the Implementation of the*

---

[1] See: https://ec. europa. eu/info/food-farming-fisheries/food-safety-and-quality/certification/quality-labels/quality-schemes-explained_en.

Trademark Law provides for the registration of geographical indication as collective/certification trademark, i.e.,

> Article 4 The geographic indications as mentioned in Article 16 of the Trademark Law may be registered upon application as certification marks or collective marks in accordance with the Trademark Law and this Regulation.
>
> Where a geographic indication is registered as a certification mark, any natural person, legal person or other organization whose goods satisfy the conditions for using the geographic indication may request the use of the certification mark, and the organization which controls the certification mark shall permit the use. Where a geographic indication is registered as a collective mark, any natural person, legal person or other organization whose goods satisfy the conditions for using the geographic indication may file a request for joining the group, association or other organization which has registered the geographic indication as a collective mark, and the group, association or other organization shall accept the natural person, legal person or other organization as a member according to its bylaws; or if the natural person, legal person or other organization chooses not to file a request for joining the group, association or other organization which has registered the geographic indication as a collective mark, the natural person, legal person or other organization is entitled to legitimately use the geographic indication, and the group, association or other organization has no right to prohibit the use. ❶

Coupled with the rising awareness of intellectual property rights, some inter-professional organizations filed applications for the registration of local snacks and business brands either as trademarks or collective trademarks. But if we check with the above regulation, trademark holders cannot prohibit the use of registered brand containing

---

❶ Regulation on the Implementation of the Trademark Law of the People's Republic of China (2014 Revision) [EB/OL]. [2021-05-01]. http://www.lawinfochina.com/display.aspx? SearchCKeyword=%C9%CC%B1%EA%B7%A8&id=17968&lib=law.

place names.In his remarks on the judicial protection of geographical indications in December 2021,the person in charge of Tribunal 3 for Civil Lawsuit of the Supreme Court stated that,in such cases when the rightsholder took any legal action,the Supreme Court shall reject it.❶

It bears some resemblance with the case of generic name,being different in nature,though.For these local snacks,business brands or local cuisine that make their presence across the country,the names have become generic,making them a byword for specific food.Therefore,if such a registered brand with graphs or symbols is not copied and infringed upon by other vendors,adopting the place name with the food itself shall not be deemed a violation of trademark right.

Section 5　Flaws of the GI system

Global practices show that the GI system does contribute to the sustainable development of agriculture and characteristic sectors. It plays a significant role in safeguarding and upgrading quality,in inheriting historical and cultural traditions, and in protecting intellectual property rights.Having said that,it is necessary to analyze some of the defects of the GI system with a view to consolidating its advantages. This book has summed up the following defects concerning the GI system practiced in China.

---

❶ 最高法回应"潼关肉夹馍"事件:严厉惩治恶意诉讼[EB/OL].(2021-12-12)[2021-12-12]. https://news.china.com/social/1007/20211212/40499519.html.

1. Complex application procedures and high cost

To start with, a universally adopted GI system is not in place. Keeping this mind, this book focuses on the *sui generis* GI system, namely,law and regulation exclusively designed for geographical indication,and its application procedures for GI protection.In countries and economic communities like the EU,India,Japan,for instance,GI is regulated by the *sui generis* laws and regulations.In China,there is no GI law at the national level.The *Regulation on the Product of Designated Origin* issued by the former State Bureau of Quality and Technical Supervision,and the *Regulation on the Protection of Geographical Indication Product* issued by the former General Administration of Quality Supervision,Inspection and Quarantine (AQSIQ) are both ministerial level regulations that have followed the principles of the *sui generis* approach.Irrespective of the level of laws and regulations,it appears that the *sui generis* approach usually implies complex application procedures.In China,Article 9 of the *Working Procedures for the Protection of GI Products* stipulates that,the applicant must be an agency,association or manufacturer designated by the local government or regional government.Article 10 states that the applicant should file the Application Form together with the following documents:

(1) document issued by the county-level or higher-level government on the setting up of an application agency or on the designation of association or manufacturer as the applicant.

(2) official letter issued by the county-level or higher-level government on the delineation of protected geographical areas of the applied product, the protected areas being generally to the town level. For farmed aquatic product, the geographical areas refer to the areas of natural waters.

(3) currently valid standard or regulations exclusively for the applied product.

(4) proof documents including:

a. introduction to the product's name, producing areas and geographical features.

b. introduction to the historical origin, production, popularity and market shares.

c. introduction to the quality characteristics such as the physical, chemical, sensory indicators and their links with the natural and human factors of the producing areas.

d. production techniques, including, raw materials, special techniques, process, safety and sanitary requirements, essential quality features, equipment and technical requirements.

e. other proof documents, like the local chronicles, awards, reports of inspection, etc.

All the documents are subject to preliminary examination by the provincial quality supervision agency before being submitted to AQSIQ, which, upon completion of a formality examination, publishes the Notice of Acceptance for a two-month objection period. Only those without objection or having been resolved can proceed to the expert review meeting convened by AQSIQ. Next, the applicant must prepare documents for the meeting-a presentation report and the specification. Even those that have passed the expert review are required to make amendments to the documents in line with experts' remarks. AQSIQ will check the documents before it publishes the Announcement of Approval for GI protection. And it by no means marks the completion of application until the applicant accomplishes the regional standard and testing systems. Only by doing so is the applicant qualified to apply for the use of the GI logo.

Obviously,it is a complex process that is generalized into the following flow chart:

designating applicant→delineating geographical areas→official letter→drafting specifications→application→proof documents→preliminary examination by provincial authority→formality examination by AQSIQ→Acceptance Notice→two-month objection period→preparation of documents for expert review→expert review→amendments to documents→submission to AQSIQ→Announcement of Approval→completion of standard and laboratory examination system→application for GI logo→AQSIQ's approval→Announcement of Approval for the use of GI logo

Each step requires considerable inputs.Some of the steps,such as the documentation and drafting of standard, may lay bare capacity problems of local producers,let alone for those from remote regions. Problems in education and knowledge of the GI system all make it hard for them to fulfil.In such cases,applicants tend to consign the task to a service agency,thereby further raising the cost of application.Moreover,the service agency hardly knows everything about the GI product thus fails to meet the requirements as well.Consequently,it affects applicant's willingness to apply and has negative impacts on the overall reputation of the GI system.

A public consultation on whether to extend GI protection to non-agricultural products carried out by the EU in 2014 shows that 80% of SMEs deem it necessary to increase investment for GI protection, 20% of producers hold that application for GI registration increases costs.Some consumers believe that extra regulation and logo requirement will cause confusion among consumers and build up commodity prices.Polarized view complains that GI protection is a form of trade protectionism that hinders free market competitions.❶

2. Time-consuming formalities

This pertains to the above problems as well.The average duration of GI registration is more than one year,i.e.,from the submission of application to the publication of the Announcement of Approval of GI protection.In exceptional case,when everything goes smoothly and is free of any objection,it might be faster,which has not considered the application for the use of the GI logo that is required of all the approved GI products. Some GI products, due to applicants' capacity problems,fail to meet the requirement on the use of GI logo,and thus are not able to use it,making the application virtually uncompleted. Time-consuming application and complex formalities directly weaken applicants' interest that are harmful to the GI system.

3. High operational cost and management problems

The GI system is a comprehensive project covering wide ranges and demanding qualified management.It is challenging for many GI producers that are required to,after the registration,furnish the quality assurance system, standard system as well as the testing system. For management purposes,it is advised to set up cooperatives and associations to enforce the specification,to oversee the use of GI logo,to carry out commercialization, and to coordinate bargaining, storage, logistics and marketing.Agri-food products and handicrafts are often based far from metropolis and suffer from talent shortages.In China,local government usually plays the leading role in applying for GI protection,

---

❶ Study on geographical indications protection for non-agricultural products in the internal market[EB/OL]. (2013-02-18)[2020-04-30]. https://ec. europa. eu/docsroom/documents/14897.

yet they often fail to provide sustained support for its management and brand building,resulting in management failures and subsequent problems.The GI system requires collaborations of all stakeholders that are expected to take part in the whole process.Equally importantly,relevant parties are encouraged to invest continuously in management and commercialization.It is probably the only way to maintain positive succession of GIs' value chain and to safeguard the brand value of GI products.

In addition to the mobilization of GI producers and sector management,quality control is of particular importance demanding adequate human resources and funding capacity.Again,it adds to the costs of the GI system.People in some EU member states even argue that the cost increase caused by GI protection outnumbers its profits.[1]

4. Degeneration of plant varieties

Primary agri-food GIs account for a large proportion in China, partly because,among others,their intrinsic quality links with the producing areas are more explicitly presented.Nevertheless,we must acknowledge that primary products like fruits and vegetables may suffer from the degeneration of plant varieties.It demands consistent modification and improvement which,to some extent,causes the somewhat instability of characteristics,and therefore has implications on consumer confidence and GIs' reputations.

5. Low added value for primary product

Primary products not only face the degeneration of plant varie-

---

[1] Study on geographical indications protection for non-agricultural products in the internal market[EB/OL].(2013-02-18)[2020-04-30]. https://ec.europa.eu/docsroom/documents/14897.

ties,the volatile market and low added value plus insufficient protection of producers' rights all give rise to problems deserving efforts to deal with.Price fluctuation is commonplace for primary products,their market performance being a function of climate,timing and yields.And even at times when the production and marketing both thrive,farmers' earning is relatively low compared to that of the downstream of the supply chain.We must keep in mind that one of the aims of GI protection is to increase the added value.Despite that a primary GI could be sold at prices higher than product alike,its premium capacity is largely influenced by the latter,its added value being unstable at all.Therefore, one of the solutions is to shift GI's focus on primary products. By checking with EU's GI list,we may soon find out that primary products account for a relatively small proportion, while most GIs, like wines and spirits, cheese, olive oil, ham, are processed foodstuffs with primary products merely as raw materials. On the contrary, countries like Japan,Korea and some Southeast Asian countries all have a long list of primary GIs that resemble the situation in China.It shows that EU member states,where the GI system was developed the earliest, have already turned their attention to the high value ones,while countries at the initial stage of GI protection tend to start with the primary products,as they usually present direct links with the natural environment,which facilitates quick findings of products with geographical characteristics.Coping with the progress,these countries may draw on the EU's experiences and,by finding out processed products with geographical ties,shift their focus accordingly.Value increase for primary GIs at wide margin could only be realized through processing.It is favorable to tackle market volatility and farmers' unstable earnings as well.Moreover,it is a demand of regional economic transformation.It helps to extend GIs' value chain and boost growth of both the upstream and downstream players of the GI sector.

Some critics argue that once deeply processed,e.g.,grinding coffee beans or juicing oranges,primary products would encounter difficulty in tracing their original status,making it impossible to fulfil any GI protection.It underscores the fact that most of the protected agricultural GIs in China are fruits in their original status or fruits undergone minor processing,e.g.,peeling,slicing,etc.Whereas in fact,the key lies with management and the credit system.This book argues that processed agri-food products are eligible to be protected as GIs to generate more returns provided their producers are honest and law-abiding,and with proper internal management as well as external supervision being put in place.

Now let us move on to the intrinsic links between processed foodstuffs and natural and human characteristics.Again,it is notable that EU's foodstuff GIs primarily consist of wines and spirits,olive oil, cheese and ham,etc.,whereas primary products only account for approximate 20% of the total number.❶What underlines this phenomenon is: first,both the raw materials and processing techniques present characteristics of the geographical origin;second,all the products are closely associated with the dietary habit of European countries.They are people's daily essentials with huge market demand.But if we turn to the Asian markets,the above GIs may not be as popular as in Europe.

---

❶   EU statistics,Quality products registers,as of 21 Dec. 2019,https://ec. europa. eu/info/food-farming-fisheries/food-safety-and-quality/certification/quality-labels/quality-products-registers_en.

It then signifies distinct approaches for other countries, blending GI policies with their own culinary culture in protecting the potential GI foodstuffs. An interesting case is the bean product - an important Chinese food having global appeals - which, being varied in forms and shapes with soybean as raw material, is one of the most popular foods in China. Bean curd(tofu), dried bean curd, jellied bean curd, thin sheet of bean curd, fermented bean curd, soya - bean milk, Yuba (dried bean milk cream in tight rolls), thick broad bean sauce, and fermented soya beans are all food options of Chinese cuisine. Meanwhile, tofu itself can be divided into the northern tofu (less soft) and southern tofu (softer). Unlike tofu, the fermented bean curd, fermented soya beans, thick broad bean sauce as well as soya sauce are produced by fermentation techniques like that of cheese in Western countries, with discrete approaches, though. Their characteristics have close ties with local natural factors such as water, temperature and humidity, along with human factors passing down from generations. With stable market shares in China, bean product can be taken as an important GI category deserving additional care. Furthermore, the following oriental fermented foods are also potential candidates for GI protection - yellow rice wine, fermented glutinous rice wine, pickled vegetables, soya sauce, vinegar - to name only a few. Meanwhile, it is noteworthy that some bean products are deemed high in sodium content that calls for further study and improvement.

So far, we have probed into the connotations of GI that are considered as relevant to the sustainable development. Next, we will analyze the inherent ties and promotional effects between GI protection and achieving the Sustainable Development Goals.

Chapter 2》
The GI system helps to achieve the SDGs

Protecting environment and making rational use of natural resources are means and ends of the GI system. Excessive exploitation of natural resources directly affects GIs' characteristics and threatens their survival. Agricultural products, for instance, are subject to density and breeding. Excessive density would result in unbalanced distribution of nutrition and quality degradation. Hence, it is one of the most important principles to regulate the density of plantation and breeding in the specification that must be observed accordingly.

To be honest, GIs' roles in rational utilization of natural resources and promotion of sustainable development are not confined to the rational use of resources. Upon detailed review of the United Nations Sustainable Development Goals (SDGs), we are convinced that GI protection is in close relation to the achievement of SDGs.

Section 1 The Sustainable Development Goals (SDGs)

The notion of sustainable development first appears in the report of *World Conservation Strategy in* 1980. In 1987 Report of the World Commission on Environment and Development (WCED):*Our Common Future* by Gro Harlem Brundtland, expert of sustainable development and public health for the United Nation (UN) General Assembly, defined sustainable development as "that satisfies our current needs without sacrificing the needs of future generations". The 2030 Agenda for Sustainable Development, adopted by all United Nations Member States in 2015, provides a shared blueprint for peace and prosperity for people and the planet, now and into the future. At its heart are the 17 Sustainable Development Goals (SDGs), which are an urgent call for action by all countries - developed and developing as well as least developed - in a global partnership. They recognize that ending poverty and other deprivations must go hand - in - hand with strategies that improve health and education, reduce inequality, and spur economic growth - all while tackling climate change and working to preserve our oceans and forests.[1] The 17 Goals of the SDGs are, respectively,

Goal 1:No Poverty. End poverty in all its forms everywhere.

Goal 2: Zero hunger. End hunger, achieve food security and im-

---

[1] Knowledge Platform[EB/OL]. [2020-07-24]. https://sustainabledevelopment.un.org.

proved nutrition and promote sustainable agriculture.

Goal 3:Good health and well-being.Ensure healthy lives and promote well-being for all at all ages.

Goal 4:Quality Education.Ensure inclusive and equitable quality education and promote lifelong learning opportunities for all.

Goal 5:Gender Equality.Achieve gender equality and empower all women and girls.

Goal 6:Clean water and sanitation.Ensure availability and sustainable management of water and sanitation for all.

Goal 7.Affordable and clean energy.Ensure access to affordable, reliable,sustainable and modern energy for all.

Goal 8.Decent work and economic growth.Promote sustained,inclusive and sustainable economic growth,full and productive employment and decent work for all.

Goal 9.Industry,innovation and infrastructure.Build resilient infrastructure,promote inclusive and sustainable industrialization and foster innovation.

Goal 10.Reduced inequality.Reduce inequality within and among countries.

Goal 11.Sustainable cities and communities.Make cities and human settlements inclusive,safe,resilient and sustainable.

Goal 12.Responsible consumption and production.Ensure sustainable consumption and production patterns.

Goal 13. Climate action. Take urgent action to combat climate change and its impacts.

Goal 14. Life below water. Conserve and sustainably use the oceans,seas and marine resources for sustainable development.

Goal 15.Life on land.Protect,restore and promote sustainable use of terrestrial ecosystems,sustainably manage forests,combat desertification, and halt and reverse degradation and halt biodiversity loss.

Goal 16. Peace,justice and strong institutions. Promote peaceful and inclusive societies for sustainable development,provide access to justice for all and build effective,accountable and inclusive institutions at all levels.

Goal 17.Partnerships for the goals.Strengthen the means of implementation and revitalize the global partnership for sustainable development.

The above seventeen goals cover almost all spectrums of human society,from poverty alleviation and eradication to education of the whole people;from health care to gender equality;from job creation to economic growth;from climate action and adoption of clean energy for the ecosystem to improving infrastructure and sustainable industrialization;from responsible production and consumption to building an inclusive society with fair justice, among others. The seventeen goals chart the course for future development of the human society.At the same time,they pose challenges to the governance capacity of every country.Solidarity and concerted efforts are required of all countries to achieve the above development goals.Inaction from any party will put the healthy development of human society and the ecosystem of our planet at risk.

The seventeen goals are in connection with both the human society and natural ecological system,with human beings as the root determing the fate of sustainable development.It calls for general consensus in realizing the grave situations and urgency to enforce the ideas of sustainable development before taking actions to achieve the goals. Given the unbalanced development levels of developing countries and developed countries,it is not groundless that a common but differentiated policy is needed that,while ensuring the right to develop for all countries,minimizes consumption of resources and negative impacts on the ecosystem of the earth.

Regarding a shared view on the course towards the SDGs,there are divergent opinions about the implementation of some of the goals, reflecting mainly on the debate between the developing countries and developed countries over the reduction of greenhouse gas emissions. The developed side holds that major developing countries such as China and India,with their emission amount ranking high on the table, should shoulder the same responsibilities on emission reduction as the key developed countries.Whilst major developing countries argue that such a demand is beyond their reach,claiming that it is both unreasonable and unrealistic,and that their practical needs must be taken into account.This argument is justified by the fact that developed countries have already passed the initial stage of industrialization when pollution used to be rampant.It was not until the late 20th Century that many developing countries started their industrialization, by now at a rising stage.

The debate over the rights and obligations for the SDGs is going on.The good news is that consensus is reached on some key areas where major developing countries including China offered the medium and long‐term objectives in reducing greenhouse gas emissions. In September 2020,President Xi Jinping made a solemn promise at the general debate of the 75th session of the United Nations General Assembly that China aims to see its carbon dioxide emissions peak before 2030 and achieve carbon neutrality before 2060.❶

Section 2　Links between the GI System and the SDGs

Now that the SDGs encompass almost all spectrums of human society,discussions about the relationship between the GI system and SDGs must incorporate GI's own characteristics and applicable scope. By analyzing the 17 Goals we may find out that some of the Goals - Goal 4 on education,Goal 6 on water sanitation,Goal 7 on clean energy,Goal 9 on industry and infrastructure,Goal 11 on city and human habitats and Goal 16 on fair justice - bear loose connections with the GI system that may hardly find its roles in achieving the goals.While for the other eleven goals, ranging from the goal for poverty eradication to those for climate action,economic growth and environmental protection,the GI system could be a dynamic force in support of the goals.Thus,this book is of the view that GI protection may contribute to the achievement of the following eleven goals,namely,

Goal 1:No Poverty.

Goal 2:Zero hunger.

Goal 3:Good health and well-being.

Goal 4:Gender Equality.

---

❶ HAN B Y. Experts hail president's speech at general debate[EB/OL]. (2020-09-24) [2022-03-21]. https://www. chinadaily. com. cn/a/202009/24/WS5f6bd5f3a31024ad0ba7b5b4. html.

Goal 8.Decent work and economic growth.
Goal 10.Reduced inequality.
Goal 12.Responsible consumption and production.
Goal 13.Climate action.
Goal 14.Life below water.
Goal 15.Life on land.
Goal 16.Partnerships for the goals.

The above eleven goals are roughly grouped into four parts:

1.Alleviating poverty and ensuring food safety (Goals 1-3);

2.Attaining economic growth and social equality (Goals 5,8,10, 12);

3. Conserving biological environment and combating climate change (Goals 13-15);

4.Enhancing international cooperation (Goal 17).

It must be clarified that such a grouping is only for analysis purpose.There are connections between each goal within the same group,to some extent intercausal.According to the official interpretation of the United Nations,poverty eradication,inequality reduction and environmental protection are at the heart of the seventeen goals.Goal 1,Goal 2 and Goal 3 aim to tackle the problem of human survival,or assurance of basic human rights.Goal 5,Goal 8,Goal 10 and Goal 12 aim,on the above basis,to render equal rights for people's development and opportunities for balanced domestic social and economic development and between countries.While Goal 13,Goal 14 and Goal 15 emphasize that the development of human society cannot be at the cost of the earth's ecosystem,and that world leaders must take actions to protect environment and save our common homeland.Finally,Goal 17 calls on global cooperation in addressing the emerging problems, resolving differences and closing the gap.

As previously discussed,geographical indications are normally in connection with agri - food products and handicrafts, having positive correlation with agriculture and food industry as well as the cultural sector.What is proposed by the GI system - inheritance,controlled exploration and in situ conservation - is highly in consistent with the idea of sustainable development and the above eleven sustainable development goals.Boosting the GI sector and following the production pattern required by the GI system will maximally protect resource endowments,inherit and develop regional characteristic industries in addition to alleviating poverty,balancing development and protecting environment - the key areas of the SDGs.The discussion will be unfolded accordingly.

Chapter 3≫
The roles of the GI system in support of poverty eradication and wellbeing of mankind

Section 1 The GI system helps to eradicate poverty

Goal 1. No poverty

Eradicating poverty is the common pursuit of all countries.The latest report of the World Bank shows that,counted by USD1.9 $ per day per person - the extreme poverty line - 734 million people live below the line that account for about 10% of the global population. "Global extreme poverty rate is expected to rise in 2020 for the first time in over 20 years as the disruption of the COVID-19 pandemic compounds the forces of conflict and climate change,which were already slowing poverty reduction progress." It is estimated that the extreme poverty population will increase by 40 million to 60 million in 2020,with the extreme poverty rate rising by 0.3 to 0. 7 percent.The World Bank further reveals that the poverty population in Asia and Pacific,South Asia and Sub-Sahara regions accounts for 95% of the global poverty population.Most of the poor people live in rural areas.They are undereducated and below 18 years old.[1]

A report by the Food and Agriculture Organization of the United Nations (FAO) released in September 2021 has painted a bleak picture on the impacts with findings as follows:

(1) The COVID-19 pandemic might have pushed an additional 83-132 million into chronic hunger in 2020, making the target of ending hunger even more distant.

(2) An unacceptably high proportion of food (14 percent) is lost along the supply chain before it even reaches the consumer.

(3) Agricultural systems bear the brunt of economic losses due to disasters.

(4) Small-scale food producers remain disadvantaged, with women producers in developing countries earning less than men even when more productive.

(5) Food price volatility has increased, due to the constraints placed by the COVID-19 pandemic and associated lockdowns.

(6) Progress remains weak in maintaining plant and animal genetic diversity for food and agriculture.

(7) Gender inequalities in land rights are pervasive.

(8) Discriminatory laws and customs remain obstacles to women's tenure

---

[1] Poverty [EB/OL]. (2020-04-16) [2020-04-20]. http://www.worldbank.org/en/topic/poverty/overview.

rights.

(9) Water stress remains alarmingly high in many regions, threatening progress towards sustainable development.

It's an alarming picture, in which progress on many SDG targets has been reversed, with a significant impact on all aspects of sustainable development and making the achievement of the 2030 Agenda even more challenging, said FAO Chief Statistician, Pietro Gennari. ❶

Causes of poverty vary from over-population to social crisis resulted from warfare or natural disasters to the extreme poverty due to harsh living conditions and remote locations, such as the so-called 'Three Regions and Three Autonomous Prefectures' in China❷. In addition, poverty caused by illness, physical disability or returning to poverty due to illness is another notable phenomenon. In his address published in June 2020 on Qiushi, President Xi Jinping pointed out that, of all the poverty population in China's rural areas, poverty caused by illness and physical disability accounts for 40.7% and 20.2% respectively.❸

In terms of the causes of poverty, Hu Lian (2017) argues they are attributed to both the direct factors and indirect factors. Economic factor, personal factor, social factor, geographical factor as well as other

---

❶ The Covid-19 pandemic sets back efforts to achieve Agenda 2030[EB/OL]. (2021-09-22)[2021-09-24]. http://www.fao.org/sustainable-development-goals/news/detail-news/en/c/1440480/.

❷ The Three Regions refer to Tibet Autonomous Region and other four regions with Tibetan populations in Qinghai, Sichuan, Gansu and Yunnan Province, as well as four regions in Xinjiang Uygur Autonomous Region. While the Three Prefectures refer to Liangshan Prefecture in Sichuan Province, Nujiang Prefecture in Yunnan Province, and Linxia Prefecture in Gansu Province. They all used to be China's national level poverty regions.

❸ 习近平. 关于全面建成小康社会补短板问题[J]. 求是, 2020(11):4-9.

fragile factors directly lead to one's poverty.While institutional and cultural factors could have repercussions on poverty through the influence of the above direct factors.He argues that economic growth itself and generalized preferential policies could hardly resolve everything.❶

Poverty is a global problem.Despite its multiple causes,there is one that deserves special attention,where the existing resources contribute little to transforming the status quo.Inadequate exploitation as a result of underdeveloped economic conditions has led to stagnating poverty short of substantial changes.Some agricultural products,given their high yields,cannot be sold at profitable prices.Some,despite their characteristics,suffer from poor market returns due to inadequate management and marketing,failing to generate earnings to lift people out of poverty.

Optimizing resource allocation and enhancing skills to increase the rewards of scarce resources are ends and means of the GI system, which,as interpreted by the EU, "can benefit the rural economy.This is particularly the case in less favorable areas,in mountain areas and in the most remote regions,where the farming sector accounts for a significant part of the economy and production costs are high". "In particular,they may contribute to areas in which the farming sector is of greater economic importance and,especially,to disadvantaged areas."❷

First and for most,the GI system optimizes the allocation of resources to the maximum degree to ensure the characteristics of quality

---

❶ 胡联.中国产业发展的减贫效应研究[M].北京:经济科学出版社,2017:57.
❷ Regulation(EU)No 1151/2012 of the European Parliament and of the Council on quality scheme for agricultural products and foodstuffs[EB/OL]. (2012-12-14)[2021-05-22]. https://eur-lex.europa.eu/legal-content/EN/TXT.

products.As stated above,some regions lack basic living conditions either because of harsh environment or remote location.Some remain in poverty despite the presence of natural resources.The truth is,however, even some barren land may conceal special natural conditions favorable for the growth of specific product.Case analysis is presented in the following paragraphs.Harsh environment,in this case,might only be a *sine qua non* of poverty occurrence. To address the problem, people may start with transforming the mindset by finding out potential natural endowment and by exploring proper means to boost the characteristic industry.The GI system has proved an effective approach.

The significant roles the GI system plays in alleviating poverty are summarized as follows:

1. By mobilizing collective efforts, poverty eradication campaign extends its coverage

GI protection is for all stakeholders.It encourages joint participation in GI's production and operation,thereby sharing the rewards and benefits.Meanwhile,the collective status of GI implies it is neither the brand of any firm nor a signboard of any entity.Every farmer,every family,every workshop or enterprise can share the benefits of GI protection if he/she has engaged in the process.It is a joint effort in building up the GI brand.Furthermore,GI's reputation is secured by every stakeholder. Maintaining characteristics is both the management requirement and interest of each producer. "Stakeholders are bound together for good or ill,which,by improving organization of producers, enhances farmers' enthusiasm in participating in policy making and community governance.It upgrades the level and scale of joint participation."[1] Extensive participation with shared benefits and risks is a distinctive advantage of the GI system and an outstanding feature that differs from other poverty alleviation tools.

2. By reducing the cost of brand building, GI's market prospect gets improved

GI's popularity is derived from its history and established market reputation.GI protection plays a role in confirming rights,regulating, protecting and developing the GI product.It recognizes and confirms the intellectual property of a GI through strict procedures.No one is entitled to infringe on the GI name.Regulated management follows to ensure GI's characteristics and to foster its growth with advanced ideas of green and sustainable development. Meanwhile, the confirmation process is a recognition of the established reputation,indicating the product has already acquired popularity prior to its application for GI protection.GI producers manage to possess their own brand without being obliged to register trademarks,which is in sharp contrast to the marketing of registered trademarks.GI product has such an inborn advantage and is therefore labeled in Europe as 'the trademark of the poor'.

3. By enhancing the roles of cooperatives,quality benefits increase

This is something special of GI's production and marketing.GI's status as a collective right implies that its production and marketing cannot be monopolized by one or two firms.Instead,it is run by the joint participation of all stakeholders.In rare cases,where the tech-

---

[1] 王笑冰. 经济发展方式转变视角下的地理标志保护[M]. 北京:中国社会科学出版社,2019:52.

niques are mastered by only one person, he is eligible to be the sole applicant for GI protection. Emilie Vandecandelaere *et al* (2020) point out that the pillars of GI are special natural resources, particular techniques and producers' willingness to take collective actions.❶ All the qualified producers can take part in GI's production. They could be either big firms or small and medium size enterprises or even workshops, along with farmers or craftsmen. Individual producer or self-employed labor is the most disadvantaged at the upstream of the supply chain and bottom of the value chain, lacking any bargaining power. In the aftermath of GI registration, individual producer is mobilized to set up cooperatives of various sizes, or even inter-professional organizations covering all stakeholders which serves, inter alias, as a means to monitor performance and to enhance the leverage of organizations. It enables to optimize allocation and restructuring of the scattered production components over a wide range. By formulating standards and unifying management, GI's quality is eventually guaranteed. By fixing the minimum purchasing prices, individual interest is secured as well; and by unifying sales prices, the collective rights of GI's origin are safeguarded. The cooperatives retain better operation when individual's status remains unchanged. It reinforces the voice of producers on the supply chain and is favorable for ensuring GI's characteristics. It creates better rewards as well. GI protection may generate more reliable benefits for the poverty-stricken areas and provide revenue assurance

---

❶ VANDECANDELAERE E, TEYSSIER C, BARJOLLE D, et al. Strengthening sustainable food systems through geographical indications-evidence from 9 worldwide case studies[J/OL]. Journal of sustainable research, 2020, 2(4): 18[2020-11-18]. https://doi.org/10.20900/jsr20200031.

for farmers that are totally dependent on the soil.

Case One. Dingtan region at Beipanjiang Town, Zhenfeng County of Guizhou Province is one of the most severely rocky desertification areas in China, where 80% of the gross area is intense rocky desert, 95% of the land is covered by rocks. The hostile environment and barren land coupled with water shortage has driven local farmers to farm among rocks. Therefore, it used to be labeled as 'an area lacking basic living conditions'. In the meantime, Dingtan region is controlled by a northern plateau tropical monsoon climate which is favorable for the growth of quality Chinese prickly ashes that are easily found among rocks under the special climate characterized by strong heat radiation, with arid land and little soil. Research shows that the dry-hot valley areas of Guizhou Karst region are suitable for the growth of Chinese prickly ash.

Upon in-depth study of its natural circumstances, the Zhenfeng County Government released a policy that 'acts according to local conditions while making effort to improve the ecological environment and farmers' gains by planting Chinese prickly ash. The GI system was taken as a project to address the Three Rural Issues❶ and a significant approach to enforce the strategic arrangement of the Three Rural Issues. Local government agencies incorporated the GI system with the regional development plan. By setting up the leading team for GI application, the designated origin of Dingtan Huajiao (Chinese prickly ash) was completed, and other GI-related issues were properly arranged. Tasks were assigned to specific groups and funds were allocated by local government, along with advocacy through media and on-

---

❶ Referring to the agriculture, farmers and rural areas.

line platforms.It all contributed to improving public awareness of the GI system.In tandem with this,GI was incorporated with standardized production and brand building.GI protection was considered effective in enhancing the popularity of local characteristic products.Producers were mobilized to take part in the process.In 2008,Dingtan Chinese prickly ash was approved as a protected geographical indication product (PGI).

A case study of Dingtan Prickly Ash Co.Ltd.,Zhenfeng County indicated that its annual processing volume was as much as 2,300MT that was worth of RMB320 million yuan.By integrating production with supply and marketing,it helped to transform surplus local labor force.At the same time,the expansion of processing scale had driven the development of glass,carton and transportation industries.With the Guanling-Xingyi highway opened to traffic,Dingtan Chinese prickly ash became the key actor of local sightseeing agriculture joined by the Beipanjiang Valley tour.As of 2008,a total of 10,200 hectare of Chinese prickly ash was planted,with an output of 11,000MT,and an eco-friendly zone worth of RMB120million yuan was set up.Dingtan Chinese prickly ash has turned into a well-known brand popular both within and beyond Guizhou Province.By creating the so-called 'Dingtan Model' in harnessing rocky desertification of the Karst region and in boosting rural economy,it has become a showpiece of rocky desertification control.❶

Chinese prickly ash is also planted in Sichuan Province.Hanyuan Huajiao (Chinese prickly ash)-a PGI approved in 2005-excelled in

---

❶ See:贵州省黔西南州贞丰县质监局地理标志产品保护交流材料。

brand building and protection. Its unit price between 2012 and 2021 mounted to RMB170yuan/kg from RMB60yuan/kg - an increase by 183%. To date, the annual output for dried Hanyuan Huajiao is 5,000MT with a value of RMB686 million yuan.Plantation of Chinese prickly ash per person is as much as 0.133hectare with a profit of RMB10,000yuan.It has sustained farmers' income rise and poverty alleviation.As many as 7,000 farmers were lifted out of poverty in 2020 by joining in the Chinese prickly ash industry - one of the successful courses for poverty eradication and rural vitalization in the mountainous areas of Hanyuan County.❶

Case Two. Situated at the southeast of Gansu Province, Lixian County is 345km from Lanzhou,capital city of Gansu Province.Valleys and ravines block traffic and contribute to the poor economy,making it a national level poverty county over time.Yet people familiar with Li County are aware that it used to be the origin of the ancient Qin culture.It has preserved a tradition to plant medicinal herbs throughout its farming civilization,among which the plantation of Lixian Dahuang (Chinese rhubarb) could be traced back to the Han Dynasty.Being a well-known producing area of quality Chinese rhubarb,Longnan City where Li County is located boasts 'a natural medicine storage', and 'home to medicines with thousand-year history'.Of all the five core medicinal herbs listed in the Compendium of Materia Medica,four are planted in Longnan.Moreover,they are known as quality materials in large quantity.❷ That said,the development of Lixian Dahuang (Li

---

❶ Source from Hanyuan County Government, December 2021.
❷ 《甘肃发展年鉴》编委会. 甘肃发展年鉴 2018[M/OL]. 北京:中国统计出版社,2018 [2021-09-13]. http://tjj. gansu. gov. cn/tjnj/2018/indexce. htm.

County Chinese rhubarb) had long remained stagnant. In 2004, Li County launched its application for GI protection as a way to enhance its market reputation.Lixian Dahuang was approved as a PGI by AQSIQ in 2005,when more efforts were made in strengthening management and in disseminating knowledge of the GI system.

Lixian County scaled up Lixian Dahuang's production and improved its standardized plantation thanks to the backing of local government.Meanwhile,the GI system has ensured its characteristics,lifted sales and earnings.Farmers eventually managed to taste the 'sweetness' of the Chinese rhubarb (being extremely bitter).As of 2018 the total output of Lixian Dahuang was as much as 944MTS. Lixian Dahuang's success encouraged producers of other local specialties to turn to the GI system,among which Lixian Apple and Lixian Huajiao (Chinese prickly ash) were some of the examples.As a means to alleviate poverty by enhancing local characteristic industry,plantation of fruits and herbal medicinal materials evolved as the pillar of local farmers' earnings.In the year 2017 Lixian Apple attained an output of 96,600 MTS and Li Xian County was granted the National Outstanding Achievement Award in Poverty Alleviation by Fruit.As of 2018 local average per-capita income rise through characteristic industry was RMB3, 100 yuan,and the per-capita disposable income of rural households was RMB6,529 yuan-a rise by almost 30% as against 2015.❶

Producing a good GI is but the first step in eradicating poverty. Successful marketing is critical to transforming the characteristic prod-

---

❶ 《甘肃发展年鉴》编委会.甘肃发展年鉴 2018[M/OL].北京:中国统计出版社,2018 [2021-09-13]. http://tjj. gansu. gov. cn/tjnj/2018/indexce. htm.

uct in farmers' hands into concrete monetary returns.Given marketing issue's extensive coverage,this book is not intended to engage in further discussions.Instead,some paradigms of GI's marketing are provided for reference only.

(1) How to address the transportation problem?

Poverty often occurs in remote areas where access to traffic is impeded by mountains and valleys.Traffic remains a big problem. "If you want to get rich,build a road first."❶ Goods can only be delivered when there is a road.Next,even when the road is completed,distance matters.The challenge posed by long distance transportation is another concern for sales management.In fact,remote mountainous areas remain a major obstacle for poverty alleviation,where many characteristic products keep unknown to the outside world.Thus,it is essential to innovate marketing strategy to cash in from new technology apart from road construction.

Coqen County is located in the heart of Qiangtang Plateau,Ngari Prefecture of Tibet Autonomous Region.It is 880km away from Lhasa and 746km from Shiquanhe Town,location of Ngari Prefectural Administrative Office.Being the most remote county of Ngari Prefecture,Coqen County suffers from adverse natural conditions and extremely poor traffic access.Nevertheless,it is endowed with rich livestock resources,among which the purple cashmere goat,a breed unique to Tibet that is strongly cold‐resistant,has a high cashmere yield,its flesh fine and tender.In view of this advantage,Coqen County was committed to developing the purple cashmere goat sector and optimizing the

---

❶ A well‐known Chinese saying.

use of grassland before applying for GI protection. Meanwhile, local government made contacts with key on-line operators such as Taobao and Jingdong to introduce and promote Coqen's local characteristic products.The genuine natural products of the Qinghai-Tibet Plateau-the 'Third Pole of the Earth' - are of strong appeal.Producers of Coqen purple cashmere goat soon received orders from across the country.

What goes hand in hand with long distance is the high logistic cost for products made in remote areas.It is common knowledge that on-line operators often do not provide free delivery there,for the delivery cost may well exceed the goods' prices.High logistic cost is the crux of the problem.In China,freight transport to remote areas predominantly relies on automobiles,which, as compared to railway and air freight,are superior either in mobility or in cost-being somewhere in between.And for such a remote county as Coqen,road transportation is not only the sole option but 'China Post',a state-run mailing company,is the only operator available that provides regular freight transport to Lhasa and other cities and counties of Tibet.To date,the majority of freight transport to counties and towns in Tibet is run by China Post. Thanks to this 'lifeline',Coqen's purple cashmere has managed to be sold to cities like Beijing, Shanghai and Xi'an. Coqen County was hence awarded Tibet's Top County for On-line Sales in 2017.

"By the end of 2019,Coqen County's sales volume,aided by the on-line platforms along with offline stores and commodity fairs,was approximately RMB31 million yuan,among which livestock sales exceeded 25 million yuan,while characteristic products like purple and gold cashmere sales was about RMB6 million yuan.In addition,efforts were made to build the Village of Top On-line Sales,a market at Men-dong Town aimed to display Coqen's characteristic products and to create more economic returns for local herdsmen.County-level public service centers and offline experience stores for e-commerce were set up as an approach to promote e-commerce into villages. 'Goods from Tibet-Coqen Channel' kicked off its on-line operation,covering all the 12 e-commerce village-level service stations.34 sessions of e-commerce training were conducted,distributing more than 2,500 Chinese-Tibetan bilingual booklets to local herdsmen.It is safe to say that by continuously raising public awareness of e-commerce, the life of local herdsmen has considerably changed. Meanwhile, local government helped to streamline the brand building strategy and established a traceability system.With the enhanced promotion via Taobao and other online platforms,goods from Coqen achieved exceptional success at domestic exhibitions and the Tibet International Expo.To ensure logistics safety,an agreement was signed between Coqen County and China Post Ngari Branch to build a new transit center at Saga County,Shigatse, where transit goods destined to Coqen by other logistics companies would be reloaded by China Post.The move aimed to ensure that all the express mails and on-line sale goods could be delivered to Lhasa within 1 or 2 days."❶

(2) How to promote GI products?

The role of promotion is significant for marketing purposes.What distinguishes GIs from other products is that they are not produced by any individual household or a single firm.Instead,they are produced by all the qualified producers within the designated areas.As far as GI's

---

❶ See:http://www.xzcq.gov.cn/cgjj_1555/202005/t20200519_3068728.html.

property right is concerned,it is of collective nature.And in terms of GI's organizational components,producers not only refer to farmers, households or small workshops,but also large‐scale firms.Therefore, GIs' commercialization is not a business of any individual entity.Then how to carry out effective promotion for GI products? Marketing of GI products generally consists of two tiers.The cooperatives,on behalf of the collective interests of GI producers,may be responsible for over-all marketing.Meanwhile,individuals and firms are also entitled to sell their products if they meet GI's requirements.In China,all the post‐approval GIs must meet the requirements on packaging and logo,implying additional cost difficult to be borne on individuals.Thus,producers are more likely to leave the sales to cooperatives whose original intent coincides with this demand.For others within the designated areas,they are entitled to sell their products as per the same GI rules,or they may leave them to the cooperatives as well.Cooperatives are entrusted with comprehensive roles‐overseeing mobilization,implementation,coordination, bargaining, communication and commercialization activities. Moreover, they are supposed to make GI protection favorable for the sustainable development of the community and local economy.❶ Hence,it is crucial for GI producers to set up cooperatives.The following cases may help explain.

A.Turrialba Cheese (Costa Rica)

In 2006,a series of studies were conducted in Costa Rica on Turrialba Cheese as an attempt to define the causal links between its qual-

---

❶ VANDECANDELAERE E, ARFINI F, BELLETTI G, et al. Linking people, places and products‐a guide for promoting quality linked to geographical origin and sustainable geographical indications[M]. Rome:FAO,2009:97.

ity and the producing areas, and to analyze market potentials and consumer demand. The study was carried out by visiting farmers and dairy processors along with chemical, physical, microbiological analysis as well as sensory examinations. 'The survey on consumers' perceptions was conducted with 201 interviews in some shopping areas in order to help define the preferred characteristics of the cheese, its reputation, consumers' characteristics and their willingness to pay. An open-ended questionnaire was used in methodolgy to enable consumers to express fully their views on the cheese, visual identification, etc. The results of the survey provided the following messages:

— confirmed the image of tradition for the cheese, with specific flavor and texture;

— identified the preferred places of purchase for consumers;

— clarified consumers' awareness and proof of a longstanding reputation: for example, 81.6% of consumers polled agree on 'Queso Turrialba', among different types of white cheese, as very distinct and recognizable.

Based on the above information, producers defined marketing plan, especially different market channels according to consumer groups and locations: distant urban centers via middlemen;

— stores at local villages and nearby cities via local sellers;

— direct selling to consumers during the fairs (especially the annual event organized by producers in Turrialba) and selling on farm, in relation to the development of tourism and the 'route of the Turrialba Cheese'.❶

---

❶ VANDECANDELAERE E, ARFINI F, BELLETTI G, et al. Linking people, places and products-a guide for promoting quality linked to geographical origin and sustainable geographical indications[M]. Rome: FAO, 2009: 107.

B.Banano de Costa Rica

The Corporación Bananera Nacional Corbana,S.A.(CORBANA) - a national banana corporation - was established in 1971 in Costa Rica. CORBANA is a public entity jointly owned by farmers,the Government and nationalized banks that supports banana growers in Costa Rica.

Beginning in 2008,three - year research was conducted by CORBANA and government agencies,research institute as well as international partners,which eventually succeeded in making Banano de Costa Rica the first registered GI in Costa Rica in 2010.It was also the first GI for banana product in South America.

Upon its registration,CORBANA formulated marketing strategy for Banano de Costa Rica,adopting new brand marketing approaches in boosting global market.By applying GI as a tool of IP protection,the government of Costa Rica enforced internationally recognized quality and safety standards to create competitive edge for domestic farmers. As far as marketing management is concerned,CORBANA has engaged in the following practices:

(a) commercialization and promotion through large events - being the official sponsor for Oslo Marathon 2008 where banana and leaflets were distributed;

(b) facility construction at the National Children Museum - educating children through entertainment that simulated the whole process of banana production.Blended with education on environmental protection and pest control,the younger population was informed of the banana industry,which is favorable for the potential banana consumers.❶

C.Comté Cheese (France)

The Inter-professional Gruyère and Comté Committee (CIGC) was set up in 1963 for the renowned Protected Denomination of Origin(PDO) of France.It is "both the representative of the actors within the supply chain and their intermediary with economic,administrative, political and academic partners. It commercially promotes Comté Cheese,defends the interests of the professional network, organizes cultural events and conducts research.Its activities include marketing management,protection and regulations of the PDO,communication, advertising and managing the internal cohesion of the network".❷

D.Hanyuan Huajiao (Chinese prickly ash)

Ever since its approval as a PGI in 2005,producers of Hanyuan Huajiao have engaged in multiple activities to extend its popularity by the following ways:

(a) promoting through national exhibitions;

(b) hosting a series of events - fairs and seminars on Chinese prickly ash,picking experience,food festivals - to strengthen its market influence;

(c) innovating marketing channels,i.e.,farmer - supermarket - direct purchase,farmer - trader - direct purchase,farmer - commerce - direct purchase,promoting manufacturers of Chinese prickly ash to enter chain

---

❶ WIPO GIs and Rural Development: a Case of Bananas [EB/OL]. [2022 - 01 - 05]. https://www. wipo. int/ipadvantage /en/details. jsp? id = 3111.

❷ VANDECANDELAERE E, ARFINI F, BELLETTI G, et al. Linking people, places and products-a guide for promoting quality linked to geographical origin and sustainable geographical indications[M]. Rome:FAO,2009:99.

stores in Chengdu, and Carrefour, Ito Yokado as well as other supermarkets and markets for local produce; in addition, the high-end Hanyuan Huajiao products - accounting for 25% of the total annual sales volume-were successfully settled in Chengdu Shuangliu International Airport and airport in Chongqing, Hangzhou and Qinhuangdao as well as the 5A scenic spots of Sichuan Province;

(d) participating in brand evaluation events to enhance its brand value;Hanyuan Huajiao made a sixfold rise in brand value within three years at the Brand Evaluation 2020 organized by China Promotion Association for Brand Construction-from RMB704 million yuan in 2016 to RMB4.97 billion yuan,making a leap forward in brand image.[1]

E. Lixian Apple

As mentioned in previous paragraphs, Lixian Apple is a PGI approved in 2008.Thanks to the support of local government and on-line operators,Lixian Apple's on-line marketing has gained momentum in recent years.New marketing tools like live webcast and live streaming commerce show advantages that are more straightforward and efficient.By logging on the 'T-mall's 11+11 Carnival 2019' ,Lixian Apple established a fast track that connected production and marketing,which was joined by network anchors, celebrities and local officials. Meanwhile,as a charity act,Lixian Apple made its debut on YouKu in support of poverty alleviation by consuming Lixian Apple,whereby its brand image was improved.On 17 September 2019,a three-hour on-line charity live webcast was conducted by Alibaba,where around 15,000 cartons of

---

[1] Source from Hanyuan County Government, December 2021.

apples were sold with a sales volume of RMB500,000 yuan.❶

The case of Lixian Apple is paradigmatic.The Internet era has ended the disconnection among production,supply and marketing,when middleman used to play the key role.The live streaming commerce emerging in recent years indefinitely bridges the gap between producers and consumers,enabling consumers to see the product from where it is made,which presents additional information before triggering their willingness to pay.The live streaming commerce is especially suitable for agricultural products in remote areas.It pays to be promoted to bring about new market opportunities for GI producers.That said,reports of fake media campaigns and credit problems remind us of the need for enhanced regulations.

Goal 2. Zero hunger

This goal aims to eliminate hunger,ensure food safety,improve nutritional conditions and promote sustainable agriculture.According to the UN report published on 30 November 2021,as many as 13.8 million people in Latin American countries were added to the hungry population for the year 2020 alone,bringing the total number to 59.7 million.The report quoted the remarks of an representative of the FAO as saying that Latin American Countries and the Caribbean Region were faced with severe food safety problems,where hungry population increased by 79% between 2014 and 2020,reaching 9.1% of the total

---

❶ 甘肃礼县:直播带货连接消费扶贫 激发脱贫攻坚新动力[EB/OL]. (2020-07-08) [2021-03-02]. http://www.chinaxiaokang.com/xianyu/yaowen/2020/0708/998715. 1_html.

population-the highest for the last 15 years.Meanwhile the global average hungry population accounted for 9.9% of the total population.❶

Food safety is crucial to mankind,whereas agriculture and food industries provide the inputs,with agriculture being the root.meanwhile agri-food products dominate the list of global GIs,ranging from fruit, vegetable,cereal,grain and nut to cheese,olive oil,ham,coffee,tea,so on and so forth.

The specific objectives of protecting designations of origin and geographical indications are securing a fair return for farmers and producers for the qualities and characteristics of a given product,or of its mode of production,and providing clear information on products with specific characteristics linked to geographical origin, thereby enabling consumers to make more informed purchasing choices. ❷

By implementing strict quality control measures,the GI system serves as a supplement to the quality assurance system to maintain GI's characteristics and ensure food safety.The advantages of the GI system in safeguarding food safety are rendered as follows.

1. Quality control starts with the sorting of seeds and breeds

The safety of agricultural products has close ties with seeds and breeds,whereas food processing safety is in relation to the raw materials

---

❶ A joint publication of FAO,IFAD,PAHO/WHO,WFP and UNICEF [EB/OL]. (2021-11-30)[2021-01-10]. https://www. fao. org/newsroom/detail/new-un-report-hunger-in-latin-america-and-the-caribbean-rose-by-13. 8-million-people-in-just-one-year/en,30/11/2021.

❷ Regulation(EU) No 1151/2012 of the European Parliament and of the Council on quality scheme for agricultural products and foodstuffs[EB/OL]. (2012-12-14)[2021-04-11]. https://eur-lex. europa. eu/legal-content/EN/TXT.

thereof.Selection of seeds and breeds,therefore,is a prerequisite for quality agri-food products.The GI system pays special attention to seeds and breeds.It is one of the essential requirements to fix the plant variety or animal breed in the specification.Once defined,producers are obliged to observe without any random changes.Now that the quality of a GI has links with natural circumstances,priority is given to the local breed or plant variety,or breeds and plant varieties that have been tested there presenting characteristics of the GI product.

As far as breeds and plant varieties are concerned,the following issues are to be discussed.

(1) Their relations with the GI system

There is no standard to follow with respect to regulations about GIs' relations with animal breeds and plant varieties.But the general rule is not to mislead consumers.For instance,France has regulated that any product name containing name of animal breed or plant variety must not mislead consumers or being suspicious of causing confusions as if the product came from the place where the name refers to.❶

In EU's regulation,the applied GI name shall not be registered if it confuses with a name of breed or plant variety to the extent that it will mislead consumers into believing that it has come from the origin of the breed or plant variety.(Article 6,EU Regulation 1152/2012)

Swiss law on GI has provided an additional clause to the conditions where animal breeds and plant varieties cannot be registered,i.e.,

---

❶ INSTITUT NATIONAL DE L'ORIGINE ET DE LA QUALITE. Guide du demandeur d'une appellation d'origine protégée (AOP) ou d'une indication géographique protégée (IGP) [EB/OL]. (2017-11-30)[2021-05-11]. https://www.inao.gouv.fr/.

Art 4b:Any danger of misleading consumers is in particular excluded where the name is homonymous with a local plant variety or animal breed that has not left its territory of origin or where the name of the plant variety or animal breed can be changed. ❶

GI practices in China have generally followed a similar course as Switzerland,where,on certain conditions,the name of local breed or plant variety can be registered. In terms of China's regulations on breeds and plant varieties,Article 18 of the *Ordinance Protecting New Plant Varieties of China*❷ (hereinafter referred to as the Ordinance) provides that a registered name shall be a generic name of the new plant variety. According to the Ordinance,the List of Protected New Agricultural Plant Varieties has been published,which contains names of plant genus or species or scientific names.All the names are generic terms,such as rice,corn,potato.Meanwhile,in January 2021,the National Committee of Generic Resources of Livestock published the *List of Generic Resources of Livestock* containing a total of 948 local breeds,cultivated breeds and their synthetic lines,introduced breeds and their synthetic lines.❸ The List has included a number of livestock named after geographical origins,such as Jinhua pig,Yanbian cattle,Altay sheep,etc. These local breeds,or original breeds,or native breeds as it is called,are mostly adapted to local natural conditions and altitudes.Once a breed containing place name is promoted to areas away from its origin,it is

---

❶ See:Ordinance on the Protection of Designations of Origin and Geographical Indications for Agricultural Products, Processed Agricultural Products, Forestry Products and Processed Forestry Products1(PDO/PGI Ordinance) of 28 May 1997 (Status as of 1 February 2019).
❷ 根据 2014 年 7 月 29 日《国务院关于修改部分行政法规的决定》第二次修订。
❸ See:http://www.chinafarming.com/axfwnh/2021/01/26/3307297899.shtml.

likely that,gradually,it may lose the function of geographical reference and reduce to a generic name,albeit the scope of quality breed is extended,which is favorable to breed improvement and output increase. Hence,total rejection of any GI application containing name of breed or plant variety may not be helpful for the quality improvement and protection of plant varieties and animal breeds.On the contrary,it may lead to,as a result of continuing promotion coupled with ever changing environment,the degradation of germplasm resources and dilution of characteristics.It is therefore in line with the aim of protecting animal and plant germplasm resources to accept applications for GI protection on certain conditions.

Wang Qingyin *et al* (2005) argue that good breeds and plant varieties are raised by sufficient genetic materials irrespective of their sources as being original,as being introduced or newly cultivated varieties or species.It could be impossible for them to recover once inbreeding or crossbreeding occurs,as their original genes are destroyed. "The conservation of genetic resources aims to maintain genetic diversity of species,genetic variation within species,and the natural reproductive capacity between species and populations in order to achieve sustainable utilization of biological resources."❶ It partly explains why the names of local native breed populations (those that are not included in the National List),which must be defined in GI's specifications, are eligible to be protected as GI products.And for the ones having been included in the National List,if their breeding and reproduction has not been promoted to other regions,it is eligible to apply for GI

---

❶ 王清印. 海水生态养殖理论与技术[M]. 北京:海洋出版社,2005:7.

protection as well. In this case, experts and GI authority would either advise the applicant to apply for name change to the competent authority of animal breeds and plant varieties or request local authorities to take protective measures for the local breeds and plant varieties to prevent from outflow and proliferation. It coincides with the idea of 'in situ conservation' encouraged in the practice of genetic resource conservation, which refers to the conservation of genetic resources at the habitat where species(population) appear, and where there is a natural or artificial ecosystem. This is a genetic conservation of population levels and a form of ecological protection. "The in‐situ conservation is the most efficient approach compared to ex situ conservation."❶

Having said that, for those that are included in the National List and have been considerably promoted off site, GI applications are normally to be rejected. It is a reminder that such GI applications, due to their proliferated productions off site, almost always imply eventual failure in protecting the intellectual property rights of the so‐called GI products, making the protection itself meaningless. The case of Wuchang Fish may help explain. An application was once filed by the municipal government of Ezhou City, Hubei Province for the GI protection of Wuchang Fish but was rejected by the national GI authority, for, despite its origin being in the geographical territory of Ezhou City, the breed itself has been commercialized to various regions outside Ezhou and has always been named and sold as Wuchang Fish across the country. Signboards of Wuchang Fish could easily be spotted at aquatic market and restaurant. Wuchang Fish has turned into a generic

---

❶ 王清印. 海水生态养殖理论与技术[M]. 北京:海洋出版社,2005:7.

fish name that has lost its original geographical reference together with the possibility for any meaningful GI protection.The only hypothetical feasibility,for the sake of GI protection,would be a nationwide prohibition of Wuchang Fish breeding on behalf of the local producers,restricting its breeding to the territory of Ezhou City,which,apparently, would be a move unrealistic.The case of Wuchang Fish shows the necessity of protecting local breeds and valuable animal and plant resources,for which GI protection system may serve as a working force. Once a local breed is severely proliferated off site,the cost to retrieval would be too high to afford.

(2) Relations between breed and variety options and possible changes

Market changes and technology progress always make newcomers come to the fore.The same is true of animal breeds and plant varieties. Cherry product of Chinese domestic origin,for instance,has given way to foreign varieties in recent years.And the lion's share of domestic apple market has been replaced by Malus Pumila Mill.It reminds us of the question about whether an existing GI would expire if the defined breed or plant variety is replaced by new ones.There is hardly any definite answer,for some replacements do not necessarily change the essential characteristics of the GI,while others may have adverse effect on the characteristics that must be taken in a cautious manner.Besides, timing is important,too.It should be based on experiments and empirical studies,rather than frequent changes at random.

Change of breed and plant variety is in relation to the variable and invariable.GI protection is,among others,for the inheritance of historical and cultural traditions.The designated geographical areas,production techniques and specifications containing requirements on breeds and plant varieties should remain relatively stable. Random changes without adequate reason are not acceptable.EU's provisions on any amendment to the specifications of PGI/PDO state that there shall be no changes to the product's name,the defined geographical areas as well as the essential characteristics of the product.[1]

At the same time, nothing is immutable. GI protection aims to maintain characteristics rather than to follow a beaten track. New breeds and plant varieties emerge as time moves on.It is possible that novel breeds and plant varieties adapted to the environment are singled out through experiments.In addition,a breed or variety is subject to,after years of growth cycle,cross breeding or degeneration that calls for purification and rejuvenation.Adjustment is always permitted if the new breeds and varieties are proved viable in the designated geographical areas,and their characteristics are presented even better.It is thus an inborn demand of GI's sustainable development. Fresh fruits like red bayberry and honey peach,for instance,have long been confined to local market due to storage problems.Some fruits,like banana and mango,must be plucked before they are ripe,their maturation being done during transportation. Scientists are improving the varieties to make them more storable,which in part addressed the problem of storage and transportation.Nevertheless,selection of breeds and varieties is a long-term task that must be addressed in practice.Early plucking or

---

[1] Amendment to a product specification,REGULATION (EU) No 1151/2012 OF THE EUROPEAN PARLIAMENT AND OF THE COUNCIL of 21 November 2012 on quality schemes for agricultural products and foodstuffs[EB/OL]. (2012-12-14)[2021-05-11]. https://eur-lex. europa. eu/legal-content/EN/TXT/? uri=CELEX%3A32012R1151.

alteration to the breed through technical means may affect the fruit's taste and flavor.Jiang Quan (2020),researcher of Beijing Academy of Agriculture and Forestry Sciences,argues that some essential characteristics of the fruit have been 'removed' because of the efforts that emphasize high yields and endurable storage.[1] It is a reminder that any cultivar improvement must be balanced to keep the original quality and flavor.

Finally,what has been defined in the specification is almost always the local breed or plant variety sorted out by long-term experiments,which has proved adaptable to the local environment.Any potential change may affect the key characteristics and consumers' knowledge of the GI product.Wang Qingyin *et al* (2005) argue, "introducing new breeds helps to improve the breeding structure and provide breeding materials,yet it may lead to genetic confounding between local breeds and foreign ones."[2]It implies that any introduction of new breed should be handled cautiously.Futog Cabbage,a GI from Serbia,may serve as an example.It is a local cabbage variety characterized by its thin leaves and sweet taste.The cabbage's production has not been scaled up and is confined to a small area.The GI system aims to protect the characteristics of this local variety and its native environment.The variety is defined in the specification that cannot be

---

[1] 于文静.买家说桃子越来越不好吃了？啥原因？——来自水蜜桃产业的调查[EB/OL].(2020-09-02)[2020-09-06]. https://baijiahao.baidu.com/s? id = 1676711377245137204&wfr=spider&for=pc.
[2] 王清印.海水生态养殖理论与技术[M].北京:海洋出版社,2005:7.

changed at will.❶

2. Specific ingredients, recipe and technique ensure GI's characteristics

Regardless of a GI's nature-whether it is an agri-food product or handicraft-its production relies on specific breed, variety, ingredients, recipe or special technique and treatment that is critical to a GI product. That said, it is important not to exaggerate the distinctiveness of GI production, which, instead of following an entirely independent management system, must first abide by the general rules. All the special requirements are incorporated to satisfy both the compulsory requirements, standards or management systems, and special technical demands of characteristic qualities. For instance, the standards and technical requirements for fruits have covered all fruit products, whose quality can be guaranteed provided that all the technical rules are observed. What distinguishes a GI fruit when it comes to special techniques is that:

a. the varieties are explicitly defined;

b. the density of plantation is strictly defined along with tree's shape, minimal planting distances and trimming requirements;

c. fertilizer and water management rules;

d. harvest timing requirement;

e. weight and size requirement for each fruit, being separated into different classes.

As a general rule, GI protection only covers the fruits classified as

---

❶ VANDECANDELAERE E, TEYSSIER C, BARJOLLE D, et al. Strengthening sustainable food systems through geographical indications-evidence from 9 worldwide case studies[J/OL]. Journal of sustainable research, 2020, 2(4):27[2020-11-18]. https://doi. org/10. 20900/jsr20200031.

Grade A and,in some cases,Grade B.Of course,specific criteria must be put in place to cope with the local context,which will not be discussed in detail.

3. Traditional techniques ensure GIs' characteristics

The GI system is committed to making rational use of natural resources and maintaining traditional techniques.It promotes less fertilizer,pesticide or food preservatives in producing healthy products with premium quality.Parallel to this commitment,the GI system is also concerned about traditional techniques.

Tradition is,according to its definition, "a way of thinking,behaving,or doing something that has been used by the people in a particular group,family,society, etc. ,for a long time". ❶

As far as techniques are concerned,tradition refers to the assembling of experiences inherited from long‑term accumulation.Traditional technique often means hand‑made or complex procedures with limited application of modern equipment.It often implies labor‑intensive with higher cost.Traditional techniques are often associated with the uniqueness of a characteristic product. "Despite the high cost of traditional approach,GI's capacity in managing price surplus makes it possible for such a production mode to acquire economic basis to sustain."❷As to the relations between GI and traditional technique,priority should be given to the assurance of characteristic quality.Modern equipment is not to be rejected as long as GI's characteristics are wholly displayed.

---

❶ Merriam‑Webster's Advanced Learner's English‑Chinese Dictionary[M]. Springfield: Merriam‑Webster Incorporated,2017.
❷ 王笑冰.经济发展方式转变视角下的地理标志保护[M].北京:中国社会科学出版社,2019:49.

Otherwise, it must be handled cautiously. When it comes to the duration of time and efficiency, the time-consuming procedures required by traditional techniques are not to be dismissed at will, nor is it necessary to pursue the so-called modified techniques. Agri-food products are creatures of water, soil and climate blended with human wisdom. Historical inheritance should be honored, and traditional techniques should be observed without random change or dismissal. Modified techniques are intended to improve efficiency. But the truth is that timing and seasons are crucial for agri-food products. Any imprudent act to accelerate the pace may be disastrous for the GI product. Shanxi Overmature (or long-aged) Vinegar(山西老陈醋), for example, is a renowned GI in China. The name itself signifies the requirement on time. Further analysis reveals that, compared to other vinegars, Shanxi Overmature Vinegar is rich in guaiacols, tetra methylpyrazine, 5-methylfurfural and benzaldehyde due to the raw materials adopted from sorghum and bran, with sorghum as the main ingredient, aided by special techniques. The above indicators are considered unique to Shanxi Overmature Vinegar.❶ According to the national standard, any commodity labeled as Shanxi Overmature Vinegar must follow a series of quality controls, among which the so-called 'ice picking in winter and sun exposure in summer' is an essential process that usually lasts for as long as 12 months. Only the vinegar produced in this way could be referred to as Shanxi Overmature Vinegar. In practice, however, some vinegar producers in Shanxi Province fail to meet this requirement and turn to adopt the so-called modified techniques instead. As they are not in con-

---

❶ See:深圳市计量质量检测研究院在 2010 中国地理标志保护论坛上分享材料。

formity with the specification for GI protection, such vinegars cannot be named as Shanxi Overmature Vinegar. That's why we could spot vinegar brands labeled as xxx aged vinegar, xxx old vinegar, xxx (a trademark) overmature vinegar, etc. Of all the vinegars produced in Shanxi Province, only 'Shanxi Overmature Vinegar' stands for the genuine aged vinegar that completely meets consumers' demand for GI's traditional technique and health notion.

Alcoholic drinks, including but not limited to, wines, spirits, beers, Chinese Baijiu, rice wine, are important components of global GI products. Despite apparent differences in raw materials and diversified techniques, alcoholic drinks account for a large proportion of GI products due to their close ties with local natural and human factors. In China, the brewing history of Chinese Baijiu is age-old with strong regional characteristics. It is well-known that 'a good drink must come from good water', which mirrors the significance of water resource of the producing areas. In fact, all the renowned Chinese Baijiu bear links with natural environment, especially water and microclimate, plus unique brewing techniques that ensure the preservation of Chinese Baijiu's characteristics. Chishui River, winding its way between Guizhou Province and Sichuan Province, is vividly called as 'the river of best Baijiu' because some of the most famous Chinese Baijiu-Moutai Chiew, Lang Jiu, Xi Jiu, to name only a few-are produced along this river.

Quality Chinese Baijiu has followed traditional technique of the so-called solid fermentation for distilled liquor, i.e., made from sorghum and other grains by solid (or semi-solid) saccharification, fermentation, distillation as well as aging and blending. It is characterized by its distinct flavor without any edible alcohol and aromatic substance out of non-fermentation way.❶

In addition to the special requirements on water and raw materials, major techniques of Chinese Baijiu include koji making, fermentation and storage. Koji making refers to the solid substance accumulated amid different raw materials aided by saccharification and starter, which, relying on fungi and strain brought into from nature, is cultivated and air-dried or dried and stored. Lai Dengyi et al. (2021) claims that Daqu-yeast for making hard liquor-plays four roles in liquor making, i. e., fungi supply, saccharification and fermentation, grain feeding effect as well as aroma generating effect. Because of the links between microorganism and natural environment, geographical conditions are crucial for liquor making. Whereas GI product highlights the importance of geographical conditions to produce Chinese Baijiu.❷ Temperature and humidity as well as the 'microenvironment' of the producing area-wind direction, terrain, vegetation-all contribute to the quality of koji.

For instance, the Luzhou-flavor Chinese Baijiu owes much to the pit and pit mud, where mud cellar of a pit is taken as the container for fermentation, where pit mud serves as the culture medium of microorganism producing aromatic substances of the liquor-the critical foundation for Luzhou-flavor Chinese Baijiu. Quality Luzhou-flavor Chinese Baijiu cannot be made without quality pit mud. It takes time for the mud to attain natural aging. Meanwhile successful experiments have been made to imitate the conditions for the natural aging of aged

---

❶ 赖登燡,王久明,余乾伟,等.白酒生产实用技术[M].2版.北京:化学工业出版社, 2021:9.

❷ 赖登燡,王久明,余乾伟,等.白酒生产实用技术[M].2版.北京:化学工业出版社, 2021:27,31.

fermentation pit to accelerate its aging process.By cultivating favorable fungi population and making it the dominant fungi in the pit mud,it produces proper aromatic substances and sustains the prolonged and viable growth of fungi groups.❶

It is worth noting that the production of Chinese Baijiu is an organic combination of natural circumstances and human factors that is typical of GI products.With a deep reverence for nature,it is an inheritance of traditional techniques and history.No wonder that many producing areas of Chinese Baijiu are rich in tourism resources that enable dual prosperities.

4. Improved inter-professional management

GI protection is a comprehensive system involving management of upstream and downstream entities and calling for,in addition to self-discipline of producers,supervision and monitoring on behalf of the industry and authority.For instance,producers of Nanxi Dried Tofu - a specialty of Sichuan Province approved as a PGI in September 2008 - has developed a working mechanism in their post-approval practices.

First,a GI protection institution was set up,consisting of government agencies,inter-professional organizations,firms and peers,each playing its distinctive role.Government agencies are responsible for the overall protection and brand promotion and planning for sectorial growth.The Committee of GI Protection for Nanxi Dried Tofu was established,and the *Regulation on the GI Protection of Nanxi Dried Tofu* was released,along with the *Assessment Rules for the Use of GI Logo of*

---

❶ 赖登燡.王久明,余乾伟,等.白酒生产实用技术[M].2版.北京:化学工业出版社,2021:59-64.

Nanxi Dried Tofu. The Food Industry Association of Nanxi County-member of the GI protection mechanism-manages the peer review and self-discipline of the industry.It also helps to manage the GI's market access,standardization,data collection and meeting arrangement.The association,mainly composed of enterprises that finance by itself,is responsible for taking independent actions.

Second,the standard system was enhanced.In addition to the specification,a regional standard for the GI product and a regional standard on the technical requirements of Nanxi Dried Tofu were released.The GI logo users,upon filing the application,are subject to on-site verification in line with the above two standards as well as food safety requirements,which,from the initial stage of GI production,ensures the GI's characteristics and its credibility.

Third,testing skills and R&D status were improved.The Sichuan Provincial (Nanxi) Bean Product Inspection Center and Sichuan Nanxi Food R&D Center were established to enhance the transformation of agricultural technology to concrete economic yields, and to strengthen the surveillance capacity for the food safety of dried tofu. The key firms were encouraged to innovate and cooperate with universities and research institutes-a plus for food safety and better development.❶

Another example is Hanyuan Huajiao (Chinese prickle ash).Upon Hanyuan Huajiao's approval as a PGI in 2005,Hanyuan County was committed to regulating the industry and upgrading the protection scheme with measures as follows,

---

❶ See:四川省宜宾市南溪质量技术监督局在 2010 中国地理标志保护论坛上分享材料。

- setting up the association for Hanyuan Huajiao responsible for experiments of fine varieties and promotion of plantation skills and branding.

- setting up a leading group for the promotion of Hanyuan Huajiao,a bureau for sectorial development,a development center and a development fund,making Hanyuan Huajiao a strategic focus and breakthrough for rural economic development of mountainous areas.

- exploring a development model that was aided by local government,driven by leading firms,joined in by farmers with socialized services.

- prioritizing training, driven by best practice, on - line platform building,technology support,plus subsidy and collaboration between enterprises and universities,making Hanyuan Huajiao an effective way to alleviate poverty for rural population at mountainous areas and a way to increase local financial revenues.[1]

The above two cases are examples of GI practices that could be drawn as lessons for other GI producers.In fact,many GI producers have explored ways adapted to local characteristic industries.Furnished GI protection measures contribute to GI's quality and safety as well as to its reputation and consumer confidence.

---

[1] Source from Hanyuan County Government, December 2021.

Section 2 The GI system benefits the health sector

Goal 3. Good health and well-being

UN statistics show that as of 2019, millions of people's health conditions were improved.Progress was made in life expectancy,reduction of pregnant women and infant mortality and anti-infectious diseases.However,it appeared stagnant in eliminating some diseases,such as malaria and tuberculosis. Over half of the world population do not have access to basic medical care,many could not afford medical cost and were stuck into abject poverty.It calls for global collaborations to realize general coverage of basic medical care,and to provide sustained funding support to address the increasing burden of non-infectious diseases including psychological diseases,and to combat the resistance to antibiotic drugs as well as air pollution and drinking water problems.[1]

Healthy living is the eternal pursuit of human society.Safe water and food along with sanitation and health service are indispensable for livelihoods.As a main category of GI products,agri-food GIs provide consumers with quality products that are mostly eco-friendly.To be honest,GI products-being in consistent with the idea of healthy con-

---

[1] Knowledge Platform[EB/OL]. [2020-07-24]. https://sustainabledevelopment.un.org.

sumption because of their optimized production measures-could better satisfy consumers' demands.Although the GI system has nothing to do with health service, GI products are in relation to genuine medicinal materials that are one of the concerns of the GI system,which helps to enhance the health care of all ages of the population.

Medicinal herbs have a long plantation history in China.Market demand for medicinal herbs remains high.It is one of the categories of GI products as well.Given that Chinese traditional medicines play an important role in domestic medicine market,plantation of herbal medicinal materials has long been a big industry having extensive impacts on millions of people.Moreover,it is closely associated with poverty alleviation.

Quality differences do exist among medicinal herbs produced in discrete regions,so are their efficacy and curative effects.It is therefore advised to adopt the so-called 'genuine medicinal materials' (道地药材) that are produced in specific regions.In fact,the idea of genuine medicinal materials corresponds to that of the GI products.To date,several genuine medicinal materials have been protected as GIs by designating producing areas to prevent from counterfeiting and to ensure their characteristics and efficacy.In addition to the case analysis for Lixian Dahuang (Chinese rhubarb) in previous paragraphs, products like Minxian Danggui (Chinese angelica), Huoshan Shihu (dendrobium), Qichun Ay Tsao (Chinese mugwort), Xixia Dogwood (cornel), Fengqiu Honeysuckle have all been protected as GIs in China.Patients manage to take the 'medicine of assurance' that is helpful for the overall progress of traditional Chinese medicines.

Plantation of medicinal herbs is worldwide.Crocus sativus, commonly known as saffron,for example,is an medicinal herbs originated in West Asia.It works in blood-activating and stasis-eliminating,in cooling blood and detoxifying,in relieving depression and calming the nerves,according to traditional Chinese medical theory.Saffron was introduced to the interior regions of China by way of the Qinghai-Tibet Plateau in ancient China.This is way saffron is called Zang Honghua, or Tibetan Saffron,in China whose plantation,however,has been extended to Shanghai and Zhejiang Province in recent years.Saffron is also produced in Afghanistan,Greece,Iran,Morocco and Nepal,to name only a few.It is an important income source for local inhabitants.In China,although saffron is also produced outside Tibet,people always prefer the name 'Tibetan saffron' for any saffron product,making 'Tibetan saffron' a virtually generic name.Consequently,when saffron producers of Tibet Autonomous Region filed the application for GI protection,they had to turn to Tibet Tibetan Saffron for registration purpose to differentiate itself with saffron produced outside Tibet.In 2017, Tibet Tibetan Saffron was registered as a PGI.

Meanwhile,the saffron sector of other countries benefits from the GI system as well.Krokos Kozanis is a renowned Greek saffron protected as PDO in Greece.In Morocco,the annual output of saffron was about 3MTS in 2008,of which 1.8MTS was produced in an area of 560 hectares.The GI process has promoted the building of a sustainable production system and generated positive impacts on the culture, economy and biodiversity as well as saffron-related rural tourism.❶

---

❶ 联合国粮农组织.可持续食品体系的自愿性标准:机遇与挑战[M].王永春,等,译. 北京:中国农业出版社,2019:89.

Taliouine Saffron is a Moroccan GI constituting 95% of national production.The GI system aims to foster local development and to hold back the outflow of rural population of the economically backward regions.Local public policies support organizational constructions of individual household,where 35 cooperatives were set up.Thanks to the sales through the cooperatives,saffron purchasing price rose five times between the year 2000 and 2014.Meanwhile,the purchasing price only increased by 40% for those that did not join the cooperatives.Accordingly,the sales volume dropped by 26% for non‐cooperatives, while that of the cooperatives rose by 10.75 times.The number of cooperatives increased from five in 2000 to thirty‐five by 2014,plus the setting up of an inter‐professional association covering all saffron producers.❶

Rooibos is an aromatic tea product of South Africa with global appeal.Produced in South Africa,it is the only tea product having health notions across the country. Scientists discovered during the 1960's‐1970's that Rooibos was rich in antioxidant content without any caffeine.Thereafter,it has been adopted to relieve symptoms like infant food allergies,dry skin,insomnia and hyperactivity.It also serves as cosmetics for skin care.Rooibos was finally registered as a PGI of South Africa in 2014 after eight‐year research and advocacy.❷

Natural mineral water can be protected as GI in China,where

---

❶ VANDECANDELAERE E,TEYSSIER C,BARJOLLE D,et al,Strengthening sustainable food systems through geographical indications‐evidence from 9 worldwide case studies[J/OL]. Journal of sustainable research,2020,2(4):8,16,30,33[2020‐11‐18]. https://doi. org/10. 20900/jsr20200031.

❷ WIPO. Disputing a name, developing a geographical indication[EB/OL]. [2022‐01‐08]. https://www. wipo. int/ipadvantage/en/details. jsp? id=2691.

healthy,clean and mineral-rich natural mineral water is affluent,especially in plateau regions and mountainous areas that are major origins of natural mineral water.Being the Third Pole of the Earth and 'Water Tower of Asia' ,Tibet is rich in glaciers,rivers and lakes,together with water sources of natural mineral water.With its water source at an altitude of 5,100 meters,Qumalong Mineral Water is originated from the north region of Damxung Fault Basin,Gongtang,Damxung County,Tibet Autonomous Region,where Nyenchen Tanglha Range is situated in the south. The mineral water, with an annual output capacity of 200,000MTS,is rich in meta silicic acid,lithium,strontium,which well meets the national standard.Qumalong Mineral Water was registered as a PGI in November 2009.The specification provides that the seven mouths of spring are located at an altitude above 5,000m,while the maximum daily pumping capacity is set at 3,000m^3.Detailed protective measures are in place to prevent the water source from being polluted.❶ Qumalong Mineral Water stands for China's GI protection for natural mineral water.It helps to provide quality and healthy drinking water while fulfilling conservation of water resources.

---

❶ For the announcement on the protection of Qumalong Mineral Water geographical indication,See:Announcement No. 109 of 2009 on the GI Protection of Qumalong Mineral Water,AQSIQ.

Chapter 4≫
The GI system enhances economic growth and social equality

Section 1 The GI system promotes gender equality

Goal 5. Gender equality

Gender equality is a symbol of social civilization. Yet gender inequality widely exists around the world. The *Little Data Book on Gender* 2019 published by the World Bank points out that despite the progress made especially in education and health,the achievement is unbalanced. Gender inequality is serious in low‑income countries,particularly in the Sub‑Sahara regions.

Gender inequality is displayed in various forms,

one of which is the job discrimination against females that deprives them of the right to work.In some underdeveloped countries,women are only engaged in household chores or simple labor,lacking the ability to achieve financial independence.It calls for joint efforts of the whole society to change this situation.Possible solutions may include the extension of female employment and improvement of their working skills to meet the discrete demand.

Handicrafts are important components of GI products in many countries.It is estimated that about 60% of Indian GIs are textile and handicraft products.[1] In China, embroider, hand knitting and pottery products can be protected as GIs.And regardless of time changes,females are,owing to their aptitudes,the key players of handicraft making.Woman's participation has enhanced GIs' inheritance and development.It plays a positive role in gender equality that is of special significance.

To sum up,GI promotes gender equality in the following respects,

1. Enhancing female employment and fostering financial independence

GIs are predominantly agri-food products and handicrafts,among which agricultural GIs are mostly cash crops, vegetables and under-forest products that often imply light physical labor fitting for female's participation.In addition, field management and food processing demand attentiveness and endurance that are supposed to be female's advantage.In fact,the food industry has employed large number of fe-

---

[1] BAGADE S B, METHA D B, Geographical Indications in India: Hitherto and challenges [J]. Research journal of pharmaceutical, biological and chemical sciences, 2014, 5(2): 1235-1236.

males.In the meantime,women account for a large proportion of the agricultural sector as well.It is safe to say that the GI industry has a direct impact on female employment that adds to their economic rewards.

2. Promoting professional education and improving woman's working skills.

The influence of GI protection is not limited to its production and marketing,it helps promote the correlated growth of packaging,logistics and tourism as well.It has the potential to generate a chain effect to the producing area and adjacent region.Light physical labor only stands for a limited part of the GI sector.To implement the specification and to fulfil the tasks of field management and marketing,it is necessary to carry out training sessions on specific skills.Otherwise,the technical requirements for GI protection could hardly be satisfied.Females could learn and master new working skills that benefit themselves and the whole family.It plays a positive role in improving female education and closing the equity gap.

3. Providing local jobs for rural housewives

Increasing number of rural migrant workers in China are returning to homeland to find jobs or start business for the sake of children's education and health care of the elderly.Women in rural areas are more often expected to look after children and take care of the old.Household duties considerably deter women from going out to work to attain financial independence.GI helps to address the problem in a sensible way,where woman manages to find a job at home that,at her own capacity,does not affect her taking care of the family.Most GI products-agri-food ones-are seasonal.And the making of handicrafts often has no requirement on venue,sometimes it could be done at home.It facilitates female employment by providing seasonal jobs or jobs that fit for working from home.Housewives may opt for jobs out of their own timing and context,engaging in the making of GIs in a flexible manner.As what a maker of Li Brocade (from Hainan Province) says, "Do my embroidery while taking care of children.Make money to bring up my family."❶

Zhenhu is a small town located at the east bank of Lake Tai of Wuxu City,Jiangsu Province.There is a traditional handwork passed down from age to age-Zhenhu Embroidery-a regional sub-branch of the renowned Suzhou Embroidery.Zhenhu used to enjoy long lake banks and crisscrossing rivers in ancient times.The special geographical location made it the main waterway linking the old town of Suzhou with other towns along Lake Tai and was highly developed in trade,facilitating the formation and growth of the embroidery sector. Moreover,Zhenhu's location on a peninsula stretching into Lake Tai at the west of Suzhou,with a long and narrow terrain surrounded by water on three sides,helps to preserve the tradition of making embroidery the key side occupation for local housewives since ancient times.Lake Tai moisturizes the town and Zhenhu's embroiders who make their living on embroidery for generations.To protect the skills handed down from ancestors and to inherit this cultural treasure,local government creatively made embroidery technique a subject of local primary schools and applied for GI protection.❷Zhenhu Embroidery has a profound historical and cultural accumulation.Extensive social involvement,

---

❶ See:2020 年 7 月 18 日 CCTV-4 的《中国新闻》。
❷ 何斌,吴森明.对加强传统手工艺品地理标志保护的建议[J].中国检验检疫,2010 (11):19-70.

thanks to the joining of 80,000 female embroiders,lays a solid foundation for the embroidery sector that is paradigmatic for job creation for women.

Qingyang Xiangbao(sachet) is a traditional handicraft of Qingyang City, Gansu Province, its making skills being listed as the First Group of National Intangible Heritages. In April 2014, Qingyang Xiangbao was registered as a PGI.The origin of Xiangbao making was closely associated with the distinctive roles between men and women in the farming culture, when the latter was supposed to be at home weaving and taking care of the family. It is a traditional custom in Qingyang where females would compete in making Xiangbao during the Dragon Boat Festival to present it as a gift of exorcism and blessing.Upon careful observation of source materials at hand,local woman would draw the outline before embroidering it.Then it follows the sequence of paper cutting of the sample,embroidering the pattern on a silk cloth with colorful yarn,and sewing it into a particular shape in which cotton and spice are filled to be a delicate embroidery.Qingyang Xiangbao stands for working families' best wishes for exorcism and blessing.It is an inheritance of original,traditional manual skills and a display of personal technique and wisdom.To date,Qingyang Xiangbao has grown to a local industry with over 200 enterprises and workshops,covering 5 districts and nearly 80 towns of Qingyang City.It was awarded 'Model Base of National Cultural Industry' in 2008.❶

---

❶ 陈亮洲. 蓬勃发展的庆阳香包民俗文化产业 [EB/OL]. (2018 - 03 - 19) [2022 - 01 - 03]. http://wtgdly. zgqingyang. gov. cn/xwzx/ hyxx/content_70981.

In addition to handicrafts, a large number of women are engaged in tea harvesting, traditional medicine making as well as other agri-food sectors in China.

Section 2　The GI system promotes regional economy

Goal 8. Decent job and economic growth

It is a prevalent phenomenon accompanying economic growth and industrialization that people in less developed areas prefer to be migrant workers in developed regions. In China, national statistics reveal that there are as many as 290 million migrant workers, of whom 170 million choose to leave their hometowns, while the rest, approximately 120 million people opt to stay on local labor market, accounting for 41% of the total number. ❶ Each migrant worker, as analyzed by the *Economic Observer*, could earn as much as RMB4,427 yuan, comparing to RMB3,500 yuan for a worker in his hometown...Nevertheless, the number of people who choose to stay home is increasing over the last decade. Statistics show that, between 2011 and 2018, the proportion of local workers increased from 37.25% to 40.12%, and the speed of its annual increase surpassed that of the migrant workers as well.

---

❶ 国家统计局. 中华人民共和国 2019 年国民经济和社会发展统计公报[EB/OL]. (2020-02-28) [2020-04-30]. http://www.stats.gov.cn/tjsj/zxfb/202002/t20200228_1728913.html.

The *Economic Observer* has quoted Li Guoxiang,researcher of Rural Development Institute of China Academy of Social Sciences,as saying that,despite the negative impact of COVID - 19 pandemic when more people opted to return to their hometowns,most people would prefer to go out as migrant workers.He hinted that by the year 2019 the rising rates of local workers were lower than that of the migrant workers,who, according to Li,prefer to go out to work for the following three reasons:

－local job opportunities are limited;

－local wages are lower;

－national policies on urbanization favor such regions as the Yangtze Delta Region and Guangdong - Hong Kong - Macau Greater Bay Areas.What determines the mobility trend is the potential of regional economic growth in the long run.Therefore,the long - term trend of more job opportunities for migrant workers will not necessarily change.❶

Migrant workers have played an important role in promoting economic growth.Yet parallel to it is the massive outflow of young labor force that leads to vacant villages and hollowing-out rural areas,where only the old and children are left.Improved well-being for rural families aided by migrant workers creates new social problems.It remains a hot topic to explore ways for rural population to work locally,to start business or find jobs nearby. 58Tongcheng and Anjuke,two on - line operators in China,released the *Report on Business of Returning Migrant Workers* 2019 - 2020,indicating that,of all the returning migrant

---

❶ 田进.2.9亿农民工的艰难选择:本地就业,还是外出打工? [N]. 经济观察报,2020-06-12.

workers,68.6% prefer to return to their hometowns to start business, while 29.8% opt to stay in cities where they are employed (neither hometown nor provincial capital).Children's education,housing price, job opportunities and family concerns are the primary factors influencing their decisions.Kong Xiangzhi et al (2019) referred to the statistics from the Ministry of Human Resources and Social Security,claiming that,for Quarter 4 in 2017,10.9% of migrant workers who returned home preferred to start their own business.As of January 2018, over 7 million migrant workers returned to their hometowns.❶

Preferential policies have been released to encourage tax deduction and exemption,interest subsidized loans and subsidies for business creation.Nevertheless,it all depends on the backing of local industries, particularly characteristic industries making use of natural resources. Kong Xiangzhi et al.(2019) points out that the four typical forms of business creation for returning migrant workers - family farm,rural online business,leisure agriculture and processing of agricultural products all rely on local characteristic resources.❷ For the less developed regions,it is a way out to eradicate poverty.

Being a city of agriculture in Hubei province,Huanggang has peculiar natural conditions with rich agricultural resources.Nevertheless,its well-known status as the origin of some characteristic products used to be overshadowed by the small scales that had implications on farmers' earnings and regional economy. Five of the eleven districts and counties of Huanggang were designated as the national level pov-

---

❶ 孔祥智,等.农业经济学[M].2版.北京:中国人民大学出版社,2019:78
❷ 孔祥智,等.农业经济学[M].2版.北京:中国人民大学出版社,2019:78-79.

erty-stricken counties, one being designated as the provincial level poverty-stricken county. To change this situation, local government was committed to enhancing product quality by prioritizing the GI strategy to boost the leaping growth of its rural economy.

First, they integrated GI protection with the industrialization of local agriculture. With GI products as the link and leading enterprises as the passage, agricultural issues were redirected by industrial ideas that aimed to coordinate farmers with market by promoting the model of 'GI + leading enterprise + farmers', which contributed to upgrading rural economic structure and alleviating poverty in mountainous areas. Luotian Chestnut, a GI product, attracted 3 processing plants after its registration. The overall chestnut plantation areas reached 70,000 hecters with an annual output of 30,000 MTS, topping the rank of counties in China. Meanwhile, the chestnut-related products attained RMB700 million-yuan worth of total value, accounting for 40% of local agricultural output, with a per capita chestnut income of RMB1,000 yuan. The chestnut sector turned into the most dynamic force for Luotian's growth.

Second, they integrated GI protection with the branding strategy, export-oriented agriculture and leisure agriculture. Thanks to Yingshan Tea-a PGI-Yingshan County developed the Mount Wuyun Tea Park that emerged as a key ecotourism site of Dabie Mountains.

Third, they incorporated GI protection with upgrading agricultural efficiency and farmers' income. As a means to strengthen the protection of characteristic products and to upgrade their quality and competitiveness, the idea of GI was blended in local manufacturing enterprises, where they "make use of the GI to scale up the industry and benefit local residents". Thanks to GI protection, Huangzhou Turnip was sold by each stick against by 'a pile' as it used to be, making it a new way for farmers to get rich.❶

Sichuan is one of the main provinces with the largest outflow of migrant workers, where millions of people would go out to find jobs every year. By improving the well-being of families, though, most migrant workers are bound to return home. The GI protection strategy, which has played a positive role in promoting local employment and income gains, was regarded as one of the solutions.

Rural population accounts for a large proportion in Sichuan Province. As of 2019, the number was 38.7 million❷, causing severe unemployment problems. Local government agencies, realizing the roles of the GI system for rural revitalization and development, campaigned for GI protection and succeeded in making Sichuan's PGI products lead the country in quantity and in exploring new ways for rural employment. Upon its registration as a PGI in 2008, Pujiang Queshe's (a tea product) plantation and production were regulated, followed by improved added value and brand popularity. Meanwhile, rural tourism gained momentum, along with the packaging and logistics sectors. As many as one million tourists paid visits annually. An increasing number of farmers turned to local jobs from the tea sector, whereby their earnings were considerably raised.

In the aftermath of GI registration in 2005, Hanyuan Huajiao (Chinese prickly ash) gained momentum by adopting the policy of act-

---

❶ See:2009年10月27日,湖北省黄冈市人民政府代表应红在地理标志产品保护实施十周年纪念会议上的发言。
❷ See:《四川省2019年国民经济和社会发展统计公报》。

ing according to local circumstances to plant Chinese prickly ash wherever possible,and industrial planning of the GI sector that unified layout of the whole county.It designated the core areas between the altitude of 1,200m and 2,500m,focusing 63 poor villages and extending to all the county's mountainous areas.Plantation of Chinese prickly ash grew to 6,927 hectares since 2012.As of 2021,the total plantation was as much as 13,600 hectares with an output volume of 25 million kilograms - equivalent to 5 million kilograms of dried Hanyuan Huajiao with a worth of RMB2.6 billion yuan. Meanwhile migrant workers from Ganzi Autonomous Prefecture,and some counties and dicturicts Liangshan Autonomous Prefecture, Yunnan Province and Guizhou Province would come to harvest Hanyuan Huajiao between July and September - creating more than 30,000 jobs with earnings totaling RMB 200 million yuan.

GI protection helps to create jobs in the following aspects.

(1) The labor-intensive nature creates more jobs

GIs stand for high value-added products that are in relation with every stakeholder of the supply chain.Being mostly agri-food products,the GI sector often demands large labor force and high labor intensity.Food processing is a typical labor-intensive sector.Whereas for agricultural products,although individual household usually does not hire extra workers,there is labor demand for harvesting,screening,sorting as well as packaging.Wang Xiaobing (2019) argues that "GIs' capacity to sustain price surplus not only increases agricultural income, but the sector also creates more jobs thanks to the labor-intensive nature."❶ Liu Zhongjun (2014) claims that "GI protection for Dujiangyan Kiwi Fruit has created jobs for 32,000 workers with annual per capita income of RMB7,000 yuan. Meanwhile, Pixian Bean Paste, also a PGI in Sichuan, has attracted as many as 100 firms joining in its production, boosting the prosperity of both upstream and downstream suppliers as well as the parallel sectors. It accentuates large scale production and cluster effect of the GI brand."❷

(2) GI-related sectors create more non-agricultural jobs

During President Xi Jinping's visit to Ningxia Hui Autonomous Region in June 2020, he addressed that "by working at home place, villagers manage to save costs for accommodation, meals and traffic, although they may earn less than working in cities. Meanwhile, they can take care of their families."❸ The influence of GI protection is not confined to local production and operation. The geographical feature of a GI product is typical cultural and tourist resource. It offers extra meaning to the GI product, along with its ecological contribution. GI protection gives rise to rural tourism and multiple cultural experiences, driving local inhabitants to take part in catering, accommodation, traffic, tourist guide and other entertainment activities that enable them to be better off at home places.

Fujian Province, home to some of the most famous teas - Anxi TieKuanyin, Wuyi Yancha (Wuyi Rock Tea), Lapsang Souchong - has a

---

❶ 王笑冰. 经济发展方式转变视角下的地理标志保护[M]. 北京: 中国社会科学出版社, 2019:37.
❷ 刘忠俊. 成都推动地理标志发展促进民众就业增收[EB/OL]. (2014-04-23)[2021-08-15] http://www.chinanews.com.cn/df/2014/04-22/6091613.shtml.
❸ "让人民群众奔着更好的日子去"——习近平总书记考察四川纪实[EB/OL]. (2020-06-11)[2021-12-04]. http://www.sohu.com/a/556107970_121400326.

rich tea culture.GI protection helps to bring its advantage in resources into full play. Good plantation and meticulous making have extended the tea sector's supply chain to tea processing industry. Starting from tea making,it proceeds to tea drinks,tea - related products and all the way to the display of tea culture,tea art,tea house and tea tourism. It forms a traditional supply chain of tea making,processing and equipment production on the one hand;and related sectors of tourism,exhibition,Expo and traffic services on the other.❶

(3) GI jobs are unfettered by gender and age

The agri - food GI sector,as far as employee is concerned,often does not have special requirement on educational background. Even traditional manual skills such as embroidery making,and weaving are suitable for females to master by training.Meanwhile,agricultural production is generally not constrained by gender and age.It means that local GI sectors may act accordingly to mobilize more people join in the process,doing whatever they can. Fuping Shibing (Fuping Dried Persimmon) is a GI produced in Fuping County, Shaanxi Province, where fresh persimmons are usually dried in the courtyard of each family.Whereas some of the skills,e.g.,kneading and reshaping,are usually done by the elderly and females.It is a traditional way preserved so far with many senior villagers joining in the process and passing on useful skills to the young.Some of them even have joined in the webcast activities to introduce Fuping Shibing,creating a novel phenomenon of the persimmon sector.

---

❶ See:福建南平顺昌县质量技术监督局地理标志产品保护交流材料。

Section 3   The GI system helps reduce inequalities

Goal 10. Reduced inequality

Goal 10 aims at reducing inequalities both within and between countries.Inequalities are widespread in both developed and developing countries.A report of the United Nations claims that unemployment with no income source caused by COVID-19 is adding to global inequalities,resulting in social and economic crisis. The COVID - 19 pandemic has led to dramatic increase of unemployment or semi-unemployment and huge losses for many sectors.It challenges countries' ability to respond and capacity to recover its economy.The least developed and other developing countries suffer more severe consequences that damage the already fragile economy and threaten the efforts made for poverty reduction.❶

In China,the Report of the 19th Session of CPC states that the socialism with Chinese characteristics is entering a new era, when the main contradictions of the society have transformed to people's increasing demand for better life verses the unbalanced and insufficient development.President Xi Jinping,at a forum with economic and social experts on Aug.24,2020,points out that China still faces outstanding

---

❶   Knowledge Platform[EB/OL]. [2020-07-24]. https://sustainabledevelopment. un. org, July 24,2020.

problems of inequalities and insufficiency. The creative ability cannot meet the demand of high-quality development. The agricultural basis is still unstable. Economic disparities exist amid urban, rural and regional development. Ecological and environmental protection has a long way to go. There are shortages in ensuring people's livelihood and social governance.❶

Zhang Zhanbin (2017) argues that inequalities are in relation to three aspects-economic inequality, social inequality and institutional inequality, whereas economic inequality includes inequality of sectors, inequality between domestic regions and inequality of dynamics.❷ Regional development is unbalanced for China's eastern, central and western regions. In some areas, the gap between the east and west is widening. By analyzing the quality of regional development, we may find that, in some regions, unbalanced industrial structure is widespread. Some sectors have consumed too many resources yet perform poorly in quality and efficiency. Meanwhile inequality between urban and rural population is more obvious in terms of income and consumption.

Causes vary when it comes to the unbalanced regional development. As discussed in previous paragraphs, backward regions are normally located in remote areas, where access to traffic is poor, where there is a shortage of human resource and backing from industries. It is true that local government would strive to attract investment, releasing preferential policies to bring in talents. The key appeal lies in its advantage in natural resources, plus low labor cost and preferential poli-

---

❶ See: 习近平总书记于 2020 年 8 月 24 日在经济社会领域专家座谈会上的讲话。
❷ 张占斌. 正确认识中国新时代的社会主要矛盾[J]. 人民论坛, 2017(31):2.

cies on land and taxation.With the tightening of environmental policies in China,mining and chemical projects are facing stringent controls.It is thus increasingly difficult to survive by adhering to these natural resources.The only way out points to the rational utilization of other local natural resources to deliver characteristic products.And sectors like cultural and tourism may get developed alongside.To sum up,the GI system may help address inequality problems in the following ways.

1. Enhancing industrial restructuring, quality benefits and scaling up of local characteristic sector

Promoting the growth of characteristic industry is one of the main objectives and advantages of the GI system.It starts with the finding of a characteristic product,followed by measures that normalize management, optimize allocation of resources,enhance quality benefits and build up the GI brand.It enhances quality benefits and scales up the characteristic industry.In the meantime,it helps to balance the environmentally harmful sector,restructuring it towards sustainable development.

Fushun,Liaoning Province,is one of the 32 resource - exhausted cities published by the State Council in 2009.Fushun used to be a city largely dependent on coal mining,implying an excessive proportion of the secondary industry and a weak primary and service sector.To foster economic transition towards sustainable development,Fushun Municipal Government was committed to restructuring industries and strengthening the role of agriculture by maximizing its advantages in extensive forest coverage with rich under-forest resources.Ten characteristic products were approved as PGIs that brought about considerable economic benefits.Meanwhile the green development by rational use of forest resources enhanced forest-related industries involving under-forest plantation,farming and processing.It has protected the ecosystem and directed the forest economy towards scaling up,standardized and industrialized growth,transforming the ecological advantage to development advantages.❶

Shiping is a remote county in Yunnan Province.Despite its inferior location,Shiping Tofu is popular in Yunnan,thanks to the unique underground water of the producing area that is used as coagulants for tofu making.Shiping Tofu has a history of 400 years and is famous for this unique characteristic. In December 2012, Shiping Tofu was approved as a PGI.❷ As of 2018,a total of 200,000 MTS,or RMB2.36 billion worth of Shiping Tofu products were produced. More than 9,000 workers were employed.In line with the layout of local government,a bean processing zone was built up,along with the Shiping Tofu Cultural and Industrial Park and Shiping Tofu Innovation Park.The Shiping Tofu sector managed to transform from scattered making to clustered production,where the industrial layout was increasingly optimized.Thanks to the technology progress,the Shiping Tofu sector advanced toward deep processing with an extension of the value chain and rise of added value.❸ Shiping Tofu is getting popular in China.It could be spotted in supermarkets across the country.It shows that the characteristic industry based on local resources has a strong vitality.Its popularity owes to the unique characteristics tied to local natural and human factors that lead to the booming of Shiping Tofu industry.The

---

❶ See:http://www. fushun. gov. cn/.
❷ See:Announcement No. 218 of 2012 on the GI Protection of Shiping Tofu,AQSIQ.
❸ 云南石屏大力发展豆腐产业[EB/OL]. (2019-10-09)[2020-04-23]. http://www. shipingdoufu. com/2019-10-09.

healthy growth of characteristic industry helps to resolve the inequality problems and provides lessons for other disadvantaged regions.

2. Boosting rural development and creating more jobs

GI's regional features imply that it is primarily geared to the needs of rural areas.The Report of the 19th Session of CPC Plenary states that the problems of agriculture,rural areas and farmers-the so-called Three Rural Problems-are essential problems of national economy and people's livelihood,which must be dealt with as the key issues of the Party that is committed to implementing the strategy of rural revitalization.In September 2018,the CPC Central Committee and the State Council jointly issued the *Plan for the Rural Revitalization Strategy*(2018-2022). On September 21,2018,the CPC Politburo convened the 8th Group Study focusing on rural revitalization,when President Xi Jinping emphasized that rural revitalization was a major strategy carried out by the 19th Session of CPC Plenary and a historical task for the construction of a modern socialist country-an impetus to tackle the Three Rural Problems in the new era.Chapter Six of the *Plan for the Rural Revitalization Strategy*(2018-2022) proposes to make decisive progress by 2035 in rural revitalization and basically realize modernization of agriculture and rural regions.It proposes that the rural structure should be fundamentally improved,rural employment quality dramatically upgraded,relative poverty further alleviated and steady steps taken towards common prosperity.Moreover,local civilization and customs are expected to reach a new height and rural governance further improved,plus a fundamental improvement in rural ecological environment and general realization of beautiful countryside that is ecological and livable.The GI system may play an important role in enforcing the

Plan for the Rural Revitalization Strategy (2018 - 2022), especially when it comes to what is stated as a quality agriculture, green development, rural culture and poverty eradication.

Land is farmers' essential source of income that is subject to many constraints, among which low productivity, small scale and high cost are the notable ones. In China, the Household Contract Responsibility System with remuneration linked to output has been in practice for over 40 years. It has played a key role in motivating farmers to end poverty and add to their earnings. That said, defects gradually emerge along with social and economic progress. It separates the working unit into one household that is too scattered, causing inefficiency in land uses. The small scale, less productive, uneconomical status is also unfitful for agricultural equipment. Jiang Shanshan (2011) argues that "farmers always get less through farming than going out to work. The key to resolve this problem is to encourage them to join in the cooperatives that empower mass production and spontaneously integrate with the market."❶ It is necessary to scale up and intensify production to overcome the less productive, inefficient way by a single family. With the Law of the People's Republic of China on Professional Farmers Cooperatives being promulgated in July 2007, farmer professional cooperatives have been set up based on the Household Contract Responsibility System with remuneration linked to output, where producers and operators or service providers of an agricultural product voluntarily get united to manage the organization in a democratic manner. The co-

---

❶ 江珊珊,黄雅虹,高定慰,等.农民收入问题调查报告[EB/OL].(2011-07-28)[2020-11-11]. https://wenku.baidu.com/view/87c0f9c10522192e453610661ed9ad51f11d54ec.html.

operatives provide services for every member,ranging from the purchase of agricultural materials to product processing,storage,marketing and logistics as well as technical assistance.As of 2017,there were 1.93 million cooperatives in China,covering more than 100 million households.❶

  The GI system encourages to establish professional farmer cooperatives for each GI product,which‐by unifying the purchase and use of agricultural materials,by unifying breeds and plant varieties,by unifying plantation,harvesting,logo and marketing‐ensure GI's characteristics and enhance the added value and competitiveness of the GI product.As discussed in the previous chapter,GI is a collective right that calls for extensive participation of farmers and other stakeholders.By inspiring common consciousness of individuals,we can give full play to GI's collective roles and collective rights.Meanwhile,good implementation of GI measures will guarantee the characteristics and raise its added value by selling at higher prices‐a reward for GI stakeholders.Global GI practices have proved it.

  Nyingchi is a city located in the southeast of Tibet Autonomous Region.It has an altitude of nearly 3,000 m, the lowest altitude in Tibet.Nyingchi is rich in water and forest resources,with plenty of trees,rivers,snow mountains and glaciers.Its natural beauty and abundant forest resources make it a perfect pastoral scenery.However,people in Nyingchi failed to enjoy much economic benefit until recent years when the Municipal Government of Nyingchi furnished the strategy of "building a quality city by developing under‐forest characteristic industry and initiating GI protections as a means to create the image of Nyingchi's regional

---

❶ 孔祥智,等.农业经济学[M].2版.北京:中国人民大学出版社,2019:180.

brand". To date, there are ten PGIs in Nyingchi, ranging from Nyingchi Pine Mushroom, Nyingchi Tianma (rhizoma gastrodiae) to Nyingchi Lingzhi (glossy Ganoderma), etc. The GI system has dramatically unleashed people's enthusiasm to join in the characteristic sector. It adds to local rural employment and contributes to sustainable rural development, let alone income gains for local farmers.

Pine mushroom is considered king of mushrooms. Gongbogyamda County, Nyingchi, has unique microclimate and rich forest resources where quality pine mushrooms grow. Yet people used to collect mushrooms and sell randomly without any management. Soon after Nyingchi Pine Mushroom was approved as a PGI, cooperatives specializing in collecting and processing were set up. A processing base was built, where freeze-drying equipment and freezers as well as logistic machines were deployed for purchasing, processing, packaging and unified marketing of pine mushrooms. As of 2020, shareholders of the cooperatives had grown from 5 to 167 with real asset value of RMB43.6 million yuan, and an annual output of RMB11 million-yuan, net annual profit RMB1.63 million yuan. The pine mushroom sector employed as many as 300 farmers whose annual per capita income rise was RMB37,000 yuan. The cooperatives created a radiation effect for 4,600 farmers from 1,600 families, adding RMB2,800 yuan to per capita income.[1]

---

[1] 西藏工布江达:深山走出"致富菇"[EB/OL].(2020-07-17)[2020-07-23]. http://tibet. news. cn. /xzwy/2020-07/17c_139219577. htm.

3. Upgrading consumption and improving insufficient consumption

Economic disparity is also reflected in insufficient consumption. Consumers' rising demand calls for improved supply chain and quality products. Zaccai. E (2012) argues that marketing management is to identify the segment market and target market.❶ Being a quality product with characteristics and a consuming product with high added value, GI's target market is the high - and - medium - income population. It meets the discrete demands of the niche market. Emilie Vandecandelaere *et al* (2020) argue that "consumers may identify something special from the GI logo and thereby inspire their willingness to pay."❷ A survey shows that consumers of EU Member States would generally pay 15% to 30% more for GI products. The case in China is similar, where GI products are normally sold at prices higher than products alike. The price surplus could be interpreted by the idea of brand impact. Yu Jixing (1996) argues that brand is more like a reputation.❸ Wei Junying and Ren Zhongfeng (2013) claim, as a generalization, brand is a guarantee and confidence to consumers and a responsibility to producers. The strength of such a hint determines the strength of brand impact and brand competitiveness.❹ GI products stand for quality local produce

---

❶ 扎卡伊. 可持续消费、生态与公平贸易[M]. 鞠美庭,展刘洋,薛菲,等,译. 北京:化学工业出版社,2012:6.

❷ VANDECANDELAERE E, TEYSSIER C, BARJOLLE D, et al. Strengthening sustainable food systems through geographical indications-evidence from 9 worldwide case studies[J/OL]. Journal of sustainable research,2020,2(4):19[2020-11-18]. https://doi.org/10.20900/jsr20200031.

❸ 俞吉兴. 市场价格[M]. 北京:中国商业出版社,1996.

❹ 卫军英,任中峰. 品牌营销[M]. 北京:首都经济贸易大学出版社,2013:21.

with characteristics.It conveys definite messages to consumers,pledging GI's quality and reputation and adding to consumer trust.The medium and high - end consumers are therefore more likely to buy GI products to satisfy their needs for green and healthy livelihoods,which, to certain extent,helps relieve insufficient consumption.

Section 4 The GI system benefits sustainable production and consumption

Goal 12. Sustainable consumption and production

In its review of the implementation for Goal 12,the United Nations states that global material consumption is scaling up,threatening the achievement of SDGs. Countries should take actions to ensure today's material consumption will not lead to excessive extraction of natural resources and damage of environment, which, inter alias, includes policies covering all economic sectors to improve the utilization of resources and to reduce waste.It states that sustainable consumption and production aim to reduce energy consumption,and upgrade quality. It aims to reduce the life - cycle resource consumption,environmental degradation and pollution to increase the net welfare benefit of economic activities.Sustainable consumption and production require comprehensive involvement and collaboration from all actors of the supply chain,including consumers' acceptance of sustainable consumption pattern,along with messages delivered through standards and labels..."[1]

This is another goal concerning resource management.Compared with Goal 1 and Goal 2,Goal 12 emphasizes the role of developed countries.As is stated by the UN, "all countries take action,with developed countries taking the lead,taking into account the development and capabilities of developing countries."[2]

Agenda 21 adopted by the Rio Summit of United Nations Conference on Environment and Development(UNCED)in 1992 deliberates the two main factors affecting global sustainable development-the excessive population increase of developing countries and excessive consumption and wastes of developed countries.Chapter 4 of *Agenda* 21 is entitled 'Changing Consumption Patterns',which focuses on the unsustainable patterns of production and consumption,studying national policies and strategies to encourage changes of the patterns.Paragraph 4.3 says, "Poverty and environmental degradation are closely interrelated.While poverty results in certain kinds of environmental stress,the major cause of the continued deterioration of the global environment is the unsustainable pattern of consumption and production,particularly in industrialized countries,which is a matter of grave concern,aggravating poverty and imbalances." Paragraph 4.5 states, "Changing consumption patterns will require a multipronged strategy focusing on demand,meeting the basic needs of the poor,and reducing wastage and the use of finite resources in the production process." Paragraph 4.8 further states, "All countries should strive to promote sustainable consumption patterns;Developed countries should take the lead in achie-

---

[1][2] Knowledge Platform[EB/OL]. [2020-07-24]. https://sustainabledevelopment.un.org.

ving sustainable consumption patterns." Paragraph 4.15 requires "reorientation of existing production and consumption patterns that have developed in industrial societies and are in turn emulated in much of the world." It points out that changing production and consumption patterns are relevant to industries,governments,households and individuals.To minimize the generation of wastes, Paragraph 4.19 calls for "Governments,together with industry,households and the public,should make a concerted effort to reduce the generation of wastes and waste products".Paragraph 4.24 argues that "without the stimulus of prices and market signals that make clear to producers and consumers the environmental costs of the consumption of energy,materials and natural resources and the generation of wastes, significant changes in consumption and production patterns seem unlikely to occur in the near future."While Paragraph 4.27 refers to the role of women,saying that "particular attention should be paid to the significant role played by women and households as consumers and the potential impacts of their combined purchasing power on the economy."❶

This book so far has probed into the roles of the GI system for resource allocations.Next,we will discuss the relations between GI and green development,sustainable production and consumption.

In China,the Report of the 19th Plenary of CPC proposes to set up a legal framework and policy guideline for green production and consumption,and to transform the economic system toward green and low-carbon development. It opposes waste and luxurious, irrational consumption.Instead,it advocates simple,moderate,green and low-carbon

---

❶ See:https://sustainabledevelopment. un. org/milestones/unced/agenda21.

lifestyles.In August 2020,President Xi Jinping made remarks on practicing economy and combating waste,pointing out that food waste is appalling and heart-broken.We must reinforce campaign and education to breed a thrift culture and create a vibe that despises waste and lauds saving.❶

  Responsible and sustainable consumption signifies minimizing the use of natural resources to reduce the negative impact on environment from human activities.It aims to meet people's needs with the least resources available.Xing Xiufeng (2013) analyzes the characteristics of a resource saving society,arguing that "the so-called resource saving society means the social and economic development should be built based on resource and energy savings.Comprehensive measures should be put in place covering all spectrums of human society to minimize resource and energy consumption so as to obtain the maximum social and economic benefits."It could be analyzed,as is claimed,by the three tiers of firms,regions and society,of which the society-a resource saving society-ranks on top.It is supposed to abandon extravagant consumption and waste.It advocates a rational,moderate,civilized way of life that is favorable for the healthy consumption mode.❷ To achieve this objective,production patterns must be improved to uplift efficiency.And consumption ideas must be transformed to pursue a green and healthy lifestyle. Next, it requires rational pursuit for material needs, which refers to the breeding of responsible and sustainable consump-

---

❶ 习近平作出重要指示强调 坚决制止餐饮浪费行为切实培养节约习惯在全社会营造浪费可耻节约为荣的氛围[EB/OL].(2020-08-11)[2021-12-04].https://baijiahao. baidu. com/s? id=1674703781602657821&wfr=spider&for=pc.

❷ 刘爱军.生态文明研究[M].济南:山东人民出版社,2013:151-152.

tion vibes to reduce waste and carbon emissions along with consumption of non‑renewable energies.

Yang Jiadong and Qin Xingfang (2000) define sustainable consumption as "being in conformity with the principle of inter‑generation justice and justice within a generation,ensuring a consumption that helps to attain sustainable development and elevating human livelihoods from lower level to higher levels".They divide sustainable consumption into three forms‑the material,spiritual and ecological forms. Meanwhile,sustainable development is interpreted by two senses‑the general sense and the narrow sense.In general,it is composed of the consumption of natural resources, production materials, commodities and labors,including traveling,cultural and service consumption.While the narrow sense only refers to commodity,labor and natural resource. "Countries at different development levels hold distinct views about environment.Wealthy countries would pay more attention to environmental protection."❶ Sun Qinan and Wang Jinnan (2001) argue that sustainable consumption refers to the goods and services purchased by a family,a company or public entity,which,while meeting their needs for food,accommodation,transportation,entertainment and communication,are ultimately expected to reduce the whole life cycle environmental damages brought about by goods and services.❷ Zaccai (2002) argues that the idea of sustainable development stems from the rising global consumption and its impact on the ecosystem.What a responsible consumer shoulders is concrete action that relies on his daily con-

---

❶ 杨家栋,秦兴方. 可持续消费引论[M]. 北京:中国经济出版社,2000:172.
❷ 孙启宏,王金南. 可持续消费[M]. 贵阳:贵州科技出版社,2001:9‑10.

duct and executive capacity.❶ Other conceptions in relation to sustainable and responsible consumption may include 'Green Consumerism' and the sharing economy. Green Consumerism calls on consumers not to buy goods that may pollute and damage the ecosystem via processing and consuming. Sun Qihong and Wang Jinnan (2001) quote John Elkington and Julia Hailes' *Guide to Green Consumers*, published in 1988, as saying that consumers are reminded of the ways to make contributions to environmental protection through their own purchasing conducts.❷ In tandem with this, sharing economy came into being in recent years and has made its presence in multiple areas of daily life. Apart from bike sharing and car sharing, sharing economy has been extended to exchange of goods, house sharing, meals sharing, so on and so forth.

The *Cambridge Dictionary* defines sharing economy as an economic system that is based on people sharing possessions and services, either for free or for payment, usually using the internet to organize this. China reportedly has the most developed sharing economy, accounting for as much as 10% of its GDP that is higher than any other country in the world. In 2020, China secured as many as 830 million sharing economy users with a trade volume of 470.6 billion euros.❸

Some sharing behaviors in daily life are not confined to on-line rental services. In Germany, for instance, the two parties may negotiate the use of an object-either a book or a drill-that is handed over time

---

❶ 扎卡伊.可持续消费、生态与公平贸易[M].鞠美庭,展刘洋,薛菲,等,译.北京:化学工业出版社,2012:3,130.
❷ 孙启宏,王金南.可持续消费[M].贵阳:贵州科技出版社,2001.
❸ 德朗格拉德.中国,共享经济王国[N].参考消息,2021-12-16(15).

on-line.The borrower does not pay for the service at all.Another example is house sharing where,at the owner's will,the tenant sometimes may not have to pay for accommodation.It means that sharing activity may not be profit oriented.Instead,it aims to make better use of idle resources to reduce waste and any consumption that is deemed unnecessary.It is claimed that sharing economy could be an activity for which the organizer provides internet platform,participants provide personal information,habits and preferences as well as desired content of the sharing act.It could be the common exchange of commodities-a book, a tool-or even clothes or a room.What's more,it could be dishes prepared by a housewife who wants to share with others.To be honest, such practices are somewhat beyond common perceptions of the sharing economy.They embody the idea of sustainable consumption and are aimed at maximizing the utilization of commodities.Now that it is less relevant to the theme of this book,it will not be discussed in detail.

The idea of sustainable consumption is entering our daily life, whereas some of the commodities may be in relation to GI products. The 26th UN Framework Convention on Climate Change Conference of the Parties (COP26) held in Glasgow,UK rendered a notable detail that displayed the carbon footprint of each dish by the supplier,which, aided by other firms,calculated the specific impact of each food on the climate.The calculation had taken the greenhouse gas emissions of every phase of food production-from plantation to processing to transportation-into account,with consideration of national and local market data.It showed that low carbon food-based on vegetation-emitted an equivalence of 0.1-0.5 kg CO_2 per kilogram,whilst high carbon food produced 1.6 kg.Low carbon foodstuffs always adopted seasonal materials that were mostly local produce undergoing short-distance transport.❶ Meanwhile local produce and local consumption are prominent advantages of GI products,which coincides with the low carbon demand.

Honestly speaking,the mindset-shaping of low carbon and environmentally friendly consumption is subject to social and economic development.*Can Kao Xiao Xi* has cited a report from the *Washington Post* in saying that about 80% of Americans in 2019 held that human activities were exacerbating climate change,yet less than 50% of the respondents agreed to make any 'substantial sacrifice' by themselves. According to a survey released by Pew Research Center,about three quarters of residents from the developed world were concerned over the impending disaster brought about by climate change.However,only 55% of Japanese would change their lifestyles to combat climate change-the lowest of all the countries surveyed.Whilst in Sweden,the figure was 85%.The report further indicated that,in general,the younger generation was more concerned about climate change than the old, whereas females were more concerned than males.❷ The result was basically in line with the findings of Yang Jiadong and Qin Xingfang (2000) that argue countries at different phase of development are at odds in terms of environment.Wealthy countries would pay more at-

---

❶ 亚当,韦斯特福尔.COP26菜单将碳足迹计算在内[N].参考消息,2021-11-08 (11).
❷ 丹尼斯,泰勒.皮尤民调发现,全球民众越来越把气候变化视为对个人的威胁[N]. 参考消息,2021-11-05(7).

tention to environmental protection.❶

Being the largest developing country, China is facing an era of mounting consumption.Despite the popularized initiatives of sustainable consumption,material pursuit is on the rise,indicating an ever-expanding consumption scale.Parallel to this is the rising waste of resources that runs in the opposite direction of sustainable consumption.Nevertheless,we must acknowledge it is a problem resulted from development that could only be addressed during the development process.

Zaccai (2012) cites multiple research findings in Europe in interpreting the relations between responsible consumption and demographic factors,which could be summarized as follows:

(1) the demographic factor is not a reliable indicator identifying responsible consumers;

(2) the responsible purchasing behavior is not subject to gender influences;

(3) the higher education seems relevant to more responsible consuming acts;

(4) the income level is the most important factor,the high-income groups being more concerned about environmental-friendliness than the low-income groups.❷

The above findings mirror the general scenarios in European countries,where responsible consumption is yet to be a common preference for the whole society.

---

❶ 杨家栋,秦兴方.可持续消费引论[M].北京:中国经济出版社,2000:172.
❷ 扎卡伊.可持续消费、生态与公平贸易[M].鞠美庭,展刘洋,薛菲,等,译.北京:化学工业出版社,2012:92.

It takes time to transform one's mindset for certain lifestyle.And it calls for concerted efforts to arouse public awareness of sustainable consumption,stimulating individual's motivation for responsible behaviors.Being a scheme highly consistent with such a commitment,the GI system practices the idea of responsible and sustainable consumption in many respects.

Firstly,GI helps to balance information asymmetries between production and consumption.One of the objectives of the GI scheme is to improve the quality assurance system of a GI product,which,inter alias, includes the setting up of a traceability system and emphasizes logo control so as to deliver transparent information.Zaccai (2012) highlights ten contradictions in relation to sustainable consumption,and one of which is that consumers are ignorant of any means to justify whether the product is made in line with sustainable consumption.He argues that it will not be effective if consumers are only reminded of the need to change their consuming habits-and to influence the market.Instead, orientation of public policies and communications could keep working. He remarks on EU's eco label,saying that,compared with the energy label,the eco label does not perform well enough,but it is helpful to reduce the information cost,namely,the time taken for consumers to find a product in conformity with the eco standard.[1] Emilie Vandecandelaere et al (2020) argue that consumers cannot precisely evaluate the quality when buying anything.Dealers may conceal defects of the product, which affects efficient running of the market force. Standardization,

---

[1] 扎卡伊. 可持续消费、生态与公平贸易[M]. 鞠美庭,展刘洋,薛菲,等,译. 北京:化学工业出版社,2012:2,6,92.

controls and labels may balance such market failures, and GI product (through logo, label) enables consumers to get 'quality' information of the product at the place of sale without any sensory examinations.❶

Information on the label and logo of a PGI/PDO is regulated by public policies aiming at protecting consumer rights, raising the credibility of the GI system and maintaining the market reputation of GI product. It "reduces consumers' cost of information and option".❷ Transparent information is helpful for consumers to obtain, before decision making, adequate information about the goods' producing areas, natural condition, reputation, ingredients as well as specific techniques. It enables consumers interested in environmental protection to prioritize their option for GI products. And despite disparities in terms of GI development, most countries have regulated the use of GI logos. Some even stipulate details of the GI label, for which producers are required to provide supplementary information on the origin of raw materials, depictions of the geographical area of origin, among others.❸

Secondly, GI protection may help to achieve fair consumption. Fair consumption refers to, as reviewed by human relations, "the equal right between each individual of this generation and offspring of later generations in his/her pursuit of quality life." No one is entitled to threaten

---

❶ VANDECANDELAERE E, TEYSSIER C, BARJOLLE D, et al. Strengthening sustainable food systems through geographical indications-evidence from 9 worldwide case studies[J/OL]. Journal of sustainable research, 2020, 2(4):4 [2020-11-18]. https://doi.org/10.20900/jsr20200031.

❷ 王笑冰. 经济发展方式转变视角下的地理标志保护[M]. 北京: 中国社会科学出版社, 2019:27.

❸ See: Article 12 of Regulations No 1151/2012 of the European Parliament and of the Council of 21 November 2012.

the well-being and consumption of others because of his own consumption-or fairness within one generation.And the consumption of this generation should not threaten the survival and consumption of later generations-or inter-generation fairness. To be honest,fair consumption is an idea demanding cognitive ability and full consciousness. As far as balancing consumption volume and dropping excessive consumption are concerned,the GI system may indirectly influence one's shopping behaviors that helps to achieve the goal of fair consumption.

  Pricing strategy plays an important role.Sun Qihong and Wang Jinnan(2001) argue that price is a favorable factor for consumption, which guides consumption and directs the behaviors of consumers and producers.A low price may lead to excessive exploitation of natural resources and unsustainable consumption,while a high price may incur decline in trade of natural resources,creating new problems for developing countries relying on export of resources.[1] Yu Jixing (1996) argues that "a reasonable price both stands for the goods' true value and status quo of market supply."He analyzes the cost of agricultural products by material cost and labor cost. Material cost contains, as he claims,the cost of production materials-seed,fertilizer,feeds,fuels,depreciation of fixed assets,etc.,while labor cost includes wages,management fees,insurances,loan interests,etc.To analyze further,labor cost could be divided into direct cost and indirect cost. For instance, plantation's direct labor cost refers to land leveling,sowing,field management,harvest,etc.,while indirect labor cost refers to labor in manure collection,labor at initial stage and operational management as well as

---

[1] 孙启宏,王金南.可持续消费[M].贵阳:贵州科技出版社,2001:18.

marketing.❶ As discussed in previous chapters, agricultural GIs are subject to controls on seed selection, on fertilizer and feed standards, on field management, on harvest and classification. All these control measures are likely to lift costs and push up prices. Presumably, agricultural GIs are sold at higher prices than products alike. Meanwhile, food and handicraft GIs usually demand extra technical requirements that also lead to higher costs. Now that GIs' target market is often high-end consumers, the consuming act for any GI product denotes his/her intent to get better service by paying more. Moreover, such services reflect the ideas of energy saving, emission reduction, consumption reduction as well as the idea of green and organic development.

According to Lai Desheng (2001), waste is generated by three sources - distribution, production and consumption.❷He claims that people would pay more attention to consumption waste than the other two. As far as consumption waste is concerned, the initiator for Zero Waste Movement Italy argues that, compared to the loss in food processing and circulation, waste at the consuming side is more severe.❸ Hannah Ritchie quoted a research paper published on *Nature* by Joseph Poore and Thomas Nemecek (2018) as saying that losses on the world food supply chain and wastes by consumers contributed to 6% of global greenhouse gas emissions.❹

---

❶ 俞吉兴. 市场价格[M]. 北京:中国商业出版社, 1996:3, 66.
❷ 赖德胜. 关注浪费[M]. 北京:中国财政经济出版社, 2001:1.
❸ 意大利"零浪费运动"发起人塞格雷:中国反对浪费食物的行动具有积极意义[EB/OL]. (2020-08-16) [2020-12-20]. https://baijiahao. baidu. com/s? id = 1675168501352290153&wfr=spider&for=pc.
❹ RITCHIE H. Food waste is responsible for 6% of global greenhouse gas emissions[EB/OL]. (2020-03-18) [2021-11-17]. https://ourworldindata. org/food-waste-emissions.

Although there is no proven evidence to back the claim that GI products may help restrain waste,it would be safe to say that,if taking consumer psychology and consumption behaviors into account,quality product with higher price is more likely to trigger consumer's cautious decision,which,in turn,may lead to less waste,and thereby reducing the potential consumption waste.

Chapter 5≫
The GI system helps to protect the ecosystem of the earth

Section 1 The GI system helps combat climate change

Goal 13. Climate action

UN report indicates that "with rising greenhouse gas emissions, climate change is occurring at rates much faster than anticipated and its effects are clearly felt worldwide. While there are positive steps in terms of the climate finance flows and the development of nationally determined contributions, far more ambitious plans and accelerated action are needed on mitigation and adaptation. Access to finance and strengthened capacities need to be scaled up at a much faster rate, particularly for the least developed countries and small island developing States."❶

Goal 13 calls on countries across the globe to take actions to combat climate change and its impacts.In addition to the rising greenhouse gas emissions resulted from industrialization,there are more human factors that have implications on global climate.Population increase,urban expansion,deforestation,extensive agriculture,contamination of ocean and sea waters all contribute to damages to the environment and climate.Climate change is no longer merely an issue in debate.The world is suffering from the pains. More and more people show concerns over possible environmental damages incurred by the goods they consume.

The United Nations Environment Programme(UNEP) cites the report of a joint research on September 1,2020,in saying that if the global food consumption system could be improved by taking actions,it might contribute as much as 20% to the goal of emission reduction by 2050.It claims that,as far as emission reduction of the food sector is concerned,the global focus has been placed on agricultural land and livestock,whereas the negative impact from food consumption and waste is often neglected.As a matter of fact,the value chain of the food system - production,processing,transportation,storage,consumption - accounts for 37% of the total greenhouse gas emissions.Unfortunately, the role of food consumption,namely opting for more sustainable reci-

---

❶ Knowledge Platform[EB/OL]. [2020-07-24]. https://sustainabledevelopment.un.org.

pes-less meat,more vegetables-has generally been disregarded.❶

In previous chapters we have discussed the advantages of the GI system in optimizing resource allocations and in improving mode of production.The following examples may help explain GI's roles in combating climate change.

Madd (Saba Senegalensis) is a yellow,wild fruit growing on the grassland or in the forest of West Africa's Burkina Faso, Senegal, Guinea and Mali,and the fruit growing in Casamance,South Senegal is called Madd de Casamance.Application for GI registration was initiated in 2017 and is expected to be the first wild fruit PGI in West Africa.A wild fruit as it is,local people have given special care to its growing environment,for it is relevant to the well-being of each individual and every family.It is reported that ever since it was picked and sold as a commodity by local people,there has been no forest fire at all,because it is "not just a moral obligation toward the environment;it is a matter of economic self-interest".The application process for PGI coordinated the interests of stakeholders,encouraging them to value such a natural endowment and play a positive role for environmental protection.❷

Pujiang Queshe-the name in Chinese referring to the tongue of a bird-is a famous tea from Sichuan Province.The forest coverage

---

❶ UNDP. Improved climate action on food systems can deliver 20 percent of global emissions reductions needed by 2050[EB/OL]. (2020-09-01)[2020-10-21]. https://www.unenvironment. org/news-and-stories/press-release/improved-climate-action-food-systems-can-deliver-20-percent-global.

❷ WIPO. Supporting environmental sustainability with GIs:the case of Madd de Casamance [EB/OL]. [2021-11-20]. https://www.wipo. int/ipadvantage/en/details. jsp? id = 11582.

in Pujiang County is 48.31%, where the soil and climate fit for tea plantation can be traced over 1000 years back to the Tang Dynasty, indicating a profound agricultural tradition. Pujiang County is also the National Ecological Construction Demonstration Area and one of the origins of Masson Pine. The GI system has contributed to the rapid growth of Pujiang Queshe industry. Firstly, a pilot project of mixed tea plantation under pine trees was accomplished, thanks to the unique natural conditions where tea trees were planted amid Masson Pine trees in mixed, irregular patterns. It is deemed favorable for tea growth because of the shades from pine trees. The mixed plantation makes it possible for tea plants to absorb sufficient nutrition with moderate exposure to sunlight. The tea's quality is thus improved together with its volume. Meanwhile, economic returns from each land unit have made gains as well, and forest coverage increases alongside, creating a win-win scenario for both the tea sector and environmental protection. Secondly, it was the nationwide pioneer in establishing the trusteeship scheme for tea fields and unified pest prevention service. In line with the pattern of 'company-cooperative-base', farmers were encouraged to leave their own fields to a firm to facilitate the unified use of fertilizer and pest prevention skills and to ensure a stable and controlled supply of fresh tea leaves. By improving the management of inputs and technical regulations, they managed to ensure Pujiang Queshe's quality and safety.❶

The roles of GI protection in combating climate change could be

---

❶ See: 成都市质量技术监督局在 2010 年中国地理标志保护与发展论坛经验交流材料。

summarized as follows.

1. Traditional technique helps to reduce greenhouse gas emissions

GI products are prone to traditional techniques and specific skills with limited application of modern equipment, which in turn reduces energy consumption and greenhouse gas emissions. Traditional technique normally refers to hand-made or made with traditional tools and recipes, implying a demand for physical labors, or complex procedures that are less productive. Notable examples in this regard may include the making of Xuan Paper, embroidery, koji - making for Chinese Baijiu, cellaring, distillery, making of rice wine and vinegar as well as vegetable oil extraction. The making of Xuan Paper - the most renowned Chinese paper product exclusively for calligraphy purpose-for instance, is regulated in its specification as follows:

Raw materials:
  Green sandalwood Processing
  Stripping, cooking, soaking, peeling, drying in the sun, and making skin base
  Grass processing
  Sorting grass, cutting, pounding, submerging, cleansing, lime washing, stacking cleansing, drying in the sun, making grass base Cooking, cleansing, spreading in the sun, cooking, cleansing, spreading in the sun, specially treating straw of sandfields

Pulp making:
  Plant skin as raw material
  Making skin base - soaking - cooking - cleansing - pressing - sorting - bleaching - cleansing-pressing-sorting-pounding-cleansing-bleaching sandalwood skin fibre
  Grass
  Specially treating straw of sandfields - cutting the straw of sandfields and removing dust-ramming-cleansing and bleaching-bleaching grass fibre

Mixing ingredients:

Smashing grass-mixing and sorting-stirring and cleansing

Skin of green sandalwood

Paper making:

Adding water to all materials-adding glue-scooping up paper-pressing-baking-selecting-cutting-obtaining end product❶

The above procedures are basically completed manually, for hand-making has contributed to Xuan Paper's characteristics that cannot be replaced by any machine. Given its low productivity, the making of Xuan Paper bucks the trend. But as it retains the paper's unique characteristics, it has won consumers' trust and survived the test of time. That said, GI production does not adhere to tradition blindly by rejecting any advanced technology and innovation. In agriculture, for example, new technology has transformed backward means and tremendously upgraded quality and efficiency of the agricultural sector. Agricultural GIs are often vanguard in adopting state-of-the-art technologies and innovative approaches. Meanwhile GI producers are required to take caution in using pesticides and fertilizers, with a view not to pursuing high yields at the cost of environmental damages. Promoting GI practices against climate change is favorable for energy saving, reduction of emissions and consumption. It inherits traditional culture and helps to reduce the negative impacts on global environment by human activities.

"Harris Tweed is the only fabric in the world governed by its own Act of Parliament. Genuine Harris Tweed bears the Orb Certifica-

---

❶ See: Announcement No. 75 of 2002 on the GI Protection of Xuan Paper, AQSIQ.

tion Mark approved by its custodians the Harris Tweed Authority.This mark guarantees that the tweed to which it is applied has been made from 100% virgin wool which has been dyed and spun on the islands and handwoven at the home of the weaver in the Outer Hebrides of Scotland.Finally, the cloth is returned to the mill on the island for washing and finishing.Only then is the cloth inspected and authenticated by the Harris Tweed Authority with the Orb Stamp."[1] The specific law protects the authenticity of Harris Tweed,which is one of the approaches for traditional handicrafts.Other examples include Bordado da Madeira (porcelain of Portugal), Solingen (cutlery of Germany), etc.[2] Wang Zuishan (2016) argues that Harris Tweed has never changed its hand twisting,dyeing and woven techniques since the last century.It is handmade,using pedal looms without any automatic or electronic equipment. Again, since its raw materials and fuels are all from nature are biodegradable,they absorb the volatile organic compounds and do not induce allergic reaction.Plus,due to its energy saving processing,the negative impact on the ecosystem is minimized.[3]

2. Local raw materials helps reduce carbon emissions and energy consumption

It is mainly in relation to food processing.The processing of agrifood GIs can be divided into two groups:Group One must entirely use local raw materials and must complete the processing in the same area

---

[1] See:https://www. harristweedboutique. com.
[2] 欧盟关于非农产品地理标志保护的研究报告认为,对这三种产品的保护不属于专门法保护,而只是规定了质量技术要求。Study on geographical indications protection for non-agricultural products in the internal market Final report [EB/OL]. (2013-02-18) [2021-12-12],https://ec. europa. eu/docsroom/documents/14897.
[3] See:http://www. 360doc. com/content/16/0403/08/30237147_54749146. shtml

where raw materials grow,such as wine and olive oil;Group Two may adopt both local and non-local materials,as is the case for Chinese Baijiu or rice wine.Group One is produced completely in the origin of raw materials where there is extremely limited logistics,which tremendously drops carbon emission and energy consumption.While Group Two adopts non-local raw materials,though,local ones often account for larger share.To analyze further,agri-food GIs are primarily sold on local market.Many of them,especially fresh ones,almost always give priority to local market and markets nearby.Shiping Tofu,for instance, was sold only in Shiping and regions in proximity to it,and Kunming-the provincial capital city-used to be the farthest city it could reach. Another example is Gangba Sheep-a GI of Tibet-which,despite surging market demand,could hardly satisfy the needs beyond Tibet as a result of restrictions on breeding areas and density of population.In fact, Gangba Sheep is not commonly spotted even on the market of Lhasa. The above cases show that on one hand,fresh agri-food products are often not storage-friendly.It calls for technical solutions to extend their market range.On the other hand,it is relevant to GIs' strict control on quantity and scale. Undoubtedly, such control measures have caused problems for commercialization. Yet GIs' scarcity and small market range could be favorable for reducing greenhouse gas emissions and, consequently,may have positive impact on climate and environment.

La Ruche Qui dit Oui❶is an online platform in France that exclusively serves local agri-food trade-a typical player of local online business.Local farmers and traders can make deals with customers directly

---

❶ See:https://laruchequiditoui.fr/fr/p/provide.

online.The platform charges for 20% from the trade volume as tax and maintenance fee,while the rest 80% of the trade volume is returned to local producers.Local offline outlets set up by the local La Ruche Qui dit Oui are responsible for collecting goods from farmers. Consumers make orders online and get the goods at local offline stores at the appointed time.With a view to promoting and protecting local specialties,it only provides agri-food products produced in the locality, i.e.,within an average distance of 43km between producing areas and the location of each outlet.La Ruche Qui dit Oui stands for a service exclusively for local producers and consumers.Everything is produced in the locality,almost all the consumers are local inhabitants,implying its outlets across France only trade discrete local produce and none of them sells identical goods as others,whilst consumers are all familiar with the goods' characteristics.Producers would only stock by orders and deliver goods to the local outlet.Consumers simply come up to the nearby outlet to get them.This business model resembles online direct sales except that both the source of goods and consumers are in the locality-a positive move for local SMEs and local farmers.Due to the limited scale of local market,this model is apparently not tailored to bulk commodities,which are expected to explore external markets.

3. Ecological agriculture relieves the impact of climate change

Sustainable agriculture is crucial for achieving the SDGs.The Common Agriculture Policy of the European Union (CAP) argues, "Agricultural activity is sustained by good environmental conditions,which allow farmers to harness natural resources,create their produce and earn a living.In turn,the money brought in by agriculture sustains farm families and rural communities,while the foods produced sustain the whole society."❶ Indeed,environmental conditions are essential for sustainable agriculture that is threatened by pollutions from industrialization.Zhang Tianyou (2018) cited the result of an ad hoc survey by the former Ministry of Agriculture over the paddy fields of 88 districts (counties) in Hunan,Hubei,Jiangxi and Sichuan Province,saying that soil contamination of some regions exceeded the prescribed limit,with the most severely polluted areas being 68% above the limit.He further quoted a Gazette published in 2014 by the former Ministry of Environmental Protection and the former Ministry of Land and Resources on the first national survey of contaminated soils,indicating that the soil's heavy metal contamination accounted for 16.1% of the total areas in China,whereas contamination of cultivated land was 19.4% above the limit,of which 1.8% was at medium level,1.1% belonged to heavy pollution.Comprehensive study of multiple surveys shows that the heavy metal contamination of cultivated land accounted for approximately 10% - 15% ,with cadmium pollution being the most prevalent.The contaminated areas are mostly agricultural lands in proximity to industrial firms,plus sewage irrigation areas as well as suburban areas of big cities. "The overall situation of heavy metal pollution is not optimistic.Contamination covers large areas but are not easily seen,so it is a tough task concerning the safety of agri-food producing areas and residents' health.It has become one of the most outstanding issues of agricultural pollution."❷

  Sustainable agriculture relies on green and ecological approaches,

---

❶ EUROPEAN COMMISSION Sustainable Agriculture in the CAP [EB/OL] [2021-01-29]. https://ec.europa.eu/info/food-farming-fisheries/sustainability/sustainable-cap_en.
❷ 张天佐.转变农业发展方式与农业绿色发展[M].北京:中国农业出版社,2018:66.

which is the only way out to combat environmental pollutions. Nevertheless, green and ecological approach often implies high investment with tardy rewards, resulting in farmers' reluctance to follow. Zhang Tianyou (2018) generalizes some of the main causes for farmers' unwillingness to take part in green agriculture, including,

(1) farmers find it hard to meet the requirements of green production due to educational problems and lack of skills;

(2) cost rise in technology deters farmers from adopting green approaches unless incentives or subsidies are put in place;

(3) farmers have little knowledge about green production and are indifferent to it.❶

It shows that there is much to do for local government and inter-professional organizations to strengthen advocacy on green production. In the meantime, there must be some forms of incentives.

Being one of the major categories of global GI practices, primary agricultural GIs can be grouped into either plantation or breeding (livestock) products. Given GI system's strict requirements on environment and techniques, many plantation GIs have obtained organic certifications, where organic fertilizers and feeds are adopted whilst synthetic fertilizers, pesticides or feed additives are dismissed to curb pollutions and reduce energy consumption from pesticides and fertilizers. It is regulated through the specification that always makes explicit requirements accordingly. Cooperatives and inter-professional organizations are key players responsible for the enforcement. Meanwhile the

---

❶ 张天佐. 转变农业发展方式与农业绿色发展[M]. 北京:中国农业出版社,2018:32-33.

administrative agencies are entitled to conduct compliance checks to make sure that mandatory requirements are met. GIs' organic approaches help reduce pollutions and recovery of ecological balances.

In consistent with fertilizer and pesticide control measures, and soil conservation practices, livestock GIs shall observe regulation on ceilings for stocking density, on feeds and on breeding environment. The specification of Damxung Yak-a GI in Tibet-may help explain, which stipulates:

1. Breed

Tibetan Plateau Yak

2. Breeding environment

Altitude: >4200m, with abundant alpine meadows, water source from Sangqu River, Laqu River, Buqu River, Xiugu River and snow melt from nearby mountains.

3. Breeding management

(1) Breeding pattern: grazing on natural grassland

(2) Feeds: natural forage grass in daytime, plus supplementary feeds of local fine and raw fodder after returning.

Key points of Breeding management:

a. Weaning for calf: start from age 6-7 months, separate calves with cows, supplement local dry grass, silage and fine feeds for calves.

b. Fattening in warm seasons: in time of grass growing, yaks are fattened by grazing on natural grassland, where only mineral substances are supplemented.

c. Requirements for slaughtering:

age 5-7 years, weight for living body of cow 180-200kg, ox 250-300kg

4. Environment and safety requirement

Abide by the compulsory requirements of national standards on feeding environment, disease prevention and controls, no damage to the environment.

5. Slaughtering,processing and storage

(1) Criteria for source of yak: healthy yak from the designated areas provided in Clause 1 and Clause 4 of this specifications.

(2) Technical requirements on slaughtering and processing:

a. Rest for slaughtering: stop feeding for 24 hours, stop drinking 3 hours before slaughtering.

b. Slaughtering mode: in line with the local traditional slaughtering method.

c. Acid removal: for 48 hours when yak body is kept at 0-5℃, relative humidity 85% -90%.❶

The breeding and feeding requirements as well as slaughtering mode are all regulated.It embodies a humanitarian spirit of nature conservation and due respect for local customs.

4. Consumption of quality GIs helps achieve SDGs

Food consumption is in relation to dietary habits.A UNEP report is cited in previous chapters that advocates turning our dietary habits to more vegetation food. FAO released the *Statistical Yearbook* 2021 on November 3,2021,claiming that although "greenhouse gas emissions on agricultural land declined by 2% between 2000 and 2019, farm - gate greenhouse gas emissions went up 11%.Around 55% of them are related to livestock".❷

It is a plain fact that some goods of animal origin are from small-scale native breeds raised under free-range or semi-free-range conditions.Large scale livestocks bred in captivity are normally not eligible to apply for GI protection because of their lack of characteristics.Mo-

---

❶ Regarding the Quality and Technical Requirements of Tibetan Plateau Yak, See: Announcement No. 128 of 2016 on the GI Protection of Damxung Yak,AQSIQ.

❷ Statistical Yearbook 2021 [EB/OL]. [2021 - 12 - 20]. https://www. fao. org/3/cb 4477en/online/cb4477en. html.

reover,they do have negative impact on greenhouse gas emissions.That said,it by no means exempts livestock GIs from environmental concerns.It is possible that some GI producers fail to observe the quantity and density requirements.Thus,it calls for sustained surveillance and continuous improvement in breeding technology to curb the negative impacts.Compared to livestock GIs,plant GI products are even larger in number,containing grains,oil crops,vegetables,fruits and various of fresh or processed vegetation foodstuffs.By setting up proper management and traceability scheme,and by reducing the negative impacts on soil,water and environment,the GI system ensures food safety.Therefore,it pays to,in tandem with enhancing public awareness on environmental protection,increase consumption of GIs by encouraging consumers to prioritize their option for GI products,which,to certain extent,contributes to reducing greenhouse gas emissions and achieving the SDGs.

In the case of Fuping Shibing (dried persimmon),for instance,its GI specification is defined as:

(1) plant variety: Fuping pointed persimmon;

(2) site conditions: silt soil from irrigation and flood, yellow soil, cinnamon soil, loessal soil; organic matter content $\geqslant 0.8\%$; pH $7.0 \sim 8.0$; altitude 400m~1000m;

(3) seedling breeding: Diospyros lotus as the rootstock,grafting propagation is done by scion picking on the disease-and-pest-free mother plant of Fuping pointed persimmon;

(4) cultivation management.

a.density: $\leqslant 840$ plants per hectare,plantation according to varied tree shapes and terrain;

b.trimming:done in winter and summer,tree shapes well-structured allowing ventilation and light transmittance;

c.fertilizer application:annual application of decomposed manure no less than 20 MTS per hectare;

d.environment and safety requirement:in conformity with the national regulation on pesticide and fertilizer applications.

(5) harvest

manual picking between mid and late October when the fruit skin appears orange red and fully ripe.

(6) processing

technological process:fruit sorting→washing and peeling→drying naturally→kneading and shaping→cutting off handle and taking off shelf→frost free persimmon→softening→frost persimmon→hanging→kneading→merging

a.fruit sorting:choosing the fruit fully ripe yet not soft,with regular fruit shape, free from disease and pests,unhurt;

b.washing and peeling:fruit base must be less than 1cm after peeling;

c.naturally drying:minimum height to the ground no less than 50cm,perfrming natural solarization in open air for 2-3 days,then coveing by tarpaulin to shield sunlight,air-dring naturally;

d.kneading and shaping:done a week after air-drying when the skin turns white,the flesh a bit soft;kneading by hand to press the flesh for softening;

e.cutting off handle and taking off shelf:done when the flesh is fully soft without hard core,water content $\leqslant 35\%$;cutting off the handle and taking the fruit off the shelf,the product being 'frost free persimmon' ;

f.softening:the dried frost free persimmon should be placed in a container with a cover,then put at cool indoor areas for 4-5 days until it returns soft;

g.storage:storage temperature must be lower than 10℃;storing either at room temperature or in the fridge;the storehouse must be clean and dry with good ventilation;mixed storage with poisonous,hazardous and smelly goods is prohibitted.❶

Presumably, it would be favorable for the reduction of carbon emissions if priority is given to GI products for more consumers' by enhancing public awareness of environmental protection and sustainable consumption.

Section 2　The GI system helps protect marine resources

Goal 14. Life below water

Goal 14 aims to protect and make sustainable use of oceans, sea waters and marine resources. UN report states, "The expansion of protected areas for marine biodiversity and existing policies and treaties that encourage responsible use of ocean resources are still insufficient to combat the adverse effects of overfishing, growing ocean acidification due to climate change and worsening coastal eutrophication. As billions of people depend on oceans for their livelihood and food source and on the transboundary nature of oceans, increased efforts and interventions are needed to conserve and sustainably use ocean resources at all levels."❷

Marine fishing and mariculture have implications on the sustainable use of ocean resources. Oceans account for 70% of the earth's

---

❶　See: Announcement No. 92 of 2008 on the GI Protection of Fuping Shibing, AQSIQ.
❷　Knowledge Platform[EB/OL]. [2020-07-24]. https://sustainabledevelopment.un.org.

surface,and rational use of ocean resources is one of the key components of sustainable development.Marine fishing has a direct bearing on human life,which,along with mariculture and aquatic processing,is usually one of the key sectors for coastal countries and regions.Chen Zuozhi (2008) argues that marine fishing is an important part of global industry that provides jobs for 200 million people and supplies about 19% of the total animal protein for mankind.❶ Accordingly, marine fishing rise is constituting notable negative impact on world ecosystem.The redoubled fishing volume poses severe threat to the survival of ocean lives,for it damages marine biodiversity.Meanwhile the expansion of mariculture exacerbates the pollution of sea waters.Some critics even argue that the side effects of mariculture exceed its actual contributions.❷ John Clark (2000) argues that mariculture is both the plaintiff of pollution and defendant of clean environment.Mariculture's success demands ample supply of clean water.Meanwhile,mariculture may aggravate contamination to the coastal sea waters,reducing their biodiversity.He further claims that global fishery catch is declining,and the output of marine food could hardly maintain the status quo unless effective environmental management is put in place.❸

Being a leading player in mariculture,China excels in mariculture areas and total output. Statistics of the FAO show that as of 2019,

---

❶ 陈作志.捕捞对北部湾海洋生态系统结构与功能的影响[D].上海:上海海洋大学,2008:1-2.
❷ MERCOLA J. Farmed Salmon = Most Toxic Food in the World, Organic Consumers Association[EB/OL]. (2018-07-25) [2021-07-03]. https://www.organicconsumers.org/news/farmed-salmon-toxic-flame-retardant.
❸ 克拉克.海岸带管理手册[M].吴克勤,等,译.北京:海洋出版社,2000:4-8.

China's mariculture output was 48.25 million MTS.❶ In the meantime, China's mariculture sector has focused on shellfish and seaweeds,leaving much room for other species.

China's mariculture sector has experienced a process from contamination to regulation to sustained improvements. Wu Jun *et al* (2013) argue that,despite the progress made in recent years,pollution of the immediate offshore sea in China is still serious.❷ However,with the environmental protection strategy being enforced,China's offshore and coastal pollution is getting improved. The 2017 *Gazette of the Quality of Maritime Environment of China* indicates that,between 2013 and 2017,the overall environment quality of the breeding areas graded as Class I and Class II accounted for 91% and 96%,respectively, showing an encouraging trend.In 2017,water quality of the total areas of maritime space below Class IV was 33,720 km^2 in summer,47,310 km^2 in autumn,showing consecutive drops.❸

Mariculture is one of the important categories of GIs covering a variety of products.In China,the protected mariculture GI products include,among others, fish, prawn and shellfish.Chengcun Hao (oyster), Taishan Manyu (eel),Yantai Haishen (sea cucumber),Sanmen Qingxie (green crab) are some of the notable ones following strict regulations and controls that aim to minimize the impacts on ecological environment.To sum up,this book is of the view that the GI system plays a role in sustainable utilization of ocean resources in the following aspects.

---

❶ See:https://www. fao. org/fishery/en/countrysector/cn/en.
❷ 吴军,陈克亮,汪宝英,等. 海岸带环境污染控制实践技术[M]. 北京:科学出版社, 2013:4.
❸ See:http://gc. mnr. gov. cn.

1. Controlled scale and breeding density minimize pollution to sea waters

It is in relation to the conception of marine environmental capacity.Wu Jun *et al* (2013) argue that "marine environmental capacity refers to the maximum load rate of pollutants of a particular maritime space in the context of sufficient utilization of the self-purification capacity of oceans that does not cause any pollution damage." "Marine economy must be controlled within the marine environmental capacity which is an important judgment basis for marine sustainable development."❶ Therefore,mariculture is supposed to control its scale within the marine environmental capacity to avert negative impact on the ocean resources.

According to the 2017 *Gazette of the Quality of Maritime Environment in China*,key pollutants of maritime space are inorganic nitrogen, active phosphate and petroleum,which are mainly caused by the eutrophication of water body and E.coli of sediment that exceed the acceptable limit.Mariculture is the major contributor. "Some farms have overly dense seedlings that deteriorate the environment.Poor marine environmental quality combined with a lack of controls and capacity to maintain a healthy environment all leads to the breakout of diseases and increasingly serious epidemics." "It indicates that resource management and improvement for off-shore environment have been undervalued with insufficient support."❷ "Drug abuse, overdose and abuse of additives are rampant in some regions' mariculture,processing

---

❶ 吴军,陈克亮,汪宝英,等.海岸带环境污染控制实践技术[M].北京:科学出版社,2013:9-11.
❷ 浙江省海洋与渔业局.海水养殖[M].杭州:浙江科学技术出版社,2006:4-5.

of aquatic products and sales as well."❶

The GI system shows ample concerns for breeding density and scales that must be regulated in the specification. The objectives are, first,to ensure adequate nutrition for aquatic products living in confined water body;second,to ensure normal quality of the water body; third,to control the pollution from excrement to a reasonable level.The breeding of Yantai Haishen (sea cucumber),a Chinese GI,for instance, requires a sea area where there are mild waves with clear water,smooth and slow tide flux.The sediment bottom should be covered by reefs, gravels,hard sand and weeds.The density of seedlings is $2-4/m^2$.Trawler is prohibited within the aquatic areas.❷ The specification of Taishan Manyu (eel), another Chinese GI, provides: the breeding area should have a good ecological environment with water quality in conformity with the national standard for mariculture....breeding density 30,000 ~ 45,000 eels/hectare;formula feeds exclusively for eels;breeding environment, prevention and control of diseases complying to relevant compulsory requirements,no damage to the environment".❸

2. Standardized production retains a safe mariculture

It is one of the mandatory requirements for China's GI producers to carry out standardized production by furnishing the GI's standard system.And despite varied practices,the idea of standardization is widely adopted for GIs across countries.It is of significance for the mariculture sector where mismanagement once prevailed.Zhang Yan *et al*(2005) ar-

---

❶ 王清印. 海水生态养殖理论与技术[M]. 北京:海洋出版社,2005:2.
❷ See:Announcement No. 32 of 2009 on the GI Protection of Yantai Haishen,AQSIQ.
❸ See:Announcement No. 175 of 2011 on the GI Protection of Taishan Manyu,AQSIQ.

gue, "many practitioners still rely on experiences when it comes to management, without any technical specifications."[1] Zhao Fajian (2005) claims that "blind pursuit for higher output is prevalent,together with casual expansion of breeding areas,poor layout,excessive density, unqualified feeds,poor management as well as abuse of antibiotics,disinfectant and water quality conditioner." "Formula feeds have unstable quality,and the coefficient of feeds is high.Feed remnants,excrement and metabolic product will cause contamination and diseases."Besides, "water treatment is overlooked,which damages the off-shore waters and causes imbalance of ecosystems."[2] It is thus meaningful to follow the measures of the GI system to standardize mariculture production that helps to reduce its pollutions.As far as the mariculture standard system is concerned, it ranges from drafting standards on breeding methodology,water environment control to R&D on feeds.Zhao Fajian (2005) proposes to improve the assurance system of mariculture,including that of the environment,of disease control,of seedlings and product quality.He proposes to develop a healthy mariculture that "covers breeding facilities,seedling cultivation,breeding density,water treatment, feed quality,drug use and general management." "It is essential to carry out R&D on quality formula feeds that are stable,appealing,absorptive and helpful in improving immunity and anti-adversity ability,combined with environment friendliness and low feed coefficient."[3] Zhang Yan *et al* (2005) claim that "feed quality not only determines the con-

---

[1] 王清印.海水生态养殖理论与技术[M].北京:海洋出版社,2005:13.
[2] 王清印.海水养殖研究新进展[M].北京:海洋出版社,2008:4-5.
[3] 王清印.海水养殖研究新进展[M].北京:海洋出版社,2008:6-9.

version rate,but also plays a decisive role in water environment."❶ It appears that a regulated mariculture and improved assurance system are the key to address the environmental problems, which precisely corresponds to the ends and means of the GI system.In practice,some mariculture GI producing areas have taken actions to fulfil the idea of eco‐friendly breeding.

3. Promoting sustainable marine fishing to safeguard marine biodiversity

FAO report indicates,illegal fishing,unreported or irregular fishing constitutes the biggest threat to sustainable fishing.Chen Zuozhi (2008) argues, "marine fishing,through its direct or indirect effect,deteriorates the marine ecosystem.In the maritime spaces where fishing and other human activities concentrate,fishing has direct impact on marine biodiversity and causes a simplified global marine food network and decrease in trophic grade of catch by deteriorating by‐catch and habitat as well as biological relations."❷ Whilst the negative impacts of marine fishing are conspicuous,viable solutions to the problem are in relation to a wide range of areas challenging the whole world.It is a due obligation and responsibility for every marine fishing state to carry out regulated planning and rational fishing to protect the marine biodiversity.

Marine Stewardship Council (MSC) defines sustainable fishing as an act that,by maintaining sufficient marine fish stocks and environ-

---

❶ 王清印. 海水生态养殖理论与技术[M]. 北京:海洋出版社,2005:16.
❷ 陈作志. 捕捞对北部湾海洋生态系统结构与功能的影响[D]. 上海:上海海洋大学, 2008:2.

ment of fish habitat, ensures the well-being of the population who make a living by fishing in the sea.❶ It refers to three aspects. Firstly, the number of fishing species must be guaranteed. Fishing should be controlled within a specific range to ensure fish stock's reproduction and their healthy growth. Secondly, fishing's impact on marine ecology must be minimized. Fishing should be cautiously conducted to make sure that population of other species and habitats in the ecosystem maintain a healthy growth. Thirdly, management must be enforced. Management measures should observe the regulations and be subject to adjustment amid environmental changes.

The GI system promotes the sustainable development of marine fishing in the following aspects, namely,

− rational planning of fishing areas;

− strict control of fishing volume;

− proper fishing schedules.

To be honest, compared to mariculture, protected GIs from marine fishing are few. Statistics show that Zhoushan Daiyu (hairtail) is the only marine fishing product registered as a certification trademark in China, indicating a shortage of case analysis. Nevertheless, the principal approaches taken by GI practitioners could be the right path for safeguarding marine biodiversity. The specification in the case of 'Bulot de la Baie de Granville', a wild gastropod mollusc registered as a PGI by the EU in February 2019, (Official Journal L35,07,02,2019), may help explain.

'Bulot de la Baie de Granville' measures between 47 mm and 70 mm. Howev-

---

❶ See: https://www.msc.org.

er, a maximum of 8 % of the batch may consists of individuals smaller than 47 mm and 15 % of individuals larger than 70 mm. 'Bulot de la Baie de Granville' smells of iodine, the sea and algae. In the mouth, after cooking, 'Bulot de la Baie de Granville' has a tender texture, a noticeable moisture content and iodic, marine and nutty flavours. It may be slightly crunchy owing to the presence of small sediments or shell debris. It does not have a muddy odour or taste.

'Bulot de la Baie de Granville' is fished on the west side of the Cotentin peninsula, in the coastal area extending from the headland of Goury in the north to the headland of Champeaux in the south. It is caught within a coastal strip of 30 nautical miles calculated from the landing points.

The landing area comprises all the coastal municipalities between the headland at Goury in the north and the headland at Champeaux in the south.

The need for vessels fishing 'bulots' to be located all along the coastal area, and these environmental considerations, are the reason for: the many slipways and landing points along the coast, and the small size of the fishing units (<12 m), enabling vessels to be taken out of the water or grounded.

The professional fishing of 'Bulot de la Baie de Granville' grew significantly in the second half of the 20th century, thanks to the availability of gear that made it possible to fish larger quantities. Consequently, this activity became professional, specialised and profitable. The specific gear used included pots to catch 'bulots' and open boxes for their transport.

As early as 1985, a resource management system (vessel size, type of gear, fishing calendar, etc.) was put in place for the 'bulot' fished in the Bay of Granville so as to preserve the resource and the small-scale nature of pot fishery.[1]

Apparently, the fishing of 'Bulot de la Baie de Granville' has adequately taken environmental concerns into account. The 44 loading

---

[1] See: SINGLE DOCUMENT 'BULOT DE LA BAIE DE GRANVILLE' EU No: PGI - FR - 02319—4. 8. 2017, Official Journal of the European Union 29. 8. 2018.

spots are all less than 30 miles from the coast.Fishing vessels must be shorter than 12m to facilitate landing.Fishing tools (a special pot) and timing are regulated as well.As a response to the prevailing westerly wind,fishing vessels are required to be stationed all along the coastal area,which in part explains the multiple loading spots.In addition,it defines the venue of sorting and cleaning activities to protect local environment.The relatively small catch ensures a stable fishing volume that is confined to a limited range.The case of 'Bulot de la Baie de Granville' is paradigmatic for marine fishing GI products.It renders best practices for GI producers as well as relevant authorities.

Section 3　The GI system helps protect terrestrial resources

Goal 15. Life on land

Goal 15 of the 2030 Agenda for Sustainable Development is dedicated to the protection,restoration and promotion of sustainable terrestrial ecosystems by managing forests,combating desertification,halting and reversing land degradation and halting biodiversity loss.In review of the global achievement in 2019,the United Nations states that "the world is falling short on 2020 targets to halt biodiversity loss," that land degradation continues,biodiversity loss is at an alarming rate,alien species and poaching continue to offset the efforts in protecting and restoring biological and species system.Organization for Economic Co -

operation and Development (OECD) warned G7 leaders that many ecosystems are moving towards irreversible states,to the point where they could only be restored at prohibitive cost.

A report of the Intergovernmental Science - Policy Platform on Biodiversity and Ecosystem Services (IPBES) claims in 2019 that changes of human habitats,especially nature reserves being taken for agriculture,climate change,aggression of alien species,excessive exploitation and pollution are the primary causes.❶

The earth is our homeland.As an essential way to achieve Goal 15,it is expected to transform the development mode and public consumption behaviors.While it is in relation to multiple areas,rational use of land resources and sustainable agriculture are the crucial components.Now that it has been discussed in precious chapters,we will move on to the roles of the GI system for maintaining biodiversity and sustainable agriculture.

Firstly,the GI system fosters conservation of forest resources.Ke Shuifa and Li Hongxun (2019) claim that 1.6 billion people around the world make living from forest-based products and services.They argue that forestry plays significant biological roles in combating climate change,protecting biodiversity,conserving water and soil.Forestry is a circular economic entity for green economy,which reproduces,recycles and degrades to make it the largest natural circular economic entity.The forest industry has followed the pattern of 'resource-prod-

---

❶ SETTELE J,DÍAZ S,NGO H T. Global assessment report on biodiversity and ecosystem services of the Intergovernmental Science-Policy Platform on Biodiversity and Ecosystem Services[EB/OL].(2019-05-04)[2022-03-24]. https://doi.org/10.5281/zenodo.3831673.

uct‑renewable resource' that has made circular use of energy and materials, with low energy consumption and low emissions. It provides mankind with the essential biomass materials and energies for a green economy.[1]

Under‑forest products are integral components of the under‑forest economy. Gu Xiaojun *et al* (2008) define under‑forest economy as a compound operation of multiple agroforestry projects under the tree canopies by making use of the resources of forest land and its ecological environment.[2] Ke Shuifa and Li Hongxun argue, "under‑forest economy and forest tourism may bring about diversified income and employment for local farmers, helping them resist market risks."[3] Water conservation, sunlight condition and soil humus supplied by the forest give rise to mushrooms, nuts, herbal medicinal materials, hive products and other under‑forest products ‑ an important source of GIs in China. Under‑forest products are subject to natural circumstances. Some products, such as pine mushroom and truffle, are completely wild that are unable to be bred artificially. Resource scarcity has resulted in their premium price and promising market prospect. Ke Shuifa and Li Hongxun summarize the success story and patterns of the under‑forest economy of Fujian Province that primarily include:

− the forest‑medicinal herbs pattern;

− the forest‑mushroom pattern;

---

[1] 柯水发,李红勋,等.林业绿色经济理论与实践[M].北京:人民日报出版社,2019:17‑20.

[2] 柯水发,李红勋,等.林业绿色经济理论与实践[M].北京:人民日报出版社,2019:169.

[3] 柯水发,李红勋,等.林业绿色经济理论与实践[M].北京:人民日报出版社,2019:22‑34.

- the forest-tourism pattern;
- the forest-hive pattern;
- the forest-poultry pattern.

The forest-mushroom pattern aims to make use of forest environment to plant fungi products,or simply make use of the under-forest flora available.While the forest-poultry pattern refers to raising chickens,ducks,gooses on forest land,where there is moderate sunlight and good ventilation as well as ample spaces with insects and grass resources.In addition,the feces and culture medium from wastes are fertilizers that foster trees and are source of feeds for aquaculture.

Gu Xiaojun (2008) argues that Pubei County of Guangxi Zhuang Autonomous Region has followed the rules that prioritize forestry in protecting the ecosystem and boost the under-forest economy.Under-forest economy was developed as zones and bases,where seven sectors were enhanced as characteristic industries.❶ The 10,000-hectare Pubei Red Mushroom (PGI)Industrial Base was one of the examples.Pubei County is home to 13,333 hectares of contiguous original secondary red vertebra forest where red mushroom grows.The red mushroom is a wild fungus,which so far cannot be bred artificially,growing in the humus layer formed over prolonged period under the special climate conditions of high humidity and temperature.In December 2013 Pubei Red Mushroom was approved as a PGI and became one of the models of forest conservation through GI protection.

Notable examples are also found in foreign GI practices.In Sene-

---

❶ 柯水发,李红勋,等.林业绿色经济理论与实践[M].北京:人民日报出版社,2019: 124-129,170.

gal,as mentioned earlier,producers of Madd de Casamance seized the opportunity of GI application to advocate the idea that only by protecting the invaluable forest asset could they ensure the characteristics of Madd de Casamance-a wild fruit product.By forming a symbiotic relationship between quality product and forest protection and personal income,local inhabitants voluntarily joined in protecting forest resources. Fortunately,it was the only forest region in Senegal that had no forest fire in 2019.❶

Under-forest economy patterns depend on the perfect environment of forest.Consequently,under-forest GIs must focus on protecting environment to make sure natural conditions are not damaged.Growth conditions must be defined in the specification,for it is a prerequisite for sustainable GI resources.In practice,people in GI producing areas are increasingly aware of the significance of environmental protection in connection with their income rise,taking actions accordingly.For instance,collectors of Nyingchi Pine Mushroom in Tibet would return the topsoil to its original position after picking the mushroom.It is said that mushroom will not grow next year unless by doing so.The same is true of the collection of Nagqu Cordyceps Sinensis(冬虫夏草).Local folks realize from experiences that only by showing respect for nature can they harvest wealth from the earth.GI protection itself is a process of protecting forest resources,and the two complement each other.

Secondly,the GI system helps prevent land degradation.It is reported

---

❶ WIPO. Supporting environmental sustainability with GIs:the case of Madd de Casamance [EB/OL]. [2021-12-05]. https://www.wipo.int/ipadvantage/en/details.jsp?id=11582.

that,parallel to urbanization and industrialization,approximately 37% of land is degrading in China,jeopardizing agricultural production.The primary cause is the excessive exploitation of land resources.Although natural factors such as draught,flood and wind as well may weaken soil quality,human conducts like excessive reclamation,inadequate use of pesticides and fertilizers all contribute to land desertification,decrease of soil fertility and soil salinization.Decrease of productivity, threat to food security,damage to ecosystem and loss of biodiversity are some of the serious consequences of land degradation.It calls for multiple measures to combat land degradation,one of which is about reducing land exploitation for agriculture and livestock husbandry.

Land productivity is not inexhaustible.It is subject to plant variety and quantity of crops as well as the duration of exploitation throughout the year.Crop rotation matters,too.It aims to increase soil fertility and balance soil nutrients.In addition,it helps prevent plant diseases and insect pests.Moreover,it improves soil's physical and chemical properties,regulating soil fertility in order to retain satisfactory yields. Since there are discrepancies when it comes to plants' demand for nutrients,some plants,such as ginseng and yam,have higher demand for soil fertility,implying the land must be suspended after each harvest. And such an interval may even last for years before the next round of cultivation.Otherwise,it will lead to a decrease in quality and output.

Similarly,overgrazing may cause grassland degradation and desert steppe that paralyze livestock production.Overgrazing used to be commonplace in many regions in China,where some of the problems were exacerbated by breeds.Goat,for instance,prefers grass roots,which does more harm to grassland than sheep.Meanwhile some damages are associated with stocking density, where excessive number per unit area could result in malnutrition and quality losses. Zhang Tianyou (2008) argues, "Being the foundation of livestock husbandry, grazing must be controlled within the capacity of grassland resources. Meat breeds or milk breeds with high economic yields suitable for dry-lot feeding or half dry-lot feeding are recommended for lamb raising. And part of the stocking is advised to be replaced by cow breeding for a diversified agriculture and a combination of grazing and dry lot feeding. By seasonal rotation of grazing, an economical livestock farming manages to get developed. It ensures the balance of grassland ecosystem without negative impact on herdsman's income."❶ As a means to protect the grassland ecosystem and to achieve sustainable development, China launched, since 2011, the subsidy and reward mechanism for the protection of grassland ecosystem in 13 provinces and autonomous regions with pastoral areas, namely, Inner Mongolia, Xinjiang, Tibet, Qinghai, Sichuan, Gansu, Ningxia and Yunnan. The number of stockings is assessed by the grassland area so as to dismiss overgrazing. Herdsmen are encouraged to graze rationally to sustain the use of grassland resources. This mechanism has played a constructive role in protecting the grassland ecosystem, "especially for the grassland ecosystem of relevant projects, where regional improvements are visible, where grass quantity and livestock load capacity have been raised in recent years". As of 2018, a subsidized incentive policy managed to keep working, when a total of RMB15.56-billion-yuan worth of annual central financial fund

---

❶ 张天佑. 转变农业发展方式与农业绿色发展[M]. 北京: 中国农业出版社, 2018: 113.

was allocated,in which RMB9.05 billion served as subsidies for grazing prohibition,RMB6.51 billion as award for grassland balance.Herdsmen per household income increased by RMB1,500 yuan,making this subsidy an important supplement to the herdsmen.❶

Livestock and poultry products are sources of agri - food GIs. There are myriad breeds of cattle,sheep,chicken,duck and goose.Some critics argue that the quality of livestock and poultry products are determined by breeds,having nothing to do with breeding environment. While others believe that, in addition to the intrinsic distinctiveness brought about by breeds,geographical conditions and climate are relevant factors as well,indicating that identical breed may present quality differences.For instance,it is a general view that sheep raised on land of salinization has unique meat without any gamy odor,which contributes to the unique characteristics of 'Yanchi Tanyang' -Tan sheep from Pond of Salt-a PGI in Ningxia Hui Autonomous Region.Similar product is found in Tibet,where 'Gamba Sheep' bears resemblance with what occurs to Yanchi Tanyang.The implication justifies GI protection for livestock and poultry products.

In previous paragraphs we have discussed that one of the advantages of the GI system is to protect the gene resource of superior breeds by confining their producing areas to their most adaptable living conditions without undue promotion and proliferation.Another advantage refers to the fair planning of stocking scale to optimize breeding methodology,retaining their characteristics and constantly improving their

---

❶ 中国优质农产品开发服务协会.中国品牌农业年鉴2018[M].北京:中国农业出版社,2019:73,99.

market premium capacities.Equally importantly,the GI system is dedicated to eliminating overgrazing to make sure that the grassland ecosystem is not damaged,land degradation does not happen,and characteristic livestock sector sustains.The ceiling of breeding density must be defined in its specification for each livestock GI.Breeding requirements are specified for the four seasons,for different ages,for grazing, supplementary feeding,fattening and slaughtering.Livestock and poultry GIs manage to prosper thanks to the control measures that enable rewards from characteristic qualities,making them one of the key products in lifting farmers and herdsmen out of poverty.Huge economic benefits are generated amid protecting the environment.

Finally, the GI system protects biodiversity. Christian Leveque (2005) argues that biodiversities is composed of the diversities of genetic resources,species and ecosystems.He quoted the definition of the United Nations *Convention on Biological Diversity* (CBD) as saying, "Biological diversity means the variability among living organisms from all sources including,inter alias,terrestrial,marine and other aquatic ecosystems and the ecological complexes of which they are part;this includes diversity within species, between species and of ecosystems."[1] Anne Maczulak (2011) argues that biological diversity refers to all species living on earth or in specific regions.If a region is rich in species and has prosperous populations,we would say this region has biological diversity.[2] GI protection can help maintain genetic genes and biological diversity.Wang Xiaobing (2019) argues that the GI sys-

---

[1] 莱韦克.生物多样性[M].邱举良,译.北京:科学出版社,2005:2-4.
[2] 马克苏拉克.生物多样性:保护濒危物种[M].李岳,田琳,等,译.北京:科学出版社,2011:1.

tem is helpful for maintaining biodiversity,especially the diversity of genetic resources.❶ As explained in previous paragraphs,GI protection shows concern for the selection of plant variety and animal breed that is favorable for maintaining genetic diversity,especially the genetic resources of livestock and poultry populations.It is one of the principles to study the links between native breeds and their natural living conditions and to designate the producing areas so as to preserve the characteristics of native breeds,refraining from unnecessary introduction or promotion.

The GI system plays a positive role in conserving biological diversity as well.GI production depends on unique and complete ecosystem.For example,the solid fermentation technique of Chinese Baijiu has strict demand for producing areas,and some of the techniques rely on the interactions between microbial populations at specific temperatures and humidity.It is safe to say that the characteristics of Chinese Baijiu are largely attributable to the unique natural environment and climate conditions of the producing areas.Once changes occur to the local ecosystem,the quality of Baijiu will inevitably be affected.Zhang Jiatao,Cui Chunling and Tong Zhongdong (2014) argue that the micro ecosystem of the producing areas of Maotai Town shows significant difference from that of other Baijiu producing areas,which are mainly reflected in the extreme presentation of thermophilic bacteria and acidophilic bacteria. The ecosystem under prolonged high temperature, with high temperature fermentation and stack fermentation,has tamed

---

❶ 王笑冰. 经济发展方式转变视角下的地理标志保护[M]. 北京:中国社会科学出版社,2019:49.

some extreme micro organisms, strengthening their thermal stability and expediting metabolic rate.❶ It renders a typical example of why it pays to conserve the ecosystem to safeguard the present and the future of GI products.

---

❶ 张嘉涛,崔春玲,童忠东,等. 白酒生产工艺与技术[M]. 北京:化学工业出版社, 2014:45.

Chapter 6≫
Partnership promotes international cooperation in geographical indications

Goal 17. Partnerships for the goals

Goal 17 aims to "strengthen the means of implementation and revitalize the global partnership for sustainable development". In its review of global achievements made by 2019, the UN report indicates that implementation made rapid progress, among which personal donations reached a record high, online population increased year by year along with the establishment of a bank of technology for the Least Developed Countries (LDCs). Nevertheless, the world faces many challenges: development aids for governments were decreasing, integration between personal donations and SDGs was inadequate, network construction was fragmented, trade conflicts were increasingly fierce. COVID-19 has serious implications on all the achievements.Remittances to low and middle-income countries were projected to fall from $ 554 billion in 2019 to $ 445 billion 2020.Global foreign direct investment was expected to decline by up to 40% in 2020.❶

The SDGs are bound up with every country without exception.It is necessary to reinforce global collaborations and draw on experiences from one another.LDCs need more help to improve their development planning and capacity building.The seventeen Goals encompass almost all social and economic spectrums, where coordination problems may arise. Based on the analysis of GI's contribution to SDGs and its association therewith,it calls on global collaborations to foster GI protection across countries.

The forty-year reform and open-door policy in China proves that development is the key to addressing all problems.Development is the theme for achieving the SDGs as well.Given the diverse natural conditions and varied political,economic,historical and cultural status,there is no single approach tailored to every country.The way forward rests in strengthened collaborations.GI's status as trade-related intellectual property right has given rise to both multinational negotiations and bilateral talks between trading partners.China has been engaged in dialogues over the GI issues and completed the negotiations with the EU for the GI Agreement.It is anticipated that China will reinforce cooperation and continue dialogues with more trading partners,thereby boosting bilateral trade and ensuring a healthy trade order.Given that GI protection did not draw global concerns until about two decades ago,it

---

❶ See:https://sdgs. org. un/goals/goal17.

is suggested that GI collaborations focus on the following issues.

Firstly, priority should be given to sharing best practices. The legal means governing GI protection varies from country to country. Some, such as the EU, Switzerland, Japan and India, have followed the *sui generis* path, promulgating laws specifically for GIs; others, like Canada, Chile, New Zealand, the United States, have adopted the trademark approach; the third approach regulates GI according to anti unfair competition law or consumer protection law. And even under the same legal regime, regulations vary in terms of protection of GI products. For instance, Switzerland does not require any submission of GI application. GI stakeholders may not apply for registration before being granted the right of protection.[1] In China, dual approaches exist, where the trademark law has provisions on protecting certification trademark of GI product, and there are ministerial level regulations specifically designed for GI protection. While legal system is an important component of global GI collaborations, it does not make much sense to compare the pros and cons of diverse legal means. WTO has shown respect for Members' options and has no preference for specific legal approach. Thus, legal system per se may not be the focus of GI cooperation. Instead, it is expected to target exchanging views and sharing best practices.

Every country is unique in its natural resources, history and culture. They have the same aspiration to boost domestic characteristic industry and increase the market share of their own specialties. Sharing

---

[1] See: https://www.ige.ch/en/protecting-your-ip/indications-of-source/protecting-geographical-indications/protection-in-switzerland.

experiences and deepening communication have reference significance for developing countries,especially the LDCs,which could be empowered to master management and operational skills and carry out practical activities.There are multiple ways of sharing practices,ranging from visits and training to joint projects,as are the cases for some Asian and African countries where the FAO and the EU made their presence in providing technical assistance.

Secondly,deepening cooperation to improve national or regional GI system and practices.The goal of GI protection is,in tandem with fulfilling the obligations of WTO/TRIPS,to achieve sustainable development and to lift more people out of poverty.Multilateral negotiations among WTO Members and timely notification of GI issues are helpful for Members to reinforce GI protection.It is helpful for Members to improve their own legal means in response to any concerns regarding geographical indication from trading partners.

It is of special significance to develop communication and cooperation on geographical indications between Asian countries.Due to historical and cultural reasons,Asian countries are normally conflict free with either European or American or Oceanian countries with respect to GI names and geographical terms.Fortunately,many Asian countries have come to realize GI's roles for regional economic growth and international trade.Legal frameworks are being set up,laws and regulations are getting published and registrations of local GI products have made their debut.It is notable that,despite multiple legal options,Asian countries are showing preference for the *sui generis* approach,releasing laws and regulations specifically for GIs.For instance, Japan promulgated the Geographical Indication (GI) Act that entered into force in June 2015.India enacted the Geographical Indications of Goods (Registration & Protection) Act as early as 1999 that came into force in September 2003.Southeast Asian countries,including but not limited to Thailand,Indonesia,Singapore,Laos,Cambodia,Vietnam have legislated against infringement of GIs as well,[1] some of which received joint assistance from FAO and the EU.

It is true that,due to capacity problems,some developing countries,the LDCs in particular,face challenges in building up the GI sector on their own.One of the ways to address the problem is to be engaged in collaborated projects.Countries and organizations with expertise and funding capacity may provide aid,ranging from visits to the geographical areas for designation purpose to sorting GI products, drafting specifications and providing enforcement aid with a view to forging local characteristic products and the GI sector as a whole.

Thirdly,it is suggested to reinforce GI cooperation between major developing countries.GI protection is of potential prospect for any major developing country, e. g., the BRICS (Brazil, Russia, India, China, South Africa),Indonesia,Vietnam,Egypt,Kenya,Mexico,Peru,to name only a few.Despite disparities in GI development levels,their ample natural resources and diversified cultures signify huge potentials for the GI sector.Indonesia,for instance,is the largest developing country in Southeast Asia with huge population and abundant tropical resources.In 2016,Indonesia enacted the Trademark and Geographical

---

[1] MALIK M. Updates on the Geographical Indications in the ASEAN Region [EB/OL]. (2019-07-02) [2021-04-25]. https://www.wipo.int/edocs/mdocs/sct/en/wipo_geo_lis_19/wipo_geo_lis_19_6.pdf.

Indication Law[1] and issued implementation regulations in 2019.[2] To date,Indonesia has registered 66 domestic GIs and 8 foreign GIs.Indonesian GIs such as coffee and pepper have been unveiled on global market.Statistics of ASEAN show that,as of January 2019,346 GIs were registered in ASEAN, including 37 foreign GIs from non - ASEAN countries.[3] In Mexico,Tequila stands for the most outstanding GI brand appealing to consumers from around the world.It remains one of the world leaders in terms of spirit GI products that may render practical experience to peers from other countries.

Fourthly,it is proposed to reinforce China - Japan - Korea GI collaborations.GI protection is closely associated with history and culture, which in part explains the conflicts over GI between the EU and other immigrant countries where product names adopting place names identical with those of the European countries are widespread.Contrary to this phenomenon,duplication of place names is limited for China,Japan and Korea despite their cultural ties.And conflicts over product names are not something prevalent at all.At the same time,compared to western cuisine,the dietary habits of the three countries share similarities,indicating that a popular food in one country,e.g.,rice wine,Wagyu,pickled cabbage,may find its consumers in another.Moreover,they are leading

---

[1] MIRANDAH D,DEVINA RP. Indonesia:Implementing regulations for geographical indications [EB/OL]. (2020-04-13) [2021-09-24]. https://www. mirandah. com/pressroom/item/indonesia - implementing - regulations - for - geographical - indications.

[2] Ministry Regulation No. 12 of 2019 implementing the specific provisions regarding geographical indications.

[3] MALIK M. Updates on the Geographical Indications in the ASEAN Region [EB/OL]. (2019-07-02) [2021-04-25]. https://www. wipo. int/edocs/mdocs/sct/en/wipo_geo_lis_19/wipo_geo_lis_19_6. pdf.

economic powers in Asia with huge trade volumes and frequent business transactions.Meanwhile, their GI systems were initiated not long ago and are on the way to perfect their own GI system through practices. GI collaborations are of special significance.By protecting the intellectual property rights of GI producers,their collaborations will facilitate trade and meet the market demand of each country.

Fifthly,it is suggested to further bilateral and multilateral consultations for the setting up of a meaningful mechanism for GIs.Reference has been made to the debate over the GI issue among WTO Members, where the so‐called 'new world' countries are at odds with the EU over the binding force of the multilateral notification and registration system of geographical indications,and with whether the high‐level protection for wines and spirits laid down in Article 23 of TRIPS should be extended to other GI products.In other words,the EU has been in its bid for high‐level protection for GI names to protect its agri‐food sectors.While the 'new world' countries,due to the influence of immigrant culture, have adopted identical or similar names with those of the EU member states for myriad products that,as is alleged by the EU,may have misled consumers into believing their true origins are from the places the names indicate.Thus,the 'new world' countries, where many GIs claimed by the EU are considered as generic names, strongly demand a 'weak' protection.GI protection is considered a hurdle to free trade and economic growth.

Prolonged negotiations over the GI issue persist at WTO/TRIPS Council without notable achievements.The stalemate of multilateral negotiations has propelled WTO Members to turn to bilateral cooperation.EU,for instance,has completed a series of negotiations and signed several GI agreements with,including but not limited to,China,Japan, Korea.Singapore,Vietnam.It is anticipated that more countries could be on the list.

  China - EU communications over geographical indication started since the late 1990s,when the former State Administration of Quality and Technical Supervision issued the *Regulations on the Designated Origin Product* based on studies of l'Appellation d'Origine Controlee (AOC) of France.Since 2001,upon the setting up of the former General Administration of Quality Supervision, Inspection and Quarantine (AQSIQ), extensive communications were conducted with the DG - Trade and DG-Agriculture of the European Union,and a series of forums and seminars were jointly held in China.AQSIQ and DG-Trade of the EU eventually signed an MoU on GI in 2005,paving the way for the EU-China 10+10 Pilot Project launched in 2006,which,upon in-depth discussions,document checks and on-site visits to GI producing areas,accomplished registrations for 10 GI products of the other Party. Experts from the EU complimented on the GI practices of AQSIQ. Meanwhile experts from China acquired first-hand information about EU practices.It is perceived as a prelude or basis for the subsequent national level negotiation of China - EU Agreement on Geographical Indications launched in 2011❶,when the Chinese side was led by the Ministry of Commerce (MOFCOM) and joined by the former Ministry of Agriculture,the former State Administration of Industry and Commerce (SAIC) and AQSIQ.The negotiations were concluded in 2019

---

❶ EU and China sign landmark agreement protecting Geographical Indications[EB/OL]. (2020-09-14)[2020-09-16]. https://ec. europa. eu/commission/presscorner/detail/en/ip_20_1602.

when the two Parties formally signed the Agreement at the China-EU Summit on September 14,2020. As a proceeding, the Agreement sets two phases for GI protection. Phase One covers 100 GI products from each Party that will be protected on the territory of the other Party according to its laws and regulations in force. Phase Two starts 4 years after the Agreement enters into force, when additional 175 GI products of each Party will be protected reciprocally.

China-EU Agreement on GI-a landmark GI agreement firstly signed at the national level by the two Parties[1]- provides protection equivalent to the high-level protection for wines and spirits stipulated by Article 23 of TRIPS. Cui Hongjian, Director of the Institute of European Studies of the China Institute of International Studies, remarks that it is the first comprehensive, high level bilateral agreement on geographical indications signed between China and other countries, and the first important trade agreement between China and EU in recent years with milestone significance for China-EU economic and trade cooperation. It consists of 14 articles and 7 annexes which lay down principles of GI protection as well as lists of GI products. It is highlighted by the large number (257+257), rich content and high-level protection. It contributes to meeting the shared demand of both Parties for quality products and well-being of the people. Further analysis reveals three signals to the world. First, it is an effective approach to foster the healthy development of China-EU economic and trade relations. Second, it signifies positive achievement in IP cooperation between China

---

[1] EU and China sign landmark agreement protecting Geographical Indications[EB/OL]. (2020-09-14)[2020-09-16]. https://ec.europa.eu/commission/presscorner/detail/en/ip_20_1602.

and the EU.Third,it gives impetus to global awareness and recognition of geographical indications.❶ Furthermore,it may have impact on global GI practices,prompting more countries to reevaluate GI's roles in boosting regional economy and sustainable development.

China has followed its own route in protecting GIs.With over twenty years' practices and progress,there is a growing consensus over the positive roles of GI protection in alleviating poverty,in promoting regional characteristic industry and in protecting GI's intellectual property rights.The signing of China-EU Agreement on GI is favorable for the overall progress of China's GI system and is expected to push forward the legislation of a GI law,which was referred to by President Xi Jinping in his address on November 30,2020.❷ Further assessment is needed when it comes to the agreement's concrete impacts on bilateral trade and trading with relevant countries.It is anticipated that,with more GIs entering each other's market,any product that conflicts with the GI names listed in the China-EU GI Agreement will be blocked by both parties.

Mutual benefit is the foundation of bilateral cooperation.Cooperation in GI benefits the economic interests of many trading partners.It pays to explore ways to blend GI protection with sustainable development to make GI a prominent carrier of sustainable development practices towards achieving greater success.

---

❶ 栾雨石,牛宁.海外网评:中欧地理标志协定正式签署释放三重信号[EB/OL]. (2020-09-15)[2021-02-22]. http://opinion.haiwainet.cn/n/2020/0915/c353596-31876382.html.

❷ 习近平.全面加强知识产权保护工作 激发创新活力推动构建发展格局[J].求是, 2021(3):4-8.

Postscript

By discussing the concept of geographical indication (GI), the GI system and related issues, the author intends to analyze the values and impacts of the GI system on achieving the Sustainable Development Goals (SDGs). In view of the theme of this book, he has skipped introduction to the diverse legal systems concerning GI protection and case analysis of IP enforcement to accentuate the theme and intensify reader's comprehension of GI's roles in promoting sustainable development, and to provide references for readers engaging in GI practices.

The GI system aims, from its very beginning, to protect the intellectual property rights of characteristic products, and to prevent from any changes of the natural conditions and special techniques. It aims to maintain and inherit the characteristic quality of GI products. For more than one century since its first practice, and for the last two decades since the establishment of the World Trade Organization (WTO) in particular, GI protection has provoked interests from around the world.An increasing number of countries and regions are correlating GIs with regional economic growth and market competitiveness, extending and consolidating GI's contributions. European countries,with France,Italy,Spain,and Greece as some of the key players,are both the origin of the GI system and regions where it was the most prominently and successfully practiced.Being an integral part of the Common Agriculture Policy (CAP) of the EU,GI serves as,along with the Organic Product and Traditional Specialty Guaranteed (TSG) and other quality schemes,a useful tool in elevating the reputations of EU's agri-food products,in protecting the characteristic quality and intellectual property rights and in increasing their global market shares. Being a latecomer,China has,during the past twenty years by drawing on the experience of global best practices,set up and improved its own GI systems that are enforced across the country.Nevertheless,there is still a gap when compared to the EU.The absence of a *sui generis* law may affect GI-related enforcement.In addition,there are notable regional imbalances in terms of policy support and public awareness of GI's roles.Hence,a unified,definite and sustainable GI strategy is needed,otherwise it may have implications on the healthy development of regional economy.

On practices in China,this book has referred to cases of best practices,whereas in fact there are unsuccessful ones as well,which are almost always associated with a lack of follow-up measures,low participation rate of stakeholders,inadequate training and promotion or weak potentiality of the product itself.

In general,the effectiveness of the GI system owes to the enforcement at producing areas and consensus of all stakeholders who are committed to implementing every measure regulated by the GI scheme. Global GI practices normally follow a 'bottom up' model where organizers at the producing area initiate, advocate, coach and discuss the issues with the producers and invite all stakeholders to join in the application process. It is an ante displacement way for enforcement purposes. People are thus more prepared to observe the guidelines. Nevertheless, it may take longer time when compared to the Chinese approach that, despite the similar 'bottom up' model initiated by local government or industry, usually focuses on the documentation of GI application done by local experts and government agencies. The advocacy, training and technical guidance are conducted in the aftermath of the registration (approval). It appears more efficient yet having its drawbacks - low public awareness prior to the registration - that leave more tasks to the implementation process. Consequently, it relies on the leading role of local government for continuous funding and capacity aids.

Having said that, China has done a remarkable job when it comes to the progress made for the GI system, which, from something unknown to a conception popular across the country, only took a couple of years. Thousands of GI products were registered and protected over the past two decades, including the Protected Geographical Indication Product, the GI Collective/Certification Trademark and Registry of Agricultural GI Product that encompass all the thirty-one provinces, autonomous regions, and cities directly under the state control (except Hong Kong, Macau and Taiwan). GI authorities, local governments and inter-governmental organizations have carried out effective nationwide promotions. Meanwhile, the legal framework for GI protection is improving. Yet for most GI producers, brand building is still a long-term task.This author is convinced that,by optimizing market environment and by boosting consumer trust,more consumers will opt for GI products,making these regional brands with historical and cultural memories a dynamic force in support of the Sustainable Development Goals.

附　录　专有名词翻译

Agreement on Trade-Related Aspects of Intellectual Property Rights (TRIPS)	《与贸易有关的知识产权协定》
Agreement between the European Union and the Government of the People's Republic of China on Cooperation on, and Protection of, Geographical Indications	《中华人民共和国政府与欧洲联盟关于地理标志保护与合作协定》
Appellation d'origine Contrôlée (AOC)	（法）原产地命名监控
Appellation d'origine/Appellation of Origin	（法/英）原产地命名
Appellation d'origine protégée (AOP)	（法）原产地命名保护
Banano de Costa Rica	哥斯达黎加香蕉
Bordado da Madeira	葡萄牙一种陶瓷产品名称
Bordeaux	波尔多（法国地名），知名葡萄酒原产地
Bulot de la Baie de Granville	（法国）格朗威尔海湾螺贝
Common Agricultural Policy (CAP)	欧盟共同农业政策
Champagne	香槟（法国地名），知名起泡葡萄酒原产地

China Approved Drug Names（CADN）	《中国药品通用名称》
Code of Conduct（CoC）	操作指南
Code of Practice（CoP）	操作规程，行业规则
Cognac	干邑（法国地名），知名葡萄蒸馏酒原产地
Comté	孔泰（法国地名），知名奶酪原产地
Convention for the Safeguarding of the Intangible Cultural Heritage	《非物质文化遗产保护公约》
COP26	《联合国气候变化框架公约》第二十六次缔约方大会
CORBANA	哥斯达黎加全国香蕉行业协会
COVID-19	新型冠状病毒肺炎
Defensive	防守型
European Union（EU）	欧洲联盟（简称"欧盟"）
EU-China 10+10 Pilot Project	中欧10+10地理标志产品互认互保试点项目
Final Act	（乌拉圭回合）最后决议
Food and Agriculture Organization of the United Nations（FAO）	联合国粮农组织
Futog Cabbage	塞尔维亚一种地理标志卷心菜
Geographical Indication（GI）	地理标志
Geographical Mark	地理标记（瑞士）
Guide du demandeur d'une appellation d'origine protégée（AOP）*ou d'une indication géographique protégée*（IGP）	（法）《受保护的原产地命名和受保护的地理标志操作指南》

Hazard Analysis and Critical Control Point (HACCP)	危害分析与关键控制点食品安全管理体系
Harris Tweed	哈里斯花呢（英国）
Indication géographique protégée (IGP)	（法）受保护的地理标志
Indication of Source	货源标记
In-situ Conservation	就地保护
Institut National de l'origine et de la Qualite (INAO)	法国国家原产地和质量管理局
International Trade Center (ITC)	国际贸易中心组织
Intergovernmental Science-Policy Platform on Biodiversity and Ecosystem Services (IPBES)	生物多样性和生态系统服务政府间科学政策平台
Know-How	专门知识，诀窍
Krokos Kozanis	希腊一种地理标志西红花名
Kweichow Moutai Chiew	贵州茅台酒
La Ruche Qui dit Oui	蜂巢，法国一农副产品网络平台
Label	标签，标记
Lapsang Souchong	正山小种（茶）
Little Data Book on Gender 2019	《2019年性别数据小手册》
Logo	标识，徽标
Madd de Casamance	塞内加尔一种地理标志水果名
Malus Pumila Mill	红富士（品种名）
Marine Stewardship Council (MSC)	海洋管理委员会
Offensive	进攻型

Organization for Economic Cooperation and Development (OECD)	经济合作与发展组织
Official Journal of the European Union	欧盟官方公报
Protected Designation of Origin	受保护的原产地命名
Protected Geographical Indication	受保护的地理标志
Rooibos	南非一种地理标志茶叶名
Saffron	西红花
Sharing Economy	共享经济
Sign	标牌,标示
Sign Distinctive	显著性标志
Solingen	德国一种刀具名
Specifications	地理标志产品的质量技术要求
Sustainable Development Goals (SDGs)	联合国可持续发展目标
sui generis	自成一类的,指专门法
Symbol	符号,记号
Taliouine	摩洛哥一种地理标志西红花名
Terroir	(法)风土
The 2030 Agenda for Sustainable Development	《2030年可持续发展议程》
Traditional Specialty Guaranteed (TSG)	传统特色保证制度(欧盟)
Trade Mark Act	《贸易标记法案》(瑞士)
Trademark and Geographical Indication Law	商标与地理标志法(印尼)
Trade-Related Intellectual Property Right	与贸易有关的知识产权
Turrialba	哥斯达黎加地名
World Trade Organization (WTO)	世界贸易组织

World Commission on Environment and Development (WCED)	世界环境与发展委员会
WTO/TRIPs Council	世界贸易组织知识产权理事会
United Nations Conference on Environment and Development (UNEP)	联合国环境与发展大会
United Nations Environment Programme (UNEP)	联合国环境规划署
United Nations Educational, Scientific and Cutural Organization (UNESCO)	联合国教科文组织